ZONING AND PROPERTY RIGHTS

A Hong Kong Case Study

To my parents.

ZONING AND PROPERTY RIGHTS

A Hong Kong Case Study

Second Edition

Lawrence Wai-chung Lai

香港大學出版社
HONG KONG UNIVERSITY PRESS

Hong Kong University Press
14/F Hing Wai Centre
7 Tin Wan Praya Road
Aberdeen, Hong Kong

© Hong Kong University Press 1996, 1998

First edition 1996
Second edition 1998

ISBN 962 209 452 X

Printed in Hong Kong by ColorPrint Production Company.

Contents

List of Photographs

Appendix Two

List of Figures

List of Tables

Preface and Acknowledgements

This book is an attempt to clarify the economic nature of zoning. It is a modified version of the author's doctoral thesis 'Property Rights Analysis of Zoning' submitted to the University of Hong Kong in February, 1994.

Zoning is in many countries the cornerstone of land use planning. Through segregating 'incompatible' land uses, integrating 'compatible' land uses and reserving land for community land uses, zoning can be regarded as a means to overcome the problems of the 'externalities' and 'public goods' of an unregulated land market. Such concepts of market failure, which stem from the Cambridge economist Arthur C. Pigou, have been challenged by the property rights economists, with Ronald Harry Coase being the most influential figure.

Within the Coasian paradigm of transaction costs (1960) and Steven N.S. Cheung's interpretation of the concept (1990) that social institutions (including the government) are outcomes of public choice to reduce such costs, this book aims to contribute to the existing intellectual discourse on zoning by establishing a coherent property rights framework of zoning, against which the existing literature of zoning is reviewed and a number of hypotheses evaluated. This framework depicts a dual character of zoning, i.e.

(a) zoning as a government means to assign exclusive property rights; and

(b) zoning as a government planning intervention instrument which attenuates private property rights over the most valuable uses of land.

The exclusive rights assignment character of zoning, often ignored by economists and planners, is able to (i) constrain 'rent dissipation' which would occur in a system of common property rights under competition and (ii) lead to the emergence of market transactions. To test the impact of zoning in this respect, planning for a natural resource, the marine fish culture zoning of Hong Kong is examined. It is discovered that in spite of increasing water pollution, marine zoning leads to the growth in fish output within the fish culture zones. This result compares strikingly with the fall in fish capture outside the zones, indicating the significant positive influence of exclusive property rights. Other results are also consistent with the positive contribution of exclusive property rights. For instance, more pollution-resistant fish species are kept in the more polluted culture zones, an investment behaviour difficult to explain under common property. It is also revealed that potentially more polluted cultured fish are sold at a discount compared with cleaner captured fish. This casts doubts on the popularized environmentalist view that the price mechanism fails to reflect the presence of pollution.

The second character of zoning, attenuating private property rights, has attracted more attention of economists. It is considered that such attenuation should not be regarded as being necessarily negative in economic terms, although this is a commonly perceived view of some economists. It is concluded that, whether the impacts of zoning in this respect are positive, neutral or negative, it is a case-by-case empirical question. Eight empirical hypotheses are evaluated by simple statistical methods. It is found that restrictions of freedom of subdivision or combination of land (via comprehensive development area concept by statutory zoning or lease conditions) are economically more beneficial in terms of land value enhancement, provided that the transaction costs of land assembly are not prohibitive. The imposition of statutory zoning on private agricultural land also appears to be beneficial in similar terms. However, other aspects of zoning, namely downzoning and planning application in general, do not appear to generate the alleged benefits of environmental improvement.

When I studied political theory as an undergraduate at the University of Hong Kong, I learnt a great deal from my teacher Stephen Davies on the dialectical way of thinking together with an appreciation of controversies. In my further studies and subsequent professional development, my choice of specialisms, economics and planning, was deliberate. Their apparent contradictions stimulated thought. Some of these thoughts, when expressed, may have been perceived as socially inconvenient but I have no regret for that. At first, I thought that the logical thinking of a planner (who is often thought to be anti-development) and an economist (who often prescribes 'policies' for growth) is necessarily mutually exclusive. This view indeed prevails among many of my peers who are town planners with a background in geography. Having accumulated further knowledge in 'property rights' and law, I now realize that a synthesis of the two disciplines is possible. As far as the former is concerned, I cannot deny that I have been heavily influenced by the writings of Professor Steven Cheung. This book is my attempt at reconciling the alleged dichotomy between 'planning' as a government regulatory device and 'economics' as a positive study of human 'maximization' behaviour under constraints (property rights being a set of special constraints).

The arguments in Chapters 1 to 3 describe some such issues in detail. Chapter 5 sets out a number of 'testable' hypotheses of the regulatory tools well known to town planners. Other than of obvious theoretical or academic interest, they should provide my professional counterparts in government and the private sector with some insights as to whether their social role is merely that of 'rent seeking' or is indeed capable of 'improving society'.

When this book was being edited, I read an article in the *South China Morning Post* written by Elizabeth Tacey, who reported on ecologists' warnings of a major environmental disaster due to cyanide fishing in the coral reefs throughout the Pacific and Indian Oceans. Such fishing was alleged to be arranged by Hong Kong based companies. An article in the *Economist* in 1993 also warned of global depletion of fisheries due to large scale commercial fishing. The day of no fish on the dinner table or remaining in the ocean may not be far away. Overfishing is indeed more an economic or, more precisely, a property rights issue than the result of environmental pollution *per se*. It occurred to me, having read the newspaper article, that the colourful fishes in streams at Shek O had long disappeared and the diverse fish species in the lagoon of Pui O and Lantau Island, had been replaced by the more aggressive and pollution-resistant Talapia species. Chapter 4, within this context of global and local collapse of habitats, should be of interest to conservationists. The readers are referred to an article in *Managerial and Decision Economics* written by the author and Professor Ben T. Yu for more institutional details.

I do not claim that the arguments or hypotheses of this book address or 'solve' all key issues of zoning as a basic planning tool. I am sure that many of the points I raise are simple, preliminary and may therefore appear somewhat highly controversial. It is my belief, however, that this study at least provides essential reference points for the development of better structured arguments and rigorously tested hypotheses.

The literature surveyed and cited in this work are documented in the footnotes and in the bibliography. The items were mostly obtained from the Main Library and Law Library of the University of Hong Kong. Hong Kong items were obtained from the "Hong Kong Collections" section of the Special Collections in the Main Library. A number of articles relating to Chapter 3 were made known to the author in correspondence with anonymous referees for the Town Planning Review.

The bulk of numerical data came from published government reports and reputable financial chronicles. They were largely obtained from the aforesaid libraries, notably the Special Collections. Some, however, were obtained from government departments, notably the Planning Department, the Environmental Protection Department, the Agriculture and Fisheries Department, and the Rating and Valuation Department. Many opinions were obtained from correspondence with referees for academic and professional journals, fish culturists, planning practitioners and the author's ex-colleagues in government.

Institutional details of the local fish culture and planning system are kept to the minimum. Such details have been competently documented and published by relevant government departments and scholars like Dr J. Richards (1980) and Dr Rudolph Wu (1985, 1988) on fish culture, Dr Catherine Lam (1988, 1990) on water pollution and Dr Roger Bristow (1981, 1984) on district planning. Bristow work's needs substantial updating to take into account the significant impacts of strategic and regional planning, amendments of the Town Planning Ordinance and the emerging role of Environmental Protection Department in the planning process. Such information can be obtained from various publications of the Planning Department available at the Department's public inquiry counter or at the Government Publications Centre. Institutional details of fish culture are also documented in Lai and Yu (1992, 1995).

I am in debt to Professor Anthony Walker, the University of Hong Kong, Professor Ben T. Yu, California State University and Associate Professor John Lea, University of Sydney for comments on the draft of this book. All faults are, of course, the author's. The kind permission to reproduce substantial parts of the author's articles published in the following journals is acknowledged: Chapter 3 — *Town Planning Review*; Chapter 4 — *Asian Economic Journal, EKISTICS*, and *Planning and Development*. In addition, parts of Chapters 1, 2 and 5 will be published in *Progress in Planning* with the kind permission of Hong Kong University Press.

Figures 2.3(c), 2.3(d), 2.10, 2.11 and 5.3 are reproduced with permission of the Director of Lands, (© Hong Kong Government Licence No. 20/95.) Figure 2.4(c) is reproduced with permission of the Director of Planning, Hong Kong government. The photographs which appear in this book are supplied by Government Information Services and published by courtesy of the Hong Kong government.

I thank Mr C.K. Cheung for his research and technical assistance in the preparation of the manuscript.

Lawrence Wai-chung Lai
September 1995
The University of Hong Kong

Preface to the Second Edition

The decision to produce the second edition of this book reflects a growing interest of the professional and academic community in the issue of property rights in town planning. In this edition, care is taken to remove errors discovered and to expand the bibliography. Footnotes are also added so as to elaborate on certain key concepts. Two appendices are added. Appendix One is on the use of aerial photographs as court evidence by the government against unauthorized development in rural New Territories. Appendix Two is a technical note on the government's housing planning model in terms of basic price theories. An appreciation of the economic concepts of the model should help understand the 'supply' aspect of the property price question, which has been a major issue in the Hong Kong Special Administrative Region Chief Executive's Policy Agenda. The author acknowledges the useful comments on Appendix One by his colleagues, Mr Leung Hing Fung, a practising barrister, and Mr Frederik Pretorius, who once served in the air surveillance unit of the South African Airforce, for his opinion on the interpretation of aerial photographs.

Lawrence Wai-chung Lai
January 1998
The University of Hong Kong

Chapter One

▲

▼

Introduction

▨ The Pigovian arguments for planning

Zoning is well-known as a key instrument in planning regulation which is environmental regulation in its broadest sense. Even planning systems without explicit zoning regulations have implicit elements of zoning[1] which is understood broadly in this book as government delineation and/or restrictions of rights over land within certain spatial confines.

Planning in terms of economic theorization is normally justified by the Pigovian welfare economics theses of market failure (Pigou 1932), notably 'externalities' (Samuelson 1958) and by extension, 'public goods' (Samuelson 1955). This Pigovian pro-intervention tradition is well received by planning practitioners and by Commonwealth academics[2] involved in the education of planners.

An externality arises where the costs suffered by a party due to the activities (production or consumption) of another are uncompensated or, conversely, where the benefits produced by the activities of one party are captured by another free of charge. The former is called a negative externality and the latter, a positive externality. Such uncompensated costs and benefits arise, and thus the market 'fails' to attain Paretian efficiency, because the profit mechanism only works according to private costs and benefits. Such uncompensated costs and benefits become therefore social costs borne or social benefits reaped by third parties. Figure 1.1 depicts graphically the externalities produced by the production activities for a product X. The demand curve D represents the social marginal valuation of the consumers for X. The supply curve S_m reflects the private marginal cost incurred in producing X. The unregulated market equilibrium is E_m with the corresponding output being Q_m and market price being P_m. S_m, however, does not take account of the social cost or social benefit which should be added on or deduced (vertically) from the S_m curve to reflect the net social marginal cost, which is represented by S_n in the case of a pure negative externality with X having no social benefit (i.e. S_p is irrelevant) or S_p in the case of a pure positive externality with X having no social cost (i.e. S_n is irrelevant). Respectively, the socially efficient equilibria are E_n and E_p, which the unregulated market would not attain. Comparing with E_n and E_p, E_m incurs inefficiency respectively for producing too much by the amount Q_m-Q_n at too low a price by P_n-P_m and too little by the amount Q_m-Q_p at too high a price by P_m-P_p. The standard Pigovian solution would be a tax which brings S_m up to S_n for a pure negative externality or a subsidy (a negative tax) which brings S_m down to S_p for a pure positive externality so that the socially efficient equilibrium E_n or E_p can be attained. Alternatively, a maximum quota of Q_n and a minimum quota of Q_p would be set for the negative and positive externalities. The Pigovian tradition typically interprets 'pollution' as a kind of negative externality.

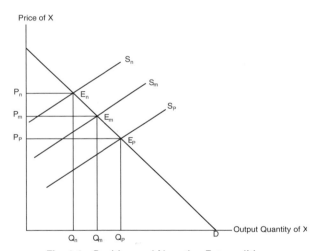

Fig. 1.1   Positive and Negative Externalities

Although the Pigovian policy solutions involve the imposition of extra constraints for market operation, they do not directly interfere with the spatial and internal aspects of production. While the planner may tend to acknowledge the existence of externalities and accept the need to tackle them, he or she is seldom given the authority to impose a pollution tax, grant an incentive subsidy or set a production quota. The planner, however, does possess a host of land use intervention tools which regulate the location, dimension, intensity, time, duration and process of the production or reception of externalities. Examples include land use restrictions, planning conditions, building codes, environmental standards, etc. Often such regulations are adopted and enforced by a zoning plan.

Public goods are those goods or services which the free market is believed to be inherently disinterested in providing an adequate amount, if any at all. The reason is that for certain types of goods, consumption is 'joint' and not exclusive. For instance, consumption of a movie is joint among viewers. The marginal cost of showing a movie to one more person is zero (up to the point of full seating). In such a situation, efficient resource allocation requires zero pricing and this deters the private sector. Besides, consumers would pretend that they have no demand for the goods in the hope that they could 'free ride' on the payment by other consumers. In the case of exclusive consumption, however, consumers will not conceal their real preferences as they would be unable to obtain the goods. The classic economic example of the free ride problem is national defence. While all citizens in a polity require collective security services, individual citizens when asked to pay for military expenditure on a voluntary basis may well deny their needs in the expectation that someone else would pay for the service. Hence there is a need for government as a coercive monopoly of violence to compel payment through the tax system and allocate resources to national defence. The same argument could be applied to many community services like education and open space.

Technically, public goods are jointly consumed, i.e. the aggregate demand curve for a public good is the vertical summation of individual demand curves (Figure 1.2). This implies joint consumption. However, the aggregate demand curve for a private good is obtained by horizontal summation, implying exclusive consumption (Figure 1.3). In many instances of planning intervention, goods which are private in nature — consumption of which is exclusive — are nevertheless treated by policy as if they are public goods. That is to say, payment for them is not directly, overtly or fully borne by the consumer through the private market but by government which in turn compels payment largely from the tax paying public through a fiscal regime. The typical examples in planning are: public housing; public open space and roads in general (largely borne by the tax paying public who pay the difference between the opportunity costs of road space and expenses, such as licence fees, registration fees, etc. recovered from vehicle users). These goods are either purely private or at least they become private above a certain technical limit of utilization when 'congestion' arises. Again zoning is a principal means to organize the spatial allocation of public goods.

Theoretical origins of planning as an interventionist endeavour

From the historical perspective, the post-World War II rise of planning as a profession dealing with the techniques, activities, procedures and management of government interventions in spatial and socio-economic affairs in

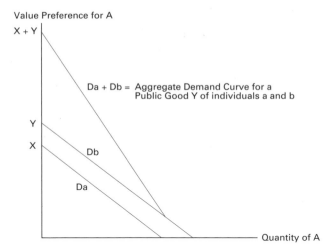

Fig. 1.2 Aggregate Demand Curve for a Public Good

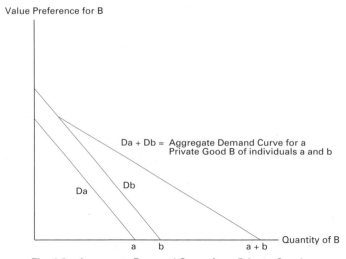

Fig. 1.3 Aggregate Demand Curve for a Private Good

terms of the issues of externalities and public goods was heavily influenced by European pre-war economic thought and political experience. It is noteworthy, for example, that when Leninist-Stalinist central economic planning and Nazi totalitarian 'National Socialism' were being pursued at all costs in the 1920s and 1930s, the Cambridge Professors of Economics, A.C. Pigou and J.M. Keynes were writing their famous interventionist treatises that revolutionized the libertarian neo-classical tradition. Pigou's *The Economics of Welfare* (1932) provides justifications for government intervention on resource allocation efficiency grounds, whereas Keynes's *The General Theory* (1936) offers 'short run' solutions to macro-economic problems of unemployment and stagnation. Political sentiments leading to the Dawes plan providing loans to the Weimer Republic and the New Deal in the USA were surely conducive to the intellectual acceptance of such free world versions of market reformation as an alternative to the Marxist market displacement model.

Post-war economic recovery in the West and the associated suburbanization process provided fertile ground for putting into practice the interventionist thoughts of Pigou and Keynes. In the developing world, there was also a similar drive towards intervention. Some countries, like the People's Republic of China, imported the Soviet planning model en bloc. Others, leaning towards the West, did almost the same under the guise of Pigovian and Keynesian economic management. In the 1950s and 1960s the planning paradigm was determinedly interventionist. Against this intellectual ethos, Frederick Von Hayek's polemic and libertarian attack in *The Road to Serfdom* (1946) and *The Constitution of Liberty* (1960) was an odd and lonely voice. Similarly, Ronald Coase's '*The Problem of Social Cost*' (1960) that disputed the Pigovian approach had little audience among planners in the British Commonwealth planning regimes.

The rise of 'property rights economics' in America, ensuing from Ronald H. Coase's seminal papers on transaction costs, particularly 'The Nature of the Firm' (1937) and 'The Problem of Social Cost' (1960), has led to the growth of anti-interventionist libertarian thinking in the field of economics in North America and Western Europe. As opposed to the Pigovian 'market failure' concept, notions like 'public failure' (Wolf 1987), 'non-market failure' and 'staatsversagen' (the German idea of state failure) (Janicke 1990) have emerged. In the field of environmental planning in particular, the concept of 'market environmentalism' (Kwong 1990) predicated on 'liberalization', 'de-regulation', 'privatization', and 'user charges' has created a new intellectual tradition competing with the Pigovian school. The demise of planned economies with the collapse of the Soviet Union and other communist regimes in Eastern Europe and success of the 'Chicago School' in capturing Nobel Prizes in economics have also produced a political and academic environment which fosters further development in this direction.

Objectives

Within the Coasian paradigm of transaction costs and Steven N.S. Cheung's interpretation of this concept (1990) that social institutions (including the government) are outcomes of public choice to reduce transaction costs, this book attempts to contribute to the existing intellectual discourse on zoning. This agenda is to be achieved by establishing a holistic property rights framework.

Within this framework, the economic literature on zoning could be critically reviewed and the dual character of zoning could be tested, on the basis of the following hypotheses:

(a) zoning as a government means to assign exclusive property rights can constrain rent dissipation, which would occur under a system of common property rights under competition, and at the same time facilitate market transactions, and hence maximize property value;

(b) zoning as a government planning intervention instrument would attenuate[3] private property rights over the best possible (most valuable) social uses of land in the following senses:

   (i) removal and/or subtraction of assigned rights over land entitlement and/or uses (whether such uses are specified or left unspecified initially) by the government act of downzoning, and other development rights (like requirements for joint development, restrictions on subdivision — with/without taking, eminent domain, compulsory resumption/ acquisition; etc.) made under the so-called process of 'forward planning'; and

   (ii) supersedure of private decision about the transfer, change or resolution of conflict of rights over land entitlement and/or uses (whether such uses are specified or left unspecified initially) by government decision made under the so-called process of 'development control', in other words, private formation of contracts are superseded by government edicts.

This book is an interdisciplinary endeavour, drawing intellectual insights from the fields of economics, planning and law. Coasian transaction costs-based property rights analysis provides the synthesis of various concepts of zoning from various disciplines. A glossary of terms is given in Appendix 1.

Organization and methodology

Establishing a coherent property rights framework

This book seeks to achieve the objectives mentioned above by establishing a coherent framework of zoning using conventional property rights paradigms in Chapter 2. This framework provides the context against which the literature on economics of zoning is reviewed in Chapter 3. The framework presented in Chapter 2 should be able to provide a more meaningful interpretation and evaluation of the zoning or using concept of Coasian ideas. However, it avoids an extreme interpretation of the Coasian paradigm as an apology against all government regulations, there being some key differences in ideas between Coase and the Coasians, which are revealed in Chapter 3. In addition, it also closes some gaps in the Coase theorization, notably the neglect of 'extension' as an ontological attribute of land.

Although the Coasian approach is positivist, some followers of Coase have formulated normative ideas which favour deregulation. In the economic discourse on zoning, while the Pigovian scholars like Baumol (1972), Crone (1983), and Fisher and Peterson (1987) continue to return analytical and empirical support for their theoretical constructs, Coasian researchers like Crecine (1967), Siegan (1970, 1972), Maser, Riker and Rosett (1977), Fischel (1978, 1979, 1980), Mark and Golberg (1981), Anderson (1982), and Benson (1984) provide directly opposite views with empirical evidence. These views are well received[4] by some real estate researchers like Harris and Douglas Moore (1984). Zoning is considered to be either undesirable or useless in improving efficiency. By implication, its abolition, or 'dezoning' or 'non-zoning' (Siegan 1970) would bring greater efficiency.

The propensity to condemn zoning categorically raises a number of fundamental questions. To begin with, why does society choose this institution?[5] Besides, how does this institution relate to Coase's presupposition of the existence of the market or, more generally, a private property rights system in his analysis of the trade of pollution rights? What is the position of this approach towards the 'non-zoning' in Houston (Siegan 1970), and the British planning system, which is said to be without zoning other than the British 'enterprise zones'[6] or the Chinese 'special economic zones?'[7] These questions are addressed in Chapter 2 which seeks to clarify the property rights nature of zoning. As mentioned above, the focus of property rights analysis is placed upon transaction costs. The conceptual framework presented here uses the most important version of the Coase Theorem to explain the dual character of zoning in terms of (a) the transformation of a state of extreme common property rights or anarchy to a state of exclusive property rights by assigning certain rights and (b) the attenuation of pre-existing rights over land. These concepts explain the institutional persistence of zoning. A series of conceptual drawings[8] are used to help explain the evolution of the concept of zoning from anarchy to a situation with government planning. The historical transition of the land pattern of Junction Road area, Kowloon, is demonstrated by a series of government 'demarcation district' plans, survey plans and town plans.

A broad definition of zoning is adopted to turn zoning into a government activity or process amenable to the empirical tests within the property rights framework. Zoning is understood broadly as government delineation and/ or restriction of exclusive property rights over land within certain spatial confines. This concept has three advantages. Firstly, it covers 'extension',[9] an ontological attribute of land apparently overlooked by Coase himself when he discusses land matters or zoning regulation. Secondly, it covers both forward planning and development control. The existing economic analysis of zoning, only deals mainly with the latter aspect of planning. Thirdly, alternative modes of government spatial regulation of land are understood as different forms of zoning. Thus, the ordinary meaning of zoning as a government planning and regulatory measure becomes a special case. The broad concept of transaction costs proposed by Demsetz is applied in order to encompass different modes of property rights.

There is an argument claiming that initial assignment of exclusive property rights over land by zoning is superior to the situation of common property rights, provided always that the transaction costs involved are not prohibitive. This argument is subject to analytical and empirical scrutiny here. The theoretical focus is that exclusive property rights can constrain rent dissipation.

The economic rationale of subsequent attenuation is conceivable within the Coasian concept of the nature of the firm as an institution that supersedes the market (Coase 1937). Whereas a private firm is always efficient due to competition[10], government as a special kind of firm or a 'super-firm'[11] may have 'inefficient' zoning policies due to political constraints.

Whether zoning as a means used by government planners to attenuate private property rights over the most valuable use of land is efficient and hence 'desirable' in terms of maximization of social wealth, subject to the constraint of transaction costs, is a question that has no *a priori* answer. It is contingent upon whether the increase in transaction costs for private landusers due to forward planning and development control are sufficiently offset by (a) the savings in the transaction costs of private solution over the transfer, change or conflict of rights over land entitlements and/or uses, and (b) the enlargement of the land market. In other words, it is more of an empirical, cost-benefit question rather than an *a priori* one. Where planning could reduce transaction costs, government as a kind of firm justifiably supersedes the market in dealing with changes of land entitlements and uses. Two groups of empirical hypotheses are derived for testing each character of zoning.

Chapter 2 also presents a succinct account of a market failure interventionist justification for zoning which is juxtaposed with the property rights explanation. It also gives the configuration of the zoning regime of Hong Kong in terms of the property rights framework to provide the context for the literature review in Chapter 3, and the empirical tests in Chapters 4 and 5. Historical details of the zoning system of Hong Kong are kept to a minimum because they have been competently documented by Bristow (1984) and Wong (1986). An institutional economics analysis of planning procedures is found in Staley (1994).

Literature review

The literature review (Lai 1994)[12] is a discourse about a host of analytical and empirical journal articles, monographs and books. Following the standard academic practice in the review of economic literature, an 'anachronic'

Photograph 1   Hong Kong in the 1960s (Courtesy of the Hong Kong Government)

Photograph 2   Hong Kong in the 1990s (Courtesy of the Hong Kong Government)

These photographs reveal the rapid pace of urban growth of Hong Kong and Kowloon as seen from the Peak.

(structural) (Leslie 1970) and 'modernist' approach is adopted to inquire into the ideas of two leading economic paradigms (Kuhn 1962) of zoning. The methodological issues of this approach[13] and a brief introduction to the two 'paradigms' or 'schools' of thought about zoning is given below. The name 'school' or 'tradition' properly applies to both groups of scholars adopting Pigovian and Coasian paradigms by virtue of their methodology and systematic treatment of the subject.

The Pigovian paradigm refers to the articulation of the concept of 'external effects' ('neighbourhood effects' or 'externalities'). As mentioned above, an externality is a kind of market failure. To reiterate, it arises where the costs suffered by a party due to the activities of another is uncompensated or, conversely, where the benefits produced by one party are captured by another without compensation. The former is called a negative externality and the latter a positive one. The Pigovian tradition typically describes pollution as a kind of negative externality. Such uncompensated costs and benefits would create economic inefficiency. The reason held by Pigovian economists is that as the market only responds to private costs and benefits, the market would fail to equate marginal value and marginal social costs, which is required as a condition for Paretian economic efficiency. They therefore argue that the state or government should intervene in the market so as to correct the inefficiency. While Pigou proposes the use of a tax (and hence the 'Pigovian tax') in the case of pollution, Buchanan and Tullock (1975) in their review of the Pigovian pollution tax scheme suggest that physical controls like quota are more suitable in some situations. The Pigovians' theorization on zoning follows this opinion. Zoning is interpreted as a kind of physical control which corrects market failure of externality. In fact, another welfare economic concept of market failure, viz public good (Samuelson 1955), can also be applied to justify land use planning. However, this has rarely been rigorously attempted.[14]

The Coasian paradigm[15] begins with Coase's attack on the concept of social cost in his 1960 paper. He illustrates that 'harmful effects' in land use are actually reciprocal[16] in terms of the parties' rights to use land. Furthermore, they can trade their rights until they reach a solution which entails joint and individual wealth maximization. In other words, the parties involved can attain the most efficient level of resource allocation where pollution, now interpreted as a factor of production[17], is also optimal. Coase's analysis is expressly stated as one in which 'the operation of a pricing system is without cost'.[18] This expression is termed as 'the cost of using the market mechanism'[19] in 'The Nature of the Firm' (1937) and later described as 'transaction costs' in the field of economics.

Coase's 1960 paper and his earlier works (Coase 1937, 1959) have stimulated in microeconomics the growth of property rights analysis with a focus on the implications of positive transaction costs on the choice of institutional arrangements: families, firms, government and the like and resource allocation.

Harold Demsetz (1967) has extended the concept of transaction costs and refer it to all costs other than those in a Robinson Crusoe (one-person) world.[20]

Zoning as a means to constrain rent dissipation

To test the social contribution of zoning as a means to assign exclusive property rights, the case of Hong Kong's Marine Fish Culture Zone (MFCZ) Ordinance, which establishes and assigns certain exclusive property rights over ocean fish, normally over-exploited as a common property, is investigated in Chapter 4 (Lai 1992, 1993[A], 1993[B]).[21] The empirical hypotheses are as follows:

(i)   the fall in rent (fish output) as a result of deteriorating (water) quality in MFCZ is less than that in common property areas (in-shore fishing grounds) due to dissipation in the latter;

(ii) the capital kept (fish reared) in more polluted zones (MFCZ) are lower in return (prices) than those in less polluted zones (MFCZ) or those kept (captured) in common property areas (off-shore fishing grounds);

(iii) the rent (queues for licences) for the more polluted zones (MFCZ) are smaller (shorter) than those for less polluted zones (MFCZ); and

(iv) more pollution-resistant capital (fish) are kept in the more polluted zones (MFCZ) than in the less polluted ones.

Economics as a science of human choice has a high level generalization: what is applicable to apples[22] and oranges, wheat and cattle,[23] bees[24] and fish is also applicable to all other scarce goods. Maximization behaviour is viewed not only as applicable to human beings, but also for animals (Hirshleifer 1977). Rules of competition for them may however vary. In the case of land resources, zoning is a means to constrain competition.

Marine zoning is investigated because in the real world, there are seldom cases of extreme common property rights over land property. The classic common property rights analysis commences with the subject of ocean fish. They are however analytical and conjectural (Gordon 1954; Scott 1955; Turvey 1964; Fullenbaum et al. 1972; Gould 1972; Smith 1972; Lawson 1988). Subsequent empirical analysis uses oysters (Angello and Donnelley 1975) as the test object. It should be pointed out that marine fish culture of Hong Kong has been neglected by property rights experts who advocate property rights assignment over common property.[25]

To evaluate zoning in terms of property rights delineation in land is consistent with the more general public choice thesis that government is the ultimate protector of the property rights of its subjects (Lai 1987).[26] Property rights over land is one of the most important property rights. Zoning cannot be discussed meaningfully in economic terms without reference to its relationship to property rights over land.

Zoning as a means to attenuate private property rights

To test the impacts of zoning as a means to attenuate private property rights, some aspects of Hong Kong's zoning practice are investigated in Chapter 5. The testable hypotheses are as follows:

(i) comprehensive development areas (CDA)[27] (and/or areas with Master Layout Plans) have less (i.e. smaller percentages of) environmental complaints than areas outside CDA (testing impact on externalities);

(ii) CDA have smaller rent variances than areas outside CDA (testing impact on externalities);

(iii) CDA development under unitary ownership is more efficient than under multiple ownership.

(iv) downzoning (reduction in plot ratio) has created a significant rise in the expected value of residential development (G.F.A.) (testing impact on externalities);

(v) planning areas with more (greater percentages of) building plans (numbers/G.F.A.) vetted under the development control (statutory planning application) process tend to have less (smaller percentages of) environmental complaints than districts with less (testing impact on externalities);

(vi) the urban-rural rent gradients have become more elastic (less steep) with the inception of statutory planning in the New Territories (testing impact on market enlargement); and

(vii) in the New Territories, the volume of land transactions have significantly increased with the inception of statutory planning (testing impact on market enlargement).

The first hypothesis, being more general, is tested by case studies whereas the other more specific hypotheses are tested by more formal analyses. While categorical judgements can be made for the tests in the preceding chapter, it is not argued that the test results in Chapter 5 are in the same sense conclusive of the general nature of zoning interpreted as a means to attenuate private property rights. As it is argued in Chapter 2 and reiterated in Chapter 3, this position is inevitable as questions on this aspect of zoning are case-specific. What is more fundamental is that these hypotheses raise meaningful questions for the policy makers about the zoning system of Hong Kong.

Conclusion

Chapter 6 discusses main methodological issues and makes recommendations for policy development and further research for Hong Kong. The discussion will be based on the implications of the results from empirical tests of rights assignment and attenuation in the preceding chapters. There is also an epilogue about the Coasian view of zoning.

The methodology adopted in carrying out the empirical tests in Chapters 4 and 5 is one of the Popperian falsification approach. This approach would only expect that the hypothesis asserted is either 'falsified' or 'not falsified' but would never claim that the hypothesis is 'confirmed'. If a hypothesis is falsified, then there are *prima facie* grounds to reject it. If it is not falsified, then there are *prima facie* grounds to accept it. In either case, there is no claim that alternative explanation is not possible. However, the fact that there could be competing explanations does not alter the interpretation of the factual results within the asserted hypothesis. It is up to the proponents of the competing explanation to prove their case or to show that their case is 'not falsifiable' by facts. An example serves to illustrate this point. If the hypothesis is that 'Peter will not come if it rains tomorrow', then this hypothesis 'is falsified' when Peter does come when it really rains. This result does not preclude the explanation that Peter comes only because he can find an umbrella.

Notes

1. The apparent lack of zoning in the United Kingdom is dealt with in Chapter 2.
2. See various articles in *Town Planning Review* 56, No. 4, 1985.
3. Unless otherwise specified, this term is used throughout the book in a positive sense without passing normative judgements regarding its desirability.
4. For a general and critical review of the American zoning system, see Dickson, A. 'A Critical Review on American Zoning System.' *Land Economics* 62, No. 4 (November 1986): 201–230.
5. Fischel asks a similar question, but he presupposes that zoning is inherently inefficient and asks the question 'if zoning is so inefficient, why does it persist'. See Fischel, William A. 'A Property Rights Approach to Municipal Zoning.' *Land Economics* 54 (February 1978), p. 65. It is considered that Fischel's answer in attempting to free ride on other people's property is too restrictive.
6. These zones are designated under s.32, para. 1 of the United Kingdom *Local Government Planning and Land Act* 1980.
7. These zones are established under the Guangdong Province Special Economic Zones Regulations, August, 1980 of the People's Republic of China.
8. For the use of conceptual drawing in economic literature, see Coase R.H. 'The Nature of the Firm.' *Economica* n.s. 4 (November 1937): 348 (reprint in *Readings in Price Theory*, published for the American Economic Association, R.D. Irwis, 1952), and Yang, Xiaobai et al. 'A Microeconomic Mechanism for Economic Growth.' *Journal of Political Economy* 99 (1991): 470. Diagramatic illustrations of economic analysis of land use zoning are best summarized in Heikkila, Eric 'Using Simple Diagrams to Illustrate the Economics of Land Use Zoning.' *Journal of Planning Education and Research* 8 (No. 3, 1989): 209–214. See Misczynski,

Dean J. 'Land-Use Controls and Property Values.' in Hagman, Donald G. and Misczynski, Dean J. ed. *Windfalls for Wipeouts: land value capture and compensation.* Chapter 5 (pp. 75–109) Washington: Planners Press, 1978; and Fischel, William A. 'A Property Rights Approach to Municipal Zoning.' *Land Economics* 54 (February 1978): 64–81, and 'Equity and Efficiency Aspects of Zoning Reform.' *Public Policy* 27 (No. 3, 1979): 301–331.

9. See Note 30, Chapter 3.

10. Coase argues that in a competitive system, there would be 'an optimum of planning'. See Coase, Ronald H., 'The Institutional Structure of Production.' Sweden: Royal Swedish Academy of Science, 1991, p. 7.

11. See Coase, R.H. 1960, op. cit., p. 17, also in Coase, R.H. 1988 op. cit., p. 117.

12. Lai, Lawrence W.C. 'The Economics of Land Use Zoning: A Literature Review and Analysis of the Work of Coase.' *Town Planning Review* 65 (No. 1, 1994): 77–98. The published version includes all the contents of Chapter 2 and the Pigovian model described in Chapter 1.

13. There are three common approaches in reviewing more than one piece of literature. The first method is to investigate texts one after another, an arrangement commonly used in encyclopaedias such as the *International Encyclopaedia of the Social Sciences* (1969). The second method is a chronological review of each author's contribution. The third and the approach adopted here is an anachronic (structural) study of various 'lines of thought', 'schools of thought' or 'traditions'. Unlike the previous two methods, this approach does not stress individual texts or authors, but their significance in a body of knowledge that merits a holistic treatment as a discipline on its own.

14. For an synoptic account, see Lai, L.W.C., 'The Role of Land Use Planning — An Economic Exposition.' *The Hong Kong Surveyor* 3 (No. 2, Fall, 1987) p. 6 and 'Some Fallacies of Incompatible Land Uses — A Libertarian Economic Exposition of the Issues of Land Use Zoning.' *The Hong Kong Surveyor* 6 (No. 2, Fall, 1990) p. 18. For informal justifications of planning in general, see Stewart, M. 'Markets, Choice and Urban Planning.' *Town Planning Review* 44 (1973): 203–220, Oxley, M.J. 'Economic theory and Urban Planning.' *Environment and Planning* A7 (1975): 497–508, Moore. T. 'Why Allow Planners To Do What They Do? A justification from economic theory.' *American Institute of Planners Journal* 44 (1978): 387–398, Klosterman, R.E. 'Arguments For and Against Planning.' *Town Planning Review* 56 (1985): 5–20 and Sager, Tore. 'Why Plan? A Multi-Rationality Foundation For Planning.' *Scandinavian Housing and Planning Research* 9, No. 2 (August 1992): 129–147. Alexander, Ernest R. *Approaches to Planning,* 2nd ed., 2nd printing. USA: Gorden and Breach Science Publishers, 1993, especially pp. 121–124. It is unfortunate that Alexander's reference to Hardin's 'tragedy of the commons' does not lead to any serious thoughts about situations where interventionist planning could reduce private property to conditions akin or close to the 'tragedy of the commons'. None of these articles or books, however, addresses the economic critique of the approach or the nature of zoning. For a recent attempt to justify the economic contribution of planning in terms of property rights, see Lai, Lawrence W.C. 'The Property Rights Justifications for Planning

and a Theory of Zoning,' *Progress in Planning: Recent Research in Urban and Regional Planning*, Pergamon Press, UK, 48 (No. 3, 1997b): 161–246.

15. Victor P. Goldberg reminds economists that Coase's idea of the reciprocal nature of costs 'bear a striking similarity' to that of John R. Commons and John M. Clark's a century ago. See Goldberg Victor P. 'Toward an Expanded Economic Theory of Contract.' *Journal of Economic Issues* (March 1976): 45–61; and 'Commons, Clark, and the Emerging Post-Coasian Law and Economics.' *Journal of Economic Issues* (December 1976): 877–893.

16. See Coase, R.H. 'The Problem of Social Cost' *The Journal of Law and Economics* (October 1960): 35, also in *The Firm, the Market and the Law*. Chicago: University of Chicago Press, 1988, p. 120. Externalities are effects involuntarily imposed/conferred on a third party to a contract. They are hence also known as 'third party effects'. A discussion of externalities or social cost therefore involve at least three parties. The example of the conflict of interest between the cattle keeper and wheat farmer (say respectively party A and party B) in Coase's 1960 paper in fact involves four parties instead of just two. The four parties create a situation where externalities are bilateral. We can imagine that party A has a contract(s) with party C, the consumer of beef or dairy products, whereas B have a contract (s) with party D, the consumer of flour. Party A is a third party to the contract between party B and party D. Party B is a third party to the contract between party A and Party C. If the property rights are so assigned that party B can exclude party A's animals from grazing on party B's land, as in the law of trespassing, it can be argued that the contract between parties B and D causes a negative externality affecting A. If the property rights are so defined that party B cannot exclude party A's animals, as in the case of some societies where cattle are regarded as sacred, party B suffers from the contract between parties A and C. Coase discusses a situation where party A and party B in such a bilateral situation are free to negotiate or re-negotiate their rights and liabilities by an additional contract. This additional contract 'internalises' the externalities imposed on the original third parties. See Lai (1997a), ibid, note 14 above.

17. See Coase, R.H. 1960, op. cit., p. 44, also in Coase, R.H. 1988 op. cit., p. 155.

18. See Coase, R.H. 1960, op. cit., p. 2, also in Coase, R.H. 1988 op. cit., p. 97.

19. See Coase, R.H. 'The Nature of the Firm' *Economica*, n.s. 4 (November 1937): 39, also in Coase, R.H. 1988, op. cit., p. 6.

20. This broad concept is adopted in this book. See Demsetz, Harold 'Towards a Theory of Property Rights.' *American Economic Review* (May 1967): 347.

21. This Chapter has been published in two journals and is forthcoming in a third one. See Lai, Lawrence W.C. 'Marine Fish Culture and Pollution — An Initial Hong Kong Empirical Study.' *EKISTICS* Vol. 59 No. 356/357 (September/October-November/December 1992): 349–356; *Asian Economic Journal* Vol. VII (No. 3, 1993), pp. 333–351, and in *Planning and Development*, Vol. 9, No. 1, 1993, pp. 11–20.

22. See Cheung, Steven N.S., 'The Fable of the Bees: An Economic Investigation.' *The Journal of Law and Economics* 16 (April 1973): 11–33.

23. See Coase, R.H. 1960, op. cit.

24. See Cheung, Steven N.S. 1973, op. cit.

25. In Kwong, Jo Ann's *Market Environmentalism: Lessons for Hong Kong*, Hong Kong: Chinese University Press, 1990, for instance, marine fish culture is surprisingly omitted.

26. Lai, Lawrence W.C. 'Democracy and Political Protection of Property Rights'. Unpublished M.Soc.Sc. (Economics) dissertation, Department of Economics, University of Hong Kong, 1987.

27. The term 'comprehensive development area' (CDA) used in this book is not restricted to those lands statutorily zoned as such in 'Outline Zoning Plans' but also refers to those 'estate' type housing development whether or not they are governed by master layout plans.

Chapter Two

The Property Rights Nature of Zoning: A Theoretical Framework

It is theory that decides what we can observe. (Einstein, letter to Heisenberg)

Introduction

This chapter presents an interpretation of zoning in terms of received property rights concepts.[1] Zoning is at the political level given a very broad meaning to encompass all spatial arrangements in a polity. Zoning, as technically understood by town planners and economists, is regarded at the economic level as a means to replace private planning of proprietors in their exercise of private property rights by government planning of planners whose decisions are based on professional judgement. This economic characterization of zoning is consistent with Ronald Coase's ideas in 'The Nature of the Firm' (1937).[2] This chapter is divided into three sections. The first section provides an account of the historical transition of common property rights towards government zoning of land, followed by an exposition of a zoning model using Pigovian interventionist concepts. The second section presents a property rights synthesis of zoning, illustrating the dual nature of zoning as a state function in (a) assigning initial exclusive property rights, thereby constraining rent dissipation in a state of common property rights; and (b) attenuating private property rights, resulting in certain kinds of costs, notably those absorbed in rent-seeking behaviour, and benefits in terms of property value enhancement and environmental improvements. The evolution of the zoning system in Hong Kong is presented in terms of property rights concepts in the third section to provide a context for the analysis.

The transition from common property towards government zoning: a historical perspective

The Classical economists like Benard Mandeville[3] and Adam Smith[4] have forcefully exalted the social value of human rationality, i.e. selfishness nicely put: human organizations exist because selfish individuals find benefits in cooperating (whether in forming a family, or a business partnership). They also believe that free competition would save human beings from the evil excesses of selfishness: an individual or a firm will honour one's promises because if one fails to do so, one will lose business forever. These liberal economic thoughts, however, presuppose the prior existence of a government protecting a system of property rights (whether capitalist or socialist) because unrestrained competition in a state of anarchy would lead to rapid depreciation in the value of the object or prize of competition. Armen Alchian produces the thesis that competition arises when two or more people in a society want more of the same good (Alchian, 1965: 127; Alchian and Demsetz 1973: 16). The conflict due to competition must be resolved in one way or another. In Alchian's view, the rules which resolve the conflict are known as property rights. The relevant property right rules in our society include those common and statutory law rules in relation to land. They evolve as a means to constrain rent dissipation.

Common property rights

Common property rights is a state of affairs in which competition over the use of a good is unrestrained by agreed rules. In this situation the income derived from such use, i.e. rent, will be absorbed by the cost of competition. An example serves to illustrate this rational economic process. Imagine a situation where gold is discovered on an unclaimed island, the worth of the gold mine is $1 billion. In the absence of property rights and presence of perfect knowledge, people from the whole world would employ every means to acquire the maximum amount of gold for themselves. In that situation, 'might makes rights'.[5] Since the ensuing violence destroys both life and property, the cost of such competition is potentially enormous and at the limit, such costs would be equal to the total value of gold reserve (for instance $1 billion life insurance, medical and funeral payment) and hence the net social worth of the gold reserve would be zero.

　　Rent dissipation is the consequence of the absorption of income derived from the use of certain goods, land in the present context, by the cost of unrestrained competition. The competitive behaviour of the participants is called rent-seeking.

However, common property rights is not a stable system because it is inconsistent with the maximization postulate. Rational human beings will seek to minimize the dissipation of rent.

> If a property is truly 'common' in the sense that it is subject to unrestrained competition for its use, with no limit set on the number of competitors, then competition will reduce the rental value of that common property to zero. But in the real world this type of 'common' property can hardly be found in the case of a scarce resource. Survival of the fittest implies that certain arrangements must be adopted to reduce rent dissipation. (Cheung 1990: 22)

The true or polar case of true common property is the state of anarchy. Thomas Hobbe's *The Leviathan* gives an excellent characterization of anarchy, where 'might makes rights' (Umbeck 1981): life is 'solitary, poor, nasty, brutish and short'[6] (Hobbes). Hence rules of competition or property rights restraining dissipation in anarchy will emerge. The institution that achieves this is called a government (Lai 1987), the primary contribution of which is the enforcement of property rights (Demsetz 1964). Land resources are more scarce than ocean resources, therefore it is natural that exclusive property rights are developed earlier on land.

Formation of communal rights[7]

Human beings differ from most animals by having government of some form. Government as an authority backed by force is a social organization that constrains rent dissipation in anarchy. When human beings are hunter-gatherers, such government may be represented by the kin chief. His or her orders and associated mores and customs are rules to maximize the collective survival ability of the kin or tribe. The hunter-gatherers treat all land on earth as common (Figure 2.1). When competition among tribes (A, B and C in Figures 2.1, 2.2 and 2.3) for land as their source of income (in terms of food and other kinds of supply) becomes critical, shifting agriculture and hunting are replaced by settled agriculture and permanent settlement. The concept of boundary of influence becomes significant. States with definite territory and restricted entry then emerge. The state can be regarded as a 'super-zone'[8] belonging to the whole community. The zone boundary is defined usually by natural features like mountain ranges or rivers. As such, it is largely irregular in shape (Figure 2.2). Within the boundary of the state, which can be regarded as a collective land property protected by the government, common ownership or 'a communal right system' may persist. Alchian and Demsetz (1973) characterize this system:

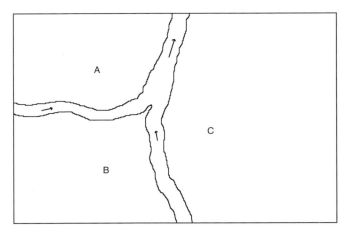

Fig. 2.1   Anarchy

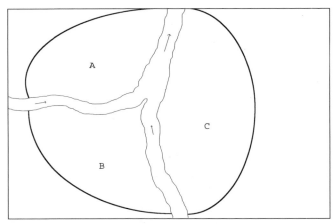

Fig. 2.2   Common Property Rights Within States as Super-zones

> Under a communal right system, each person has a private (exclusive)
> right to use of a resource once it is captured, but only a communal
> (non-exclusive) right to the same resource before it is taken. (Alchain
> and Demsetz 1974: 22) [Brackets mine].

The definition of Alchian and Demsetz actually presupposes the existence
of a government of some form that would protect both the private and
communal rights to the enjoyment of the resource and assumes away the
anarchic or Hobbesian situation where any captured rights may be forcibly
taken away: violence dictates who gets what (Umbeck 1981). Such communal
property rights envisaged by Alchian and Demsetz allow resources to be acquired
on a first-come-first-served basis. Resources are allocated, so to speak, by 'waiting'
(Barzel 1974).

The deserts occupied by the Hun Kahns are classic examples of super-zones[9] with near universal intra-communal rights. The Indians of the Labrador Peninsula who allowed free hunting on land owned by them collectively is well documented by Eleanor Leacock.[10] An example of the modern equivalent is the Libyan province of Tripolitania (Bottomley 1963).[11] The first-come-first-served rules are nevertheless inadequate when competition becomes more acute.

The rise of private property rights

Government usually creates 'sub-zones' by subdividing the states into areas retaining communal rights and areas with more sophisticated exclusive property rights, as division of labour entails spatial specialization in land uses. Indiscriminate application of communal rights becomes inappropriate. Typically, areas with sophisticated exclusive property rights are more urban and accessible. There, competition for 'scarce' land is keen and specialization in land uses is more intense. Communal rights are left either *de jure*, according to some rules prescribed by the state,[12] or *de facto*, where prescribed exclusive property rights rules become virtually unenforceable, in the rural and more remote areas. With such areal differentiation of the state's territory, land use zones naturally emerge. It is conceivable that the state's territory is broadly differentiated into towns or 'urban zones' and the countryside or 'agricultural zones'.

Within the former, there may be further differentiation between communal and institutional zones. From historical records, it is apparent that the zones with higher value, especially those in townships, are invariably smaller in size and more regular in shape (Figures 2.3(a), 2.3(b) and 2.3(c)). This reduces the transaction costs of the exchange of land rights and hence helps to expand the land market.

As regards the sophisticated exclusive property rights over land, the development of the doctrine of estates in feudal England and the evolution of the private land rights system in feudal China are cases in point. Feudalism, or indeed any system of political division of the state, can be regarded as a national zoning system decentralizing production decisions.

Complicated rules for the delineation, interpretation and enforcement are evolved to deal with the two different systems of land rights.[13] Sophisticated land law arises to delineate rights and to adjudicate disputes. The classic example of the most developed exclusive property rights or 'private property rights' over land is the fee simple absolute[14] in English land law and its equivalent in Chinese land law. Under private property rights,[15] the holder of the estate of fee simple has an exclusive right to use and to derive income from land within clearly delineated boundary, i.e. a zone without government-prescribed uses. The income obtained from the zone and the zone itself can be freely

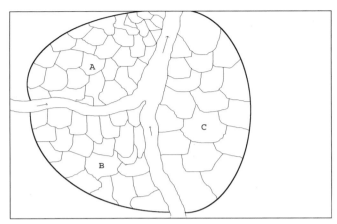

(a)   Subdivision of Private Land

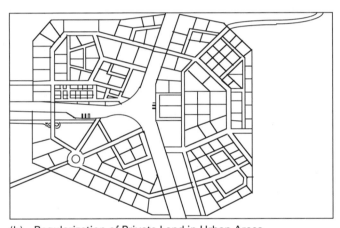

(b)   Regularization of Private Land in Urban Areas

Fig. 2.3(a) and (b)   Rise of Private Property Rights

disposed (alienated/transferred) in whole or in part (subdivision of land) or in combination with another piece of land (land assembly) for similar purposes. On-site planning by the landowner may be involved in the enjoyment of his private property rights. For instance, the landlord may decide to assign some portions of his property for wheat farming and others for cattle grazing. Where conflicts of rights to the land cannot be resolved by private negotiation, the court deals with them, developing as a result the tort law of nuisance in England. In China, conflicts were resolved arbitrarily by the bureaucracy instead of a common law system. With society becoming more developed and competition over land more intense, communal property rights over land are gradually replaced by more sophisticated exclusive property rights leading towards the formation of private property rights. The enclosure movement

Fig. 2.3(c)   Irregular Land Parcels (Junction Road Area Before Urbanization)

(Modified extract from DD Sheet No. S.D.1 Sheet 6, courtesy of the Lands Department, Hong Kong Government.)

This extract was part of 'Demarcation Survey' conducted by Indian surveyors after the New Territories was leased to the British in 1897. Note the highly irregular and intensively subdivided pattern of lots of land characteristic of Chinese customary landownership. The symbol X denotes the location of Hau Wong Temple.

in England[16] is a classic example. The Chinese people also have a long history of 'privatizing' land resources: feudalism was established in 2698 B.C. and domestication of fish started as early as 2000 B.C. (Lin 1940).[17] This was achieved by converting lakes under communal rights into private property, by excavating privately owned land or simply by combining fish culture and paddy farming on private land. The sophisticated 'zoning' pattern of agricultural land in China, which survive in parts of the New Territories in Hong Kong, bears witness to the evolution of this institution of exclusive property rights over land.[18] Sam Bass Warner's study (1962) of the suburbanization of Boston in the late nineteenth century indicates that several suburban land use patterns, often attributed to planning, in fact emerged without any planned zoning at all. While this case is often cited as a case showing the redundancy of planned zoning, it could equally be properly regarded as a prelude to planned zoning.

The rise of interventionist zoning: the replacement of private planning by government planning

Zoning, as boundary delineation and hence an integral part of the formulation of private property rights over land, becomes inadequate when the law of tort appears to fail to address the problem of conflict of rights over land[19] as a result of industrialization. Civil litigation using the tort law is expensive and cannot effectively deal with environmental problems involving a large number of parties. The notion of planned zoning prescribing uses for specific land areas emerges. Conceptually, this can be carried out initially by contract between government and individuals. In the case of Hong Kong, this has been put into practice since 1842 whereas lands zoned in terms of restrictive covenants or 'lease conditions' by the Land Authority are allocated as leasehold lots contractually by competitive auction or tender or by direct grant to individuals. The lease is a civil contract between the government and the proprietor. Either party may renegotiate the user clauses, tenancy period or premium involved in lease modification. To the extent that the leaseholds are allocated in accordance with a pre-specified street layout block plan (Figure 2.3(d)), an embryonic element of planning is involved. The engineers, often from the military, who produced such layout plans were the urban planners in practice before the modern professional town planners came into existence. Thus we may conceive the land disposal and management system that has evolved since 1842 as a kind of 'planning by contract' or consent.

Alternatively, such contractual obligations restricting use, intensity or boundary of development can be made by private individuals enforceable by the state as in the case of Houston (Siegan 1970). However, in the case where such exante zoning is not possible, deficient or is considered out of date,

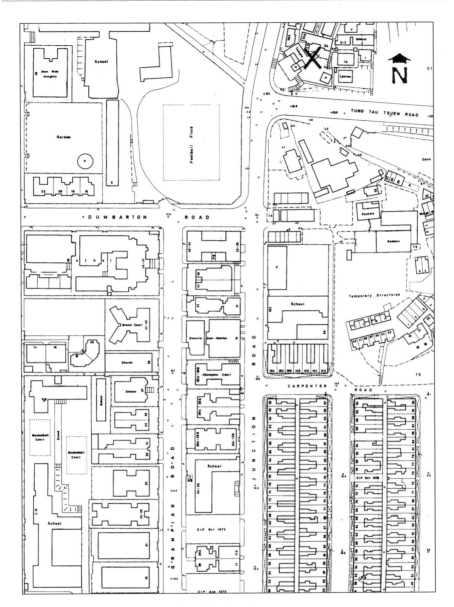

Fig. 2.3(d)   Regular Land Parcels (Junction Road)

(Modified extract from 1:1000 Survey Sheet 11-NW-15B, courtesy of the Lands Department, Hong Kong Government.)

This extract shows the modern rectilinear delineation of land property which compares strikingly with the 'indigenous' landownership pattern as shown in Figure 2.3(c). While the exact mechanism of transforming the state of affairs in Figure 2.3(c) to Figure 2.4(d) is unclear, the 'modern' practice adopted for new town development was by way of Letters A/B resumption. The symbol X denotes Hau Wing Temple as a reference point for comparison. Junction Road appears to have been developed on the basis of the pre-existing footpath found in Figure 2.3(c).

this is carried out by the conscious process of forward planning which involves as a zoning plan an end product (Figure 2.3(d)),[20] showing different prescribed types of uses for land in different location (Figure 2.4). Such prescribed uses override the uses chosen by the landlord under private property rights and are accompanied by restriction on the scale and intensity of development. Any change in the chosen use must be consistent with the designated types of uses, scale, and intensity of development.

(a)   Planned Zoning Reinforcing Pre-existing Land Use Pattern

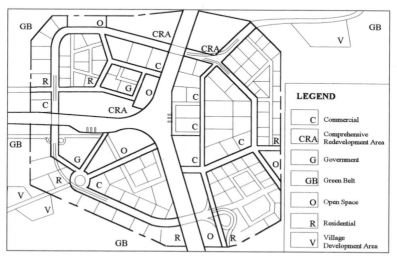

(b)   Planned Zoning Altering Pre-existing Urban Land Use Pattern and Involving Rural Area

Fig. 2.4(a) and (b)   Emergence of Government Zoning

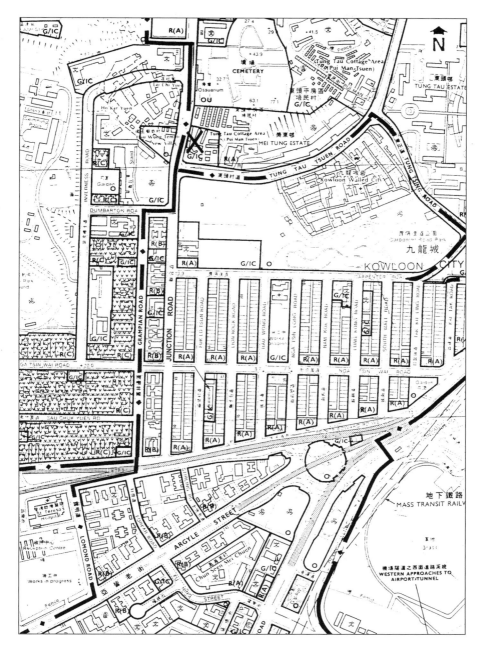

Fig. 2.4(c)   Planned Zoning Reinforcing Pre-existing Land Use Pattern

(Modified composite extracts of Outline Zoning Plans S/K8/8, S/K10/6 and LK/18/10A, courtesy of the Planning Department, Hong Kong Government.)

Note the Residential (Group) (R(C)) and Residential (Group B) (R(B)) zoning of the Grampian and Junction Road area, The symbol X denotes the location of Hau Wong Temple, zoned Government/Institution/Community (G/IC) in the statutory town plan.

Whether the chosen uses are consistent with the designated ones are determined by the planners in the development control process. A zone as such is therefore 'a zone with government-prescribed uses and development intensity.' While such prescription may or may not be the same as the existing uses on land, it is usually the case that the state-imposed uses and intensity of development follow the pre-existing one, taking into account the pre-existing zone boundaries planned by the owners. Planned zoning in Boston mentioned above is a case in point. This is nevertheless an attenuation of private property rights because the 'opportunity set' of rights are restricted to the uses specified by the planner. Apart from the infringement of the right to choose the best type of uses[21] within the zone, private property rights can be attenuated by the various measures prescribed for the zone:

(a) the rights of freedom to use and derive income from land can be attenuated by restrictions on the scale and intensity of development like density controls, plot ratio controls,[22] parking requirements, open space requirements, site coverage restrictions or development moratoria for conservation purposes, etc.;

(b) the rights to alienate land can be attenuated by requirement of joint development with the property of other owners (as in the case of the 'Comprehensive Development Area' designation under the Hong Kong Town Planning Ordinance which will be explained in later chapters) or; prohibition and control over subdivision of land.

While such restrictions on land use, development intensity and development boundary[23] are imposed by forward planning, they are implemented in the development control process. Through this process, the landowner or user may apply, or is required to apply, for an intended change in use, intensity of development, variation in the extension and scale of development. In essence, the freedom of the landowner in exercising their private property rights in this process is superseded by government determination.[24] In practical planning terms, this denotes the replacement of the developers' private solution by one involving government interference. A typology of property rights and methods of their attenuation is shown in Figure 2.5.

The British zoning system

It is a common view that the British town and country planning regime has no zoning elements,[25] other than a few 'enterprise zones'. This view can be seen to be incorrect. Not to mention the broad concept of zoning implicit in land law regarding boundary delineation, one can conceive each local planning area as one zone within which all development with a few exceptions, must go through the development control (planning application) procedure. The

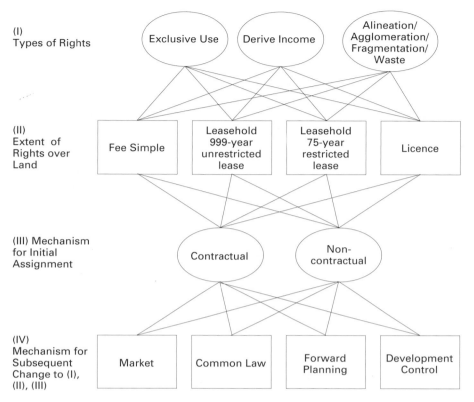

Fig. 2.5 Typology of Property Rights

British planning system therefore creates zones without clearly prescribed uses prior to planning. Implicit in the British development control system are forward planning considerations, rendering the absence of zoning apparent rather than real.

Pigovian justifications for zoning

This section presents Pigovian justifications[26] for government zoning, to provide reference points for juxtaposition with concepts about the nature of zoning based on the property rights reasoning presented above. While the land use types involved are described in Hong Kong terminology, the model itself is general enough to encapsulate the common features of most zoning systems in the world.

The most popular use of the social cost concept in land use planning is that some land uses are inherently incompatible and hence they need to be segregated by zoning. Consider three classes of activities: industrial, residential and commercial. In the absence of planning, we may imagine a possible world or natural state of random distribution of such activities as schematically depicted in Figure 2.6. Implicitly, the parties involved are not able to come to a better solution by mutual agreement as in the wheat farming example described by Coase in 'The Problem of Social Cost'.[27] The apparently chaotic land use and building patterns of the Kowloon Walled City (Photograph 3), the sovereignty over which was uncertain until resolved by the Land Commission, are often ascribed by planners to be the outcome of lack of planning control.

						Legend	
R	C	I	R	R	C		
I	I	R	I	C	R	R	Residential
R	C	I	C	I	C	I	Industial
C	R	C	I	R	I	C	Commercial

Fig. 2.6   Natural State of Random Spatial Distribution of Activities

Land use planning is meant to prevent this natural state of random land uses, and hence associated chaos, from occurring. Zoning is conceptually a two-step process. Firstly, activities are grouped into classes, i.e. land use zones, which are given certain identity labels like 'Industrial (I)', 'Residential (R)' and 'Commercial (C)', as depicted in Figure 2.7. Secondly, such land use zones are rationally arranged[28] in spatial terms on a zoning plan with the purpose of preventing uses which are considered incompatible from interfering with each other. Uses which are considered mutually beneficial and hence compatible as in the case of Residential and Commercial may be put side by side. An example is given in Figure 2.8. The Industrial Zone is segregated from the Residential Zone in the upwind direction with a Commercial Zone as a buffer, with the objective of minimizing environmental nuisance of the Industrial Zone. A buffer, ideally, creates positive externalities between two uses which exert negative externalities upon each other. In other words, the planner seeks to:

(i)   separate incompatible production and consumption activities via exclusive use zoning with or without buffer areas;

(ii) integrate compatible production and consumption activities via mixed use zoning; and

(iii) stipulate positive and restrict negative external effects via development control measures such as planning conditions, development bonus, environmental performance standards and moratoria.

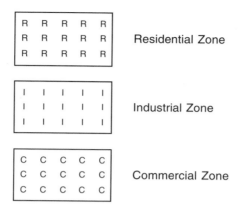

Fig. 2.7   Grouping of Activities into Classes or Zones

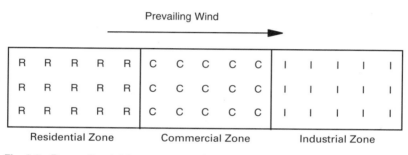

Fig. 2.8   Proper Spatial Arrangement of Land Use Zones Without Public Goods

The professional competence of the land use planner in the above process, 'forward planning' as opposed to the subsequent 'development control' stage, can be assessed in terms of (a) the accuracy in reserving the right quantity of land for each type of land use zones at the right time at the right location and (b) the appropriateness of spatial arrangement in such zones. In Hong Kong, the town planner takes care of these aspects by referring to the administrative policy document, the Hong Kong Planning Standards and Guidelines (HKPSG), in their professional practice. 'Poor planning' is usually an evaluative judgement regarding these quantitative land reservation and qualitative spatial arrangements.

In the Hong Kong planning system where open space and community facilities are financed by government in accordance with the planning stand-ards,[29] it is easy to introduce a 'public good' argument for zoning as well: zoning is a means by which the town planner reserves adequate land in suitable location for development of open space (zoned 'O') and community facilities (zoned 'GIC'). In addition roads and mass transit railways are also treated as 'public goods'.[30] Diagrammatically, this is shown in Figure 2.9, which modifies

Figure 2.8. The 'O' and 'GIC' zones are introduced and used as buffers. The area is also served by a public road and a mass transit railway. The reserves for the road and the railway are zoned on the statutory town plan. In other words, the planner also seeks to:

(iv) reserve land via zoning or require planning conditions for uses such as open space and natural reserve[31] which produce positive externalities.

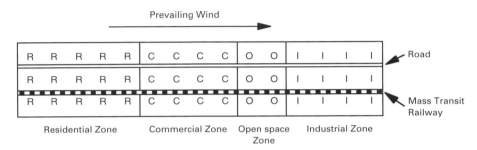

Fig. 2.9 Proper Spatial Arrangement of Land Use Zones With Public Goods

Photograph 3 Kowloon Walled City Before Demolition (Courtesy of the Hong Kong Government)

This photograph is often used to illustrate the effect of planning intervention or government-led urban renewal projects. However, it could equally be used to illustrate the outcome of unclear specification of private property rights as there is no lease control for this area. Refer to Figures 2.10 and 2.11 for the land pattern.

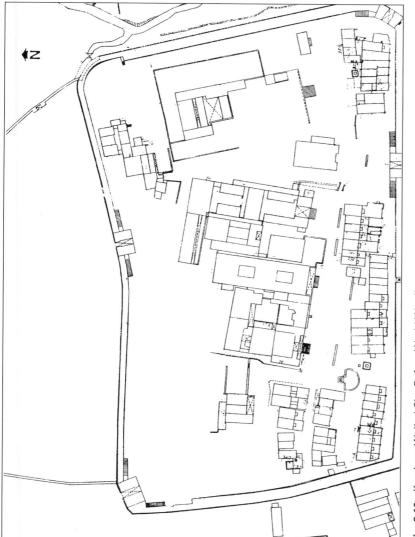

Fig. 2.10 Kowloon Walled City Before World War II

(Extract from Survey Sheet No. 137-NE-3 published in the year between 1922 and 1935, courtesy of the Lands Department, Hong Kong Government.)

This is the earliest Crown land survey record of the Walled City, the jurisdiction over which had been a contentious political issue until the 1984 Sino-British Joint Declaration. Then the city was mainly agarian with property ownership resembling the walled-settlements in other parts of the New Territories.

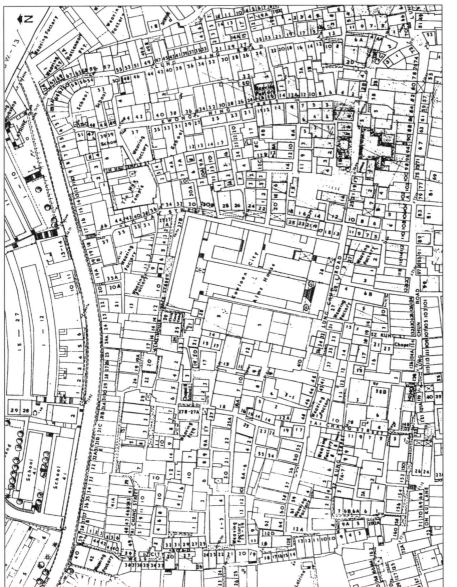

Fig. 2.11 Kowloon Walled City in 1961

(Modified extract from Survey Sheet No. 180-NW-1, courtesy of the Lands Department, Hong Kong Government.)

Note the intensive subdivision of land compared with the situation shown in Figure 2.10. Such uncontrolled subdivision manifested vertically in the form of haphazard and congested high-rise development as shown in Photograph 3. The superstructure of the City Walled has been zoned 'Open Space' (O) in the statutory town plan (see Figure 2.4(c)) and demolished except the Alms House, for development into a garden.

A property rights synthesis of zoning

Formation of private property rights by zoning

The state that emerges as a super zone within which individuals are protected is an apparatus to constrain rent dissipation under anarchy. Land within the state is further 'subzoned' as a result of spatial specialization in land uses due to division of labour. Private property rights supersede in due course communal property rights, further restraining rent dissipation and reducing the transaction costs of the land market through a process of regularizing land boundaries: a processing of rezoning. Private property rights permit the maximum degree of freedom of individual choice and decision making in the state is completely decentralized.

Private property rights are attenuated by government zoning controls which substitute private planning and decisions of individuals or firms about enjoyment and transfer of land rights with government planning decisions. Decision making in the state becomes more centralized as far as land matters are concerned. Such controls range from *contractual* obligations to *statutory* obligations restricting the use, intensity and boundary of development. Contractual obligations may be made between the state and individuals, as in the case of Hong Kong's leasehold system, described as 'planning by contract', as argued in the preceding sections before the inception of statutory zoning; or among individuals, as in the case of 'non-zoning' in Houston[32] (Siegan 1970). In Hong Kong, lands are zoned by the restrictive covenants or 'conditions' specified initially by the Crown lease (see the last section of this chapter), whereas lands in Houston are zoned in terms of restrictive covenants made by private negotiation, sub-division control which are 'zoning-like requirements' and a building code. Statutory obligations, imposed by planners, may be universally applied to all developments, as in the case of the British 'non-zoning' planning system, or selectively 'zoned' in the case of most zoning systems in the world including those in Hong Kong and New York. All the above variants of zoning, involve different degrees of private property rights attenuation. The Houston land system with subdivision restrictions is actually more restrictive than the 999-year unrestricted lease of Hong Kong which does not restrict subdivision. In any case, the concept of zoning adopted in this book finds it more meaningful to speak of different forms of zoning involving various degrees of private property right attenuation than to characterize planning systems in terms of a simple dichotomy between 'zoning' and 'non-zoning'. Otherwise one would find that 'non-zoning' in Houston must be accompanied by untidy qualifications in order to distinguish it from 'non-zoning' in the British planning system. This broad concept of zoning naturally encompasses Ellickson's land use control methods of
(1) 'mandatory public regulations' (zoning); and
(2) 'consensual private agreements' (covenants) (Ellickson 1973).

This characterization of zoning has evolved from a means of protecting the individuals collectively within a state to a means of attenuating individuals rights. It is consistent with the property rights concept that an institution, like the planning system, is a result of public choice.

To the extent that any land market presupposes the existence of land with clearly delineated boundary, zoning is implicit in all systems of property rights[33] over land protected by the state.[34] Without such boundary delineation, the transaction costs of measurement (valuation, land surveying etc.) and enforcement of rights over land would be prohibitively high, if possible at all. As such, zoning is significant as an attribute of property rights that constrains rent dissipation. This aspect of zoning has been neglected because theorists seldom relate establishment of property rights over land (communal, private or socialist), to the question of boundary delineation and the significance attached to the boundary by the state.[35] In a nutshell, the ontological attribute of 'extension'[36] in land has been neglected. When the 'market environmentalists' makes a plea for establishing private property rights over natural resources like forests and fish, they are indeed advocating zoning in one way or another by the state. Theorization about the impact of the private property rights upon rent dissipation is becoming more and more sophisticated. However, empirical testing of theoretical propositions are rare. This scarcity of empirical investigation is natural: there are few instances, especially in land matters, where goods and resources are held in a state of anarchy,[37] or under communal property rights.[38]

Zoning, however, is commonly perceived by planners as an interventionist instrument of government in ordering land uses. It seems that the economist's restrictive view of zoning may be influenced by the planner's perception of the concept, if not Coase's omission to apply Coase Theorem thoroughly.[39] Being pre-occupied with the effect of planning upon private property rights attenuation, the economists seldom consider the role of zoning in delineating private property rights and in establishing and enlarging the land market. This aspect is considered in Chapter 3.

The Pigovian exposition of land use zoning in the forward planning stage can be incorporated here without theoretical inconsistency. Like Coase's example of the newly discovered cave,[40] the rights of a newly formed piece of land must be clearly delineated if rent dissipation is to be constrained. One way to do so is by zoning, which provides an initial delineation of using rights.

The case of marine culture zone in Hong Kong provides a rare and hitherto neglected opportunity[41] for empirical analysis. Coastal fish capture in Hong Kong has been rapidly declining over the years. This phenomenon has been ascribed to the deterioration in water quality due to drastic increase in untreated domestic and industrial sewage as a result of rapid population and economic growth. There could be, however, an alternative explanation for the loss of fish yield: overfishing, which is a predictable economic outcome as ocean fish is a common property. An investigation is included in Chapter 4. It is not suggested that no equivalent analysis can be carried out for land property. In the case of Hong Kong, initial rights are allocated by land contract through price competition or direct grant rights from the early days of colonization. Such rights are subsequently attenuated by government zoning in modern times.

Attenuation of private property rights by zoning

It should be noticed that whether the property rights initially assigned by the state via zoning is 'optimal' or 'arbitrary', it is immaterial in applying the 'Invariance' version of the Coase Theorem, which is defined by Cheung as follows:

> If property rights are clearly delineated and if all costs of transactions are zero, then resource use will be the same regardless of who owns the property rights. (Cheung 1990: 11)

The reason is simple. If subsequent change in use or transfer of rights is left entirely to the market or if planning permission is always given costlessly, the market will resolve conflicts of interests in the absence of transaction costs and land will always be used in the best possible ways.

Where subsequent change is disallowed, land may not be used in the best possible ways. This has not been thought through by most market environmentalists who are preocccupied by the initial assignment of property rights. They should have asked the question: what would happen after the initial rights have been allocated? Where an area or zone is designated initially for commercial tree planting, can it be subsequently changed to wheat farming or market gardening if the latter becomes more valuable in the market? Where part of the seabed is zoned initially for commercial fish culture, can it be subsequently changed to oyster farming or raising seals, if the latter becomes more valuable? Where the countryside is zoned as green belts, conservation areas or country parks, can they be rezoned later for more profitable uses, like lumbering or suburban housing?

In the real world, of course, the planning system is not perfectly permissive. It does not work costlessly either. Therefore private property rights are either incomplete (where they are established by zoning *per se*) or attenuated (where they are superseded by subsequent zoning). Some rent will inevitably be dissipated.

Therefore, it will not be positive and meaningful to ask if zoning, as government intervention in the land market, assigns incomplete or attenuates private property rights because, clearly, it does. It will be more meaningful to ask if the cost of such attenuation is greater or smaller than the alternative of leaving the matter entirely to the unregulated market. This way of thinking is simply comparing the opportunity cost of alternative institutional arrangements, namely decisions made freely by individuals and firms *vis-à-vis* decisions made by planners.

Thus whether zoning is 'good' or 'bad', 'effective' or 'ineffective' must be a case-specific, content-specific, system-specific, and comparative question. It is not a general categorical or universal question. In other words, this question can only be meaningfully evaluated in terms of (a) the differences in the institutional design of different zoning systems or (b) changes in rights assignment within a given zoning system. This apparently unexciting but logical perspective is not yet popular among planning researchers. However, it does not mean that some generalizations predicated on inductive thinking is impossible. Three aspects are discussed in the following sections. Section A examines the extent of loss of value due to development control, with particular reference to planning application. A comparison is made between the UK system of 'non-zoning' and the Hong Kong system. Sections B and C briefly discuss the impact of zoning on land values and externalities respectively.

(A) *Extent of rent-dissipation in development control and planning applications*

Firstly, the choice of the extent of development control is significant in evaluating the potential rent dissipation of the landowners' property right. Development control is the process through which the intent of zoning is safeguarded. Typically, it involves the need for planning applications.

While both the Coasian and Pigovian economists tend to evaluate the impact of zoning regulation as being given or exogenously determined by government, in practice, any zoning system must allow certain degree of flexibility to respond to the forces of the market. From the theoretical point of view, Pigovian theorization does not eliminate the market *en bloc* but to 'correct' it. The property rights theoretical explanation is that planning control reduces the transaction costs of the land market under private property rights and complete displacement of private property rights is only an extreme possibility.

In terms of flexibility, the British planning system represents one extreme. The system apparently has no zoning in the sense that all development (except a few exempted classes of uses) within the Council district which is in fact a super-zone, other than some special areas, must go through the planning application procedure. In this procedure, the planner or the District Council, filled by politicians, has great discretionary power and is only constrained by the procedural law of natural justice. The planner may refuse or approve the application with or without planning conditions or obligations. The criteria of success in planning application are left almost entirely to the planner. While rent-seeking is not unlimited as a third party cannot participate in the planning application procedure, and appeal can be made to the Secretary of State for the Environment, this situation creates a great scope of rent-seeking due to uncertainty about the rules of this non-price competition.[42] Mills describes a rent-seeking development control system as one which 'involves case-by-case deliberation in the merits of landowners proposals' (Mills 1989: 6–7). This kind of 'zoning lotteries' is exactly the British 'non-zoning' mechanism. Rent-seeking may be *ex ante*, through which politicians invest real resources in an attempt to secure rent due to regulation. It may also be *ex post*, through which developers invest real resources in an attempt to capture a larger share of the rent for themselves (Gifford 1987). While some scholars, like Jeffrey Jowell (1977) are very optimistic about the 'selling of planning permissions' on the grounds that no corruption is revealed, the prevailing economist view[43] is always one which is predicated on maximization behaviour. In the extreme situation, the gain by the applicant may be completely dissipated by the costs absorbed in the process, notably the delay in lobbying and/or the burden of the planning conditions/obligations. The only social group which reaps benefits could well be the planning consultants (Tullock 1994). Anticipating this consequence, landowners may simply not make any application. Various 'deregulation' policies introduced by the Conservative Government since the 1970s may be interpreted as an attempt to constrain rent-seeking in the process. They include:[44]

(a) presumption in favour of development;[45]
(b) establishment of 'enterprise zones';[46]
(c) introduction of the Use Classes Orders;[47] and
(d) using the appeal process to support Central Government's liberalization policy.[48]

China's Special Economic Zones can be similarly regarded as zones of private property rights while the orthodox socialist concepts of property rights are reserved for areas outside the zones.

The Hong Kong zoning system represents another extreme. All private land in Hong Kong are held contractually under Crown leases which are very permissive. Such leases are allocated to private owners by competitive auction or tender. In effects, rights are allocated by contract. Leasehold lots can be regarded as zones with different degrees of freedom of uses as specified by the lease 'conditions'. These contractual zones in time become subject to statutory zones superimposed upon them.

Intended development within a statutory zone, shown on a map based Outline Zoning Plan accompanied by an Explanatory Statement, and a schedule of 'Notes' which contains for each zone two columns of uses (Column 1 and Column 2) (Table 2.1), falls into four categories: the use is either one

Table 2.1 An Example of Column 1 and Column 2 Uses for a Commercial/Residential Zone

Column 1 *Uses always permitted*	Column 2 *Uses that may be permitted with or without conditions on application to the Town Planning Board*
Bank	Beauty Parlour
Barber Shop	Broadcasting, Television and/or Film
Canteen	Studio
Clinic/Polyclinic	Commercial Bathouse/Massage Parlour
Educational Institution (not elsewhere specified)	Government Refuse Collection Point
Fast Food Shop	Off-course Betting Centre
Flat	Petrol Filling Station
Government Use (not elsewhere specified)	Place of Recreation, Sports or Culture
House	Public Transport Terminus or Station
Market	Religious Institution
Money Exchange	School
Pawn Shop	Service Apartment
Photographic Studio	
Place of Public Entertainment	
Police Post/Police Reporting Centre	
Post Office	
Private Club	
Private Swimming Pool	
Public Car Park	
Public Convenience	
Public Library	
Public Utility Installation	
Residential Institution	
Restaurant	
Retail Shop	
Service Trades	
Showroom excluding Motor-vehicle Showroom	
Social Welfare Facility	
Utility Installation for Private Project	

Source: Notes of the draft Mai Po and Fairview Park Outline Zoning Plan No. S/YL-MP/1

which is (i) always permitted in all zones, as listed in the cover of the Notes; (ii) always permitted in the zone in question, as listed in 'Column 1' of the Notes; (iii) may be permitted through s.16 planning application with or without planning conditions, as listed in 'Column 2' of the Notes; or (iv) definitely not permitted under the existing zoning plan. In the last situation, however, any person (whether he is the landowner or not) may apply for rezoning. Rent-seeking activities are therefore restricted to specific 'Column 2' uses in the planning application procedure or any use in the rezoning exercise. These categories of plan-governed uses override the uses contractually permitted in the lease where they are in conflict. Otherwise, the landowner still enjoy much freedom as:

(a) the zones are very broad, allowing many uses under Column 1,

(b) many zones are mixed-use, as in the case of 'Commercial/Residential' (C/R) or 'Industrial/ Office' (I/O) use;

(c) all zones can be developed under very permissive building regulations which allow high-rise development; and

(d) some zones, like the Residential zones, always permit certain uses on the first three storey of development.

As regards potential rent-seeking in the planning or rezoning application process, constraints are introduced by a balanced representation on the Town Planning Board of business, professional, and government interests. The government itself is constrained by a policy of balanced budget, the size of which is dependent on the size of Gross Domestic Product (GDP), and would therefore balance its discretion to attenuate private property rights on one hand and the return on land sales and lease modifications on the other. In other words there is a balance of interests between the Planning Authority and the Land Authority. These inherent checks on the planner's discretionary power constrain the extent of rent dissipation from within the government. Could this system be further improved to constrain rent-seeking? While Samuel Staley (1994) has identified reducing delay in the planning application procedure as a key issue,[49] the author has identified at least one other possibility. At present, s.16 planning application may be refused on the ground that the use stated in the application is incompatible with the environment in general or specific development in the vicinity. This appears to be irrational since the use itself is entered into 'Column 2'. This indicates that it is by nature compatible with the adjoining uses. A more proper view is that discretionary power in the planning application should be restricted to determine the intensity and design aspects of the use rather than the use *per se*. This would greatly reduce the uncertainty about the use of land and how to channel resources for technical design matter.

Where an intended development is inconsistent with the 'conditions' (re-strictive covenants) of the Crown Leases[50] or where joint development is necessary, and a statutory plan is not yet prepared, the landowner can always apply to the Land Authority for a 'lease modification' or a change in the 'user'. While such an application now requires inter-departmental consulta-tion, the Land Authority has great discretion to act on their own decision and tends to approve the proposed change because this would entail a premium payable by the applicant.

Lease allocation with restrictive covenants by competitive auction and ten-der and subsequent permission to change user is in reality a scenario of initial assignment of rights by zoning by consent[51] and subsequent change and trans-fer of rights by the market, i.e. the ideal case envisaged by Coase. It is also similar to the so-called 'non-zoning' in Houston (Siegan 1970) or the concepts of leasing and selling zoning restrictions, 'fungibility of zoning' or 'salable zoning'[52] (Nelson 1977; Fischel 1978, 1979) and the auction of development or zoning rights[53] (Mills 1989). This market solution is nevertheless gradually being superseded by planning discretion exercised in the planning application procedure, as the areas not covered by statutory zoning plans are drying up rapidly.

Where zoning restrictions imposed on existing land property have extra stipulations about the boundary of development, further opportunity for rent dissipation is introduced. These stipulations may be (i) prohibition or restrictions on sub-division or site coverage; or (ii) requirement for joint development with the property of other owners. The former attenuates the freedom of use and alienation of rights. The latter in effect allows freedom to use one's own land contingent on the consent of another and is more severe in terms of dissipation. In Hong Kong, such requirement can be and has been made in statutory zoning plans via the 'Comprehensive Development Area' (CDA) designation with the expressed intent to prevent 'piecemeal' redevelopment (Photographs 4 and 5). This concept requires the submission of a Master Layout Plan for the approval of Town Planning Board. If one has to see if this is justified in terms of efficiency regardless of equity, one should decide whether the aggregated value loss in individual rights are sufficiently offset by the total value gain from comprehensive development. Under the building regulations of Hong Kong, larger and more regular sites such as those prescribed by CDA zoning can in fact achieve greater plot ratio and hence greater amount of gross floor area. Thus on the grounds of allocative efficiency, there is a *prima facie* case in support of the attenuation of private property rights. However development of CDA zoning is not costless. The zone creates difficulty for individual landowners because their investment horizons and expected returns may not necessarily be the same for all parts of their land or as those of other owners.[54]

The stipulation of negative prohibition against sub-division is less restrictive than positive requirements for joint development (as in the CDA concept) because in the second situation the landowner suddenly loses his or her autonomy in deciding the fate of *any* part of his or her land. As Cheung says in the *New Palgrave,*

> private property rights offer the unique advantage of allowing individual property owners to option of NOT JOINING an organization. (Cheung 1987: 57)

The CDA concept compromises such an option in land because the owner would have no option not to join with others if he or she wants to develop land. The success of CDA under single ownership in various rezoning of public utility property (originally used as dockyards or power houses) and the failure of the Tsim Sha Tsui CDA scheme under multiple ownership both lend support to this theory. In the Tsim Sha Tsui scheme, a number of developed leasehold lots in the old commercial hub of Tsim Sha Tsui were

Photograph 4   Sheung Wan in the 1960s (Courtesy of the Hong Kong Government)

Photograph 5   Sheung Wan in the 1990s (Courtesy of the Hong Kong Government)

These photographs, showing the urban transformation of the Sheung Wan waterfront area, illustrates the phenomenon of 'piecemeal redevelopment' not favoured by town planners.

grouped into a CDA in order to render possible development only if the lots were jointly redeveloped according to an approved Master Layout Plan.

The transaction costs involved in reaching a land assembly agreement in Hong Kong where land titles are stratified are phenomenal[55] and could easily frustrate the planners' intent for orderly comprehensive redevelopment: there could simply be no private redevelopment at all.

Realizing such difficulties, the government of Hong Kong, instigate a Land Development Corporation (officially abbreviated LDC[56]) which has the statutory power under the Crown Land Resumption Ordinance to resume land for its CDA schemes which are approved by the Town Planning Board. Such schemes are to be implemented by LDC in joint venture with private developers. While the LDC Ordinance requires the LDC to operate 'according to prudent commercial principles', the company is not a private firm and hence LDC's joint venture schemes are akin to those 'socialist trading companies' or 'transideological companies'.[57] As far as the landowners are concerned, they are compensated according to the Pointe Gourde Rule,[58] constructing the object of profit making redevelopment schemes as if it is for 'public purpose'. This common law rule pegs the value of compensation at the existing level of the existing use but not the full potential value of land. This effectively allows LDC to appropriate the rent of redevelopment and transfer it to LDC and its partners. While such arbitrary transfer of wealth has nothing to do with re-source allocation, it has led to two types of costs:

(a) the political costs of rent-seeking and confrontation; and

(b) the threat to the institution of private property rights based on Crown Leases — in effect Government is in breach of her promise[59] of security of tenure by terminating the lease before expiry without due compensation, which would lead to uncertainty in the land market.

Empirically, CDA zoning does apparently achieve higher land value and is therefore *prima facie* beneficial on economic grounds. This can be tested by a comparison of the sales prices of Kornhill, a CDA development in Quarry Bay District, with the general property value of Quarry Bay (Chapter 5). The sales prices of the CDA property at Kornhill have a premium above those of the district in general, which may be due to the beneficial impact of CDA zoning.

(B) Impact on land values

Secondly, the impact on zoning could be capitalized in the value of land affected. Zoning intervention may, in some circumstances, enhance land value. One situation is where previously unclearly specified rights become clearly delineated by zoning. An example is the case of the interim Development Permission Area (DPA) Zoning in the New Territories. In the DPA plans, there are large tracts of land for which their uses are not specified. On these tracts of land, all developments and changes in use require planning approval — i.e. in the same position as 'non-zoning' in the British system. The Government is now preparing rural Outline Zoning Plans to specify the uses of these tracts of land. It can be predicted that this specification or 'rezoning' would enlarge the land market by reducing transaction costs (Chapter 5).

(C) Impact on externalities

Thirdly, zoning could affect the physical manifestation of externalities. Coase in the 'Federal Communications Commission' (1959) actually provides explanation for the transaction costs of zoning. He argues that the transaction costs of information and negotiation are so high that even the civil law does not work, zoning regulation should be made more efficient.

> if many people are harmed and there are several sources of pollution, it is more difficult to reach a satisfactory solution through the market. When the transfer of rights has to come about as a result of market transactions carried out between large numbers of people or organizations acting jointly, the process of negotiation may be so difficult and time-consuming as to make such transfers a practical impossibility. Even the enforcement of rights through the courts may not be easy. It may be costly to discover who it is that is causing the trouble. And, when it is not in the interest of any single person or organization to bring suit, the problems involved in arranging joint actions represent a further obstacle. As a practical matter, the market may become too costly to operate. (Coase 1959: 29)

In their analysis of zoning, the Coasians do not test the relationship between zoning and externalities directly but instead examine indirectly the interdependence of land values and zoning policies. Land values are taken by the Coasians to be the proxy of externalities. This is conceptually erroneous because whether land values reflect or fail to reflect (internalize) externalities does not alter the Coasian (or Pigovian) view of zoning. A better approach is to observe whether zoning measures and procedures reduce the incidence of nuisance.

It might be expected that if the planning application system could have beneficial results on the environment, the incidence of nuisance complaints would then be negatively correlated with the number of successful planning applications. A comparison of the environmental complaints and planning permission statistics[60] for the three main areas of Hong Kong, namely Hong Kong Island, Kowloon and the New Territories is included in Chapter 5 to test this hypothesis.

The zoning system of Hong Kong: a synoptic account

This section presents in brief the configuration of Hong Kong as it evolves over time in terms of property rights concepts. This would provide a context for the arguments and empirical tests in the following chapters. The territory of Hong Kong consists of three geographical areas: (a) Hong Kong Island, (b) Kowloon Peninsula and (c) New Kowloon and the New Territories. Most indigenous villages are found in the New Territories. They were mainly agrarian. Fishermen living on junks occupied various sheltered harbours along the coast line. The villages can be regarded as 'zones' with well-defined and exclusive spheres of influence. The most fertile land has been occupied by the settlers who came from North China, fleeing the Mongols in the 1200s. Some of them built fortified settlements with moats. The late comers, notably the Hakka, occupy the hillslopes and they have their own areas of influence. Within all these settlements, the Chinese system of private property rights over land, rectified by royal decrees and taxed annually, once prevailed. Land boundaries are largely irregular. Outside the settlements, land was exploited in accordance with communal rules. Both the exclusive and communal areas were protected in theory by Imperial troops and police, which became ineffective from time to time. Such land was used as common grazing ground, sources of timber, charcoal burning, burial and water gathering.[61] Competition for water supply led to violence from time to time. Violence was resolved by treaties among villages and evidence of such treaties is borne by the survival of 'treaty areas'.

The British acquired by might Hong Kong Island in 1842 under the Treaty of Nanking, and Kowloon Peninsula in 1862 under the Treaty of Peking. Finally, they obtained from Imperial China a 100-year lease of the New Kowloon and the New Territories in 1897. The British adopted a dualist land policy, which makes a distinction between land on Hong Kong Island, Kowloon and New Kowloon on the one hand, and the New Territories on the other. All land was declared Crown Land. Land on Hong Kong Island, Kowloon and New Kowloon (Figure 2.10) was regularized into land lots which were then allocated as leaseholds (Figure 2.11) to private users by competitive auction or tender and to charities or government departments by grant at nominal costs. Such leasehold land can be regarded as zones with definite boundary or 'as zoned' in terms of the conditions of the leases. Leasehold can be regarded as zones with full private rights subject to the conditions of the lease.[62] These zones are allocated by contract between the government and citizens. The land in the New Territories, however, was left intact and 'leased back' to the villagers after a comprehensive survey which clarified land entitlements.[63] The leasehold system can be said to have created zoning by contract or deemed contract.

Law and order was quickly established and the land market has flourished ever since except during Japanese occupation from December 1941 to August 1945. Land speculation began as early as 1843 when the first auction was carried out.[64]

Zoning as a *non-contractual obligation* imposed by town planners was legally introduced into Hong Kong by the Town Planning Ordinance of 1939. Actual preparation of the statutory plans commenced after the end of the Second World War. The map-based statutory Outline Zoning Plans were superimposed on the pre-existing leasehold zones (Figure 2.11). The zoned uses prescribed by the statutory Outline Zoning Plans were intended to override the conditions (or terms) of the lease where they were in conflict. In 1959 a new section 16(1)(d) was introduced to the Building (Administration) Regulations 1956 which required the refusal of building consent when a proposed development did not conform to the land-use zoning of the plans. The legal effect of this concept was tested in the Singway Case[65] in which all the statutory plans at that time were declared null and void. The case involved the validity of height control stipulation in a town plan without indicating the legal effect of the regulation. Then Notes, expressly declared as being part of the statutory zoning plans, were introduced. These 'notes' clearly specify which uses are always permitted in all zones, always permitted in a given zone or may be permitted (with or without planning conditions) on an Outline Zoning Plan upon a planning application under s.16 of the Ordinance. Private urban land zoned for open space or Government/Institution/ Community (GIC) uses can be resumed and compensated under s.4(2) of the Ordinance.

For land newly reclaimed from the sea or obtained by terracing hill slopes, the statutory zoning plans could serve as the vehicle which determines the initial assignment of private property rights. However, in practice, these rights are assigned by non-statutory development plans, namely Outline Development Plans or Layout Plans. According to these administrative plans, the conditions of the land leases are drafted and allocated by either auction, tender or grant. It is not until recently[66] that statutory plans were prepared as departmental plans more or less at the same time.

The initial assignment of private property right by non-statutory plans were most extensive in the development of high-density new towns (Photographs 6 and 7), which were formed partly by reclamation and partly by terracing. Resumption of the land held by indigenous villagers is also significant. In this context, the zoning in development plans serve the purpose of regularizing the land boundary of pre-existing privately held agricultural leases. Rural land was acquired by the government with the 'Letter A / Letter B' resumption to which the landowners surrender 5 units of rural land in exchange of a future claim of 2 units urban land in the new town according to a pre-determined schedule of prices.[67] A Letter A/B is a certificate issued by the government to the rural landowner for such exchange of rights.

Photograph 6   Sha Tin in the 1970s (Courtesy of the Hong Kong Government)

Photograph 7   Sha Tin in the 1980s (Courtesy of the Hong Kong Government)

The letter A/B system of private land exchange and massive utilization of Crown Land had been able to turn Sha Tin into a new town of nearly 0.5 million population in only about 10 years.

Until the late 1980s, there were only non-statutory town plans for parts of the rural area of the New Territories. As agriculture was virtually abandoned in the early 1980s due to rapid rise in the opportunity cost of labour and land,[68] farm land became fallow and used extensively for open storage of containers, building materials and scrap vehicles.[69] The property rights of the villagers to do so under the conditions of the agricultural lease were confirmed in the Melhado Case.[70] This case involved judicial interpretation about the right under agricultural leaseholds to put land under such uses. This is now being tackled on environmental grounds by the Planning Department which has obtained clear legal power[71] to prepare statutory plans all over Hong Kong. This in effect nullifies the private property rights of agricultural leaseholders to open storage affirmed by the Melhado Case.

Interim statutory Development Permission Area (DPA) Plans have been prepared to cover most village land in the New Territories. Except a few specified areas, the development potentials for most land within the DPA are unspecified and every proposed development requires prior planning approval. This creates the kind of uncertainty confronting the British land-owners under the 'non-zoning' situation. The government is, however, trying to remove uncertainty by preparing rural Outline Zoning Plans to supersede the DPA plans in due course.

Land, including the seabed, not held by private owners or government departments is called unallocated Crown Land. They can be allocated as soon as a development plan and the corresponding leases for developers or en-gineering conditions (for government departments) are prepared. About 70 percent of such land, however, would not be allocated under the existing country park and water supply policies. The Country Parks were put under statutory protection of the Country Park Ordinance, which in effect intro-duces explicit statutory zones on the countryside of Hong Kong. Any development within the country parks needs prior approval of the Country Park Board. (In the statutory Outline Zoning Plans, these country park zones were once expressed generally as 'Green Belt' zones.) Development with the Country Parks do not require planning approval of the Town Planning Board.

Notes

1. The concepts adopted in this chapter stem largely from the American 'property rights economics' or 'institutional economics' developed by scholars like Armen Alchian, Ronald Coase, and Steven N.S. Cheung.
2. Coase, Ronald, H. 'The Nature of the Firm.' *Economica*. n.s. 4 (November 1937): 386–405.
3. Mandeville, B., *The Fable of the Bees*. London: Oxford University Press, 1924.
4. Smith, A., *The Theory of Moral Sentiments*. Oxford: Clarendon Press, 1976.

5. Umbeck, J. 'Might Makes Rights: A Theory of the Formation and Initial Distribution of property Rights.' *Economic Inquiry* (January 1981): 38–59.

6. As quoted in Berki, R.N. *The History of Political Thought: A Short Introduction.* London, Melbourne and Toronto: Rowman and Littlefield, 1976, pp. 134–135.

7. Alchian's expression of 'communal rights' is adopted here in lieu of 'common property rights', which is better reserved for describing anarchy. Anarchy entails the use of violence when the level of competition escalates as the number of competitors increases.

8. This is consistent with Coase's argument in the 'Problem of Social Cost' that a government is a 'super-firm' (Coase, Ronald, H. 'The Problem of Social Cost.' *The Journal of Law and Economics* (October 1960), pp. 17; also in Coase, Ronald, H. *The Firm, The Market and The Law.* Chicago: University of Chicago Press, 1988, pp. 117).

9. The concept of a 'super-zone' is borrowed from Coase's characterization of government as a 'super firm', which has also been used by Cheung to describe the whole Soviet economy as a big firm. As regards zoning specifically, Lafferty and Frech III's concept of the 'entire town as a zone', which is a broader zone embodying zones at the 'neighbourhood' level is conceptually akin to the abstraction used here. See Lafferty, Ronald N. and Frech III, H.E. 'Community Environment and the Market Value of Single-Family Homes: The Effect of the Dispersion of Land Uses.' *Journal of Law and Economics* Vol. 21, No. 2 (October 1978): 381–394. Sir Patrick Abercrombie describes 'zoning' as 'the dedication of a certain area to a certain use' in his *Town and Country Planning*. See Abercrombie, Professor Sir Patrick *Town and Country Planning*. London, New York and Toronto: Oxford University Press, 2nd ed. 1933, p. 139.

10. See Demsetz, Harold 'Towards a Theory of Property Rights.' *American Economic Review* (May 1967): 351.

11. A good account of the spread of the desert (or 'desertification) in sub-Saharan Africa is given in Burton, John's Epilogue to Cheung, Steven N.S. *The Myth of Social Cost* (Hobart Paper 82) London: The Institute of Economic Affairs, 1978, pp. 84–88.

12. In China, the 'nine squares' system [井田制] dividing land into 9 lots with 8 private and outer lots and one central communal lots is a good example. The system degenerated ultimately as no one had any interest in working on the 'communal' lots.

13. Note that colonization by tribal states like the Huns led simply to the spread of their communal rights over conquered territory. European colonization on the other hand usually was accompanied by the implantation of an exclusive property rights land system which co-existed with indigenous communal rights. The history of the settlement in Australia is a good example. The traditional communal rights of the aborigines have been respected by the law. In the case of the New Territories of Hong Kong where private property rights under Chinese imperial laws and customs were well-established, the indigenous exclusive rights have been rectified by the British administration.

14. For the sake of simplicity of argument, land, in subsequent discussion of this section, refers to fee simple, unless otherwise specified.

15. The economic nature of private property rights is best described in Cheung, Steven N.S. 'A Theory of Price Control.' *The Journal of Law and Economics* 17 (April 1974): 53–71. Coase's view is that rights, once assigned, can be freely 'acquired, subdivided and combined' (Coase 1988: 12).

16. The enclosure movement itself is mentioned as a behaviour which reduces transaction costs by Armen Alchian and Harold Demsetz (1973: 22).

17. There is a story about high officials enclosing river beds surrounding the capital of the Sung Empire, for the purpose of landscaping and fish culture, an act alleged to have caused flooding. The 'externalities' created were rectified ultimately by an order of injunction by one of the most famous judges in Chinese history. The event occurred around 1100 A.D. and can be regarded as the first recorded case of 'development control' in China.

18. Like the Romans who drained marshes, the Chinese also knew how to create private land by reclamation. As early as 1279 A.D., the new settlers in Hong Kong conducted their reclamation project in San Tin, New Territories, which have created the environment of Mai Po Marshes — which is now managed by the World Wild Fund as a 'natural' habitat of international significance. The tidal shrimp/fish ponds with sluice gates or 'Kei Wei' in the Marshes were actually built by villagers in the period 1941 to 1949.

19. See Atwood, James R. 'An Economic Analysis of Land Use Conflicts.' *Stanford Law Review* 21 (January 1969): 293–315; McAuslan, P. *Land Law and Planning: Case Materials and Text.* London: Widenfeld and Nicholson, 1975, and *The Ideologies of Planning Law.* Oxford: Pergamon Press, 1980.

20. Modern zoning originated in Germany in the late nineteenth century (Nelson 1977: 8, Alexander 1993: 21). In the United Kingdom, the planning acts of 1909, 1919 and 1932 conferred zoning power on local authorities (Grant 1982: 78–79). In the United States, nuisance control was put on a statutory basis in 1885 in California to discriminate against Chinese immigrants. Zoning is however said to have begun in 1916 with the New York City Zoning Ordinance. Zoning was declared constitutional by the United States Supreme Court in the Euclid Case in 1926 (Delafons 1969). See Wong, Sydney Chun Cheung, 'Zoning Control and Property Right in Hong Kong.' Unpublished M.Sc. dissertation, University of Wales Institute of Science and Technology, September 1986, pp. 17–18.

21. In America, the Euclid Case covers conflicts of land use, leaving the question of the intensity of use or development to the Standard Zoning Act. In Hong Kong, the legality of plot ratio restrictions as a type of intensity or density control is blessed in the Crozet Case and affirmed in the CC Tse Case. Crozet Ltd. v AG. HCMP 409/73 and CC Tse (Estate) Ltd. v AG. HCMP 604/81.

22. The plot ratio controls are largely but not necessarily associated with density controls, and are treated as distinct by planners. See Mandelker, Daniel R. 'The Basic Philosophy of Zoning: Incentive or Restraint', in *Planning and Control of Land Development.* Charlottesville: Michie Co., 1990, pp. 203–211.

23. The expressions of 'land use', 'intensity' and 'boundary' are more general than the three fold classification of 'allowable use', 'density' and 'lot size' of Grieson, Ronald E. and White, James R. See Grieson, Ronald E. and White, Jame R. 'The Effects

of Zoning on Structure and Land Markets.' *Journal of Urban Economics* 10 (1981): 271–285.

24. The theoretical framework adopted here differs from Wigglesworth's naive conspiracy theory of planning (1982) as a means to erode private property rights of the dominated class or the 'structural analysis' of Keung (1980). See Wigglesworth, John Michael 'Planning Law and Administration in Hong Kong: with particular reference to the position in the United Kingdom.' Unpublished Ph.D. thesis, University of Hong Kong, January 1986.

25. It is a common view that the British town and country planning regime has no zoning elements (See for instance Ball, Simon and Bell, Stuart. *Environmental Law.* London: Blackstone, 1991, Chapter 9. Since the 'nationalization of development rights' in 1947, the zoning plan has gradually evolved from a physical layout plan system to the local structure development plan system in which all development proposals are considered on their individual merits), other than a few 'enterprise zones'. This view is incorrect. Not to mention the broad concept of zoning implicit in land law regarding boundary delineation, one can conceive each local planning area as one zone within which all development with a few exceptions, must go through the development control (planning application) procedure. The British planning system therefore creates zones without clearly prescribed uses. Implicit in the British development control system are forward planning considerations, rendering the absence of zoning apparent rather than real.

26. Lai, Lawrence W.C. 'An Economic Exposition of Land Use Planning' *The Hong Kong Surveyor* 3, No. 2 (July 1987): 6–9 and 'Some Fallacies of Incompatible Land Uses — A Libertarian Economic Exposition of the Issues of Land Use Zoning.' *The Hong Kong Surveyor* 6 (No. 2, Fall 1990): 18–22. c.f. p. 14 ante.

27. Coase, Ronald, H. 'The Problem of Social Cost.' *The Journal of Law and Economics* (October 1960): 1–44.

28. The question of compatibility of zones is not absolute and relative to specific development uses, intensity, technology, and normative judgements. See Lai, Lawrence W.C. 1987, op. cit., pp. 6–9.

29. These population-based standards, also contained in *HKPSG*, can be regarded as criteria for rationing public funds to various government funded or subsidized uses like schools and hospitals.

30. For a transaction cost critique of this concept, see Lai, Lawrence W.C. 'The Pricing of Lighthouses and Roads: Transaction Costs, Public Goods and Planning Intervention.' *Planning and Development* 7 (No. 1, 1991): 36–40. See Charles Tiebout's concept about joint consumption of local public goods and choice of residence. Tiebuot, Charles. 'A Pure Theory of Local Expenditure.' *Journal of Political Economy* 64, No. 5 (October 1986): 416–424.

31. The most important statutory zones in Hong Kong are country parks, once expressed in town plans as a kind of Green Belt.

32. The other method is 'the redefinition of property right and their private enforcement' (nuisance law). The state is ultimately involved in the enforcement of all these methods and land boundary question is always involved.

33. In Coase's parable of the wheat field, a fee simple or its equivalent is implied.

34. Political concepts like 'sovereignty', 'constituency', etc. are territorial based, hence implying boundary delineation.

35. Note that colonization can occur at any level of development of the exclusive property rights in the mother country. The Mongols transplanted their communal property rights to China after they overthrew the Sung Dynasty, the European private property rights to America, Africa and South East Asia.

36. 'Extension' is a better expression than 'physical attributes' because it is more general and encompassing in philosophical terms. In Runes' *Dictionary of Philosophy*, it reads: Physical space, considered as a single concrete, continuum as contrasted with the abstract conceptual space of mathematics. The distinction between extension and 'space' in the abstract sense is clearly drawn by Descartes (1596–1650) in *The Principles of Philosophy*, part II, Princ. IV–XV. See Runes, Dagobert D. ed., *Dictionary of Philosophy*. Totowa, New Jersey: Littlefield, Adams & Co., 1960, p. 105.

37. c.f. Umbeck's thesis with Carlifornia Gold Rush as context. (Umbeck J., 'Might Makes Rights: A Theory of the Formation and Initial Distribution of property Rights.' *Economic Inquiry* (January 1981): 38–59.

38. c.f. Bottomley's research on the desertification of Tripolitannia in Libyia (Bottomley 1963, op. cit.)

39. See Chapter 2.

40. Coase, Ronald, H. 'The Federal Communications Commission.' *Journal of Law and Economics* (October 1959), p. 25.

41. See Chapter 3.

42. See Pearce, B.J. 'Property Rights vs. Development Control: A Preliminary Evaluation of Alternative Planning Policy Instruments.' *Town Planning Review* 52, (No. 1, 1981): 47–60.

43. See for instance Benson, Bruce (1984), Gifford,, Adam Jr. (1987), Mills, David E. (1989) and Peltzman, S. (1977). Peltzman argues that 'the essential commodity being transacted in the political market is a transfer of wealth.' (Peltzman, S. 'The Growth of Government' *The Journal of Law and Economics*, April 1976, pp. 212.)

44. An excellent account of these are given in Chapter 9 in Ball, Simon and Bell, Stuart. *Environmental Law*. London: Blackstone, 1991, pp. 159–208.

45. DoE Circular 14/85, reproduced in Policy Guidance Note 2 para. 15. The effect of new s.54A of the Town and Country Planning Act 1990 on this is uncertain. See Mynors, Charles. 'The Planning and Compensation Act 1991: (3) Development Plans, Minerals and Waste Disposal.' *The Planner* (13 September 1991): 7–9.

46. United Kingdom Local Government Act 1985

47. See Home, Robert *Planning Use Classes*. Oxford: BSP Professional Books, 1989.

48. See Pearce, B.J. 'The Changing Role of Planning Appeals' in D. Cross and M.E. Whiteheads eds. *Development and Planning*. U.K.: Policy Journals, 1989.

49. Staley has worked out the cost of delay for typical development projects in Hong Kong. 'If development were delayed for one year, *added costs per project* on Hong Kong Island could range from HK$241 million for a 500,000 square foot commercial office building to HK$603 million for a 1 million square foot office building, depending on prevailing interest rates. If all new office space added on

Hong Kong Island in 1991 were subject to a one-year delay, the added costs for financing new developments would exceed HK$1 billion. A one-year delay could add between HK$480 per square foot to HK$603 per square foot to the cost of commercial development, depending on prevailing interest rates. Similarly, a one-year delay in the construction of new residential units could add HK$1.1 billion to the cost of developing a 5 million square foot residential estate. Overall, the added costs to residential construction could vary from HK$250 per square foot to HK$300 per square foot, depending on prevailing interest rates.' See Staley, Samuel *Planning, Uncertainty and Economic Development in Hong Kong: A Critical Evaluation of the Comprehensive Review of the Town Planning Ordinance.* Hong Kong: Hong Kong Centre for Economic Research, University of Hong Kong, 1992, executive summary p. iii (later published as *Planning Rules and Urban Economic Performance: The Case of Hong Kong.* The Chinese University Press, 1994).

50. There is a broad distinction between the old 999-year 'unrestricted leases' and the modern 'restricted leases'. The former has little restriction on use other than exclusion of obnoxious trades and is therefore very close to a legal fee simple.

51. See analysis above, pp. 28–29.

53. See Nelson, Robert H. *Zoning and Property Rights, An Analysis of the American System of Land-Use Regulation.* Cambridge: MIT Press, 1977; and Fischel, William A. 'A Property Rights Approach to Municipal Zoning.' *Land Economics* 54 (February 1978): 73–76, and 'Equity and Efficiency Aspects of Zoning Reform.' *Public Policy* 27, No. 3 (Summer 1979): 321–329. There is, however, no assumption in this book that there is a trade off between 'benefits to community' and 'benefits to landowners'. Nor is Fischel's concept that 'selling zoning is analogous to sell health inspections to restaurants' (Fischel 1979: 327). The presupposition of clear delineation of rights in a Coasian bargaining solution does not assume a way but indeed requires state enforcement. The proper interpretation of 'selling zoning' is to allow restrictions on land use, intensity and boundary of development to be settled contractually rather than by edict. Such contracts are nevertheless enforceable by the state.

53. See Mills, David E. 'Is Zoning a Negative-Sum Game?' *Land Economics* 65 (No. 1, 1989): 10–11.

54. Reuter's view about potential justifications for municipal zoning in terms of lot size restrictions is rather surprising. He argues: 'the establishment of *restrictions on land use and minimum lot size might circumvent somewhat the prisoner's dilemma aspects* of the assembly of large parcels of land for large-scale industrial or commercial purposes, thereby promoting more efficient private development of urban property. Requiring large lot sizes and limiting the allowable forms of land uses in various sections of the city should reduce the probability that a small group of property owners, each of whom is demanding a relatively high price for his property in an attempt to obtain a disproportionate share of the profits of a proposed new development, could make the initiation of a potentially Pareto optimal project economically infeasible'. (Reuter 1973: 337). Quite on the contrary, minimum lot sizes as in the case of CDA zoning in Hong Kong poses the problem of 'holding up' unless compulsory resumption is a credible threat. Contrast Reuter's view

with Grieson and White's view that 'large-lot zoning' is equivalent to a two-part tariff. Grieson, Ronald E. and White, James R. 1981, op. cit.

55. For instance, a typical 30-storey residential tower development in Hong Kong may contain as many as 480 titles.

56. In the field of Development Economics, LDC refers to 'Less Developed Countries'.

57. See Wong, K.C. 'A Theory of Joint Venture Partnership in Property Investment.' Unpublished Ph.D. thesis. Hong Kong: Department of Surveying, University of Hong Kong, February 1992.

58. See Willoughby, P.G. 'Let The Land-Owner Beware.' *Hong Kong Law Lectures* (1978): 185–191. Whether Pointe Gourde Rule should be used to facilitate resumption of land for commercial object is a key issue here.

59. See Dunham, Allison 'Promises Respecting The Use of Land.' *Journal of Law and Economics* 8 (1965): 133–165. See also Lai, Lawrence W.C. 'Urban Renewal and the Land Develoment Corporation,' in Choi Po-King and Ho Lok-Sang eds. *The Other Hong Kong Report 1993*. Hong Kong: Chinese University Press, 1993, pp. 175–191.

60. A time lag of three years has been allowed for successful planning applications to take into account the time of actual building development.

61. For the impact of these economic activities on the ecology, see Thrower, Stella L. *Hong Kong Country Parks*. Hong Kong: Hong Kong Government Information Services Department, 1984.

62. Land titles in the New Territories are organized in a very complicated manner. The land lots in the proper of New Territories are generally re-granted in the form of 'Block Crown Leases' for 477 Demarcation Districts (DDs) or, in the case of New Kowloon between the Kowloon Range and Boundary Street, Survey Districts (SDs). These lots were identified, surveyed, classified (broadly into house and agricultural lots), numbered, and recorded in DD or SD plans by Indian engineers before the turn of the century. They are according called 'DD lots' or 'SD lots'. Usually, one DD or SD has one, but sometimes more than one, such cadastral plan. DD and SD plans are registered as public records which are the legal basis for land transaction and other matters. Lands subject to the Block Crown Lease arrangement on some outlying islands, like Ma Wan and Cheung Chau, have their own systems of lot classification. There are also village house lots which are not shown in the DD or SD plans, though they are also part of the Block Crown lease system. For a detailed discussion of the leasehold system as a planning system, see Lai, Lawrence W.C., 'The Leasehold System as a Means of Planning by Contract: the Hong Kong Case,' unpublished research monograph, Department of Real Estate and Construction, the University of Hong Kong, 1 August 1997e, 24 pp.

63. This dualist land policy can be explained in terms of property rights analysis. As the New Territories were seen as one leasehold obtained from China, the British would certainly avoid creating major change in the land system of this piece of territory. On the other hand, the Hong Kong Island and Kowloon were regarded, until 1984, as a private property of the Crown. Hence, the British are motivated to adopt a more efficient land system. This attitude is expressed in the Abercrombie

Report prepared by Sir Patrick Abercrombie in 1946, which envisages that major urban development shall be outside the New Territories proper. Now town development in the New Territories in the 70s and 80s represented a policy by default due to immense immigration from China after the Second World War. See Lai, Lawrence W.C., 'Reflections on the Abercrombie Report 1948: A Strategic Plan for Colonial Hong Kong', unpublished research monograph, Department of Real Estate and Construction, the University of Hong Kong, August, 1997f.

64. See Tregear, R.R. and Berry, L. *The Development of Hong Kong and Kowloon as told on Maps.* Hong Kong: University of Hong Kong/ Macmillan, 1959.

65. Singway Co Ltd v AG [1974] HKLR 275.

66. The Hung Hom Bay reclamation is a case in point.

67. Pope, R.D. 'A History of Letter A/B and Land Exchange Policy' *The Hong Kong Surveyor* Vol. 1, No. 1 (May 1985): 7–9.

68. See Lai, Lawrence W.C. 'Some Economic Aspects of Agriculture in the New Territories' *Planning and Development* 7 (No. 1, 1991): 42–44.

69. The Container Port of Hong Kong ranks number one in the world. See Lai, Lawrence W.C. 'Planning for Container Storage in Hong Kong.' *Planning and Development* 8, No. 1 (1992): 14–16.

70. AG v Melhado Investment Ltd [1983] HKLR 327.

71. It was believed the pre-existing legislation did not apply to the rural areas. While this has been untested in court, the author's opinion is that 'potential urban areas' in the preamble of the old ordinance is sufficient for the use of this power even in the past. See Appendix 1.

Chapter Three

Limitations of Coasian Paradigm of Zoning: A Literature Review

> In my long life I have known some great economists but I have never counted myself among their number nor walked in their company. I have made no innovations in high theory. (Coase 1991)

Two paradigms of zoning

There are two competing paradigms of zoning, understood as a kind of government regulatory measure, in terms of economic theorization. Firstly, there is the Pigovian paradigm developed on the basis of Professor Arthur C. Pigou's thesis 'The Economics of Welfare' first published in 1920. Then comes the Coasian paradigm developed mainly on the basis of Ronald Coase's Nobel Prize paper 'The Problem of Social Cost' of 1960. The Pigovian paradigm is said to be interventionist, perceiving a positive role for government or state regulation of the land market whereas the Coasian paradigm is constantly casting doubts about such regulation. Some scholars take a step further to assert the view that market solutions are superior in terms of economic efficiency. In short the Pigovian paradigm is one for zoning whereas the Coasian paradigm is against zoning.

Generally, the above dichotomy in economic interpretation of zoning is mainly discerned in American literature and less obvious in British literature where discussion of zoning, apparently absent from the planning system, is subsumed under the broad concept of 'planning' ('town planning', 'town and country planning', 'urban planning'). In Britain, while most traditional texts on the economics of planning, exemplified by William Lean's *Aspects of Land Economics* (1966, Chapter 14) and *Economics of Land Use Planning* (1969, Chapter 1) adopt the Pigovian justification for planning, conventional texts on planning do not explicitly refer to formal Pigovian analysis. The equivalent of the Pigovian versus Coasian debate in British literature is the discussion within the planning profession about conventional dichotomy of 'plan' versus 'market' (Dunlop 1969; Kaser 1971), 'planning' versus 'price mechanism' (Lean 1966, 1969), 'libertarian planning' versus 'development control' (Sorensen and Day 1981) as informed by Hayek or 'property rights' (Pearce 1981) as policy alternatives to the status quo of planning regulation, and various non-economic 'arguments against planning'. In Britain, Friedrich von Hayek's[1] influence, or reaction against such influence, is more strongly felt, probably due to von Hayek's polemic literature attacking the 'drastic provisions'[2] of the British Town and Country Planning Act of 1947. The key feature of British articulation of 'property rights' is treating 'property rights' as categorically distinct from 'development control' or other regulatory measures instead of regarding 'market' and 'plan' as alternative modes of property rights, or rules of competition.

It is perhaps odd from the economist's point of view that in Sorensen and Day's discussion (1981) of externalities, Hayek's works[3], which challenge the concept of externalities, are extensively used but no reference is made to Coase's 1960 seminal paper on the concept. Similarly, B.J. Pearce's citation (1980, 1981)[4] of Pigou's work on externalities is not followed by any reference to Coase, although the works on property rights inspired by and ensuing from Coase's 1960 paper, those of Harold Demsetz (1967) and Steven N.S. Cheung (1978), are utilized.[5] Klosterman's exposition (1985) of the economic arguments for planning adopts the standard Pigovian concept without mentioning their stereotype Coasian antithesis. Graham Hallett's *Urban Land Economics* (1979) as a textbook gives reference to Coase's analysis of externalities very briefly and does not relate the matter to zoning. Philip Cooke's *Theories of Planning and Spatial Development* (1983), a leading work on planning theories, is illustrative of the proposition that Coase's writings have little influence in British academic circle. K.G. Willis' book *The Economics of Town and Country Planning* (1980) is probably unique in bringing home in much greater detail the messages of the emigrant prophet. However, in the discussion of M.E. Avrin's empirical test on zoning (1977), little indication is made of the intellectual influence of Coase. It seems therefore that the extensive epilogue of John Burton in Steven Cheung's *The Myth of Social Cost* (1978: 71–91), cited in Pearce's treatises, remains the clearest exposition of Coase's economic concept in the British academic realm.

It is surely a challenging question to the sociologist of knowledge why Coase has not been very prominent in the British literature on planning on the one hand and patently not well received in the British literature on jurisprudence on the other.[6]

The American based Pigou-Coase debate on zoning can be traced back to as early as 1958 when Allison Dunham of the University of Chicago Law

School stated in, 'City Planning: An Analysis of the Content of the Master Plan', appearing in the *Journal of Law and Economics*, the justification of planning.

Dunham's paper is an apology for the consistency of 'The Standard City Planning Enabling Act' which provided for zoning, among other measures, with the stated intent of promoting the 'health, safety, morals, order, convenience, prosperity, and general welfare, as well as *efficiency* and economy in the process of development' (italics mine, following Dunham 1958). This intent follows the *ratio decidendi* of the United States Supreme Court ruling in *Village of Euclid v Amber Realty Co.* [272 U.S. 365 (1926)] that zoning is constitutional, and apparently has been copied by the Hong Kong legislator. The current Town Planning Ordinance of Hong Kong, passed in 1939, states in the preamble that planning caters for the '*health, safety* and *convenience* and *general welfare* of the community' [italics mine]. Dunham argues:

> Much of the enabling legislation for zoning recognizes (the) distinction between an external cost and an external benefit. Such legislation speaks of 'securing' or 'preserving', 'avoiding' or 'preventing' certain enumerated evils as the purpose for which zoning is permitted. (Dunham 1958: 182) [brackets mine]

> What is needed in planning is a philosophy delineating the reasons for interference by central planners with the decisions of others. This paper has suggested a line which distinguishes those factors which market allocation of resources would take into account from those which considerations of efficiency and economy ignore. Central planner interference is consistent with a market economy when it limits its consideration to the external impact on neighbouring land. (Dunham 1958: 186) [Italics and brackets mine]

Coase and the Coasians

Directed straight at Pigou,[7] Coase's 'The Problem of Social Cost' presented what has been subsequently described as the 'invariance' and most popular version of the 'Coase Theorem' (an invention of George Stigler) the notion that

> If property rights are clearly delineated and if all costs of transactions are zero, then resource use will be the same regardless of who owns the property rights. (Cheung 1990: 11)

The most important version of the 'Coase Theorem' however lies elsewhere in his 'The Federal Communications Commission' (1959) where he succinctly concludes:

The delimitation of rights is an essential prelude to market transactions (Coase 1959: 27, as quoted in Cheung 1990: 10).

Coase uses the example of the potential economic conflict of interest in the rights to use land between a cattle raiser and a wheat farmer to argue that if transaction costs are zero, then both parties can internalize their conflict by a trade of their rights. Resource allocation is the same whether the law of tort holds either party liable. Coase's parable is to capture Pigou's notion of the divergence between the private and social product, which covers the legal concept of 'nuisance', and the environmental concept of 'pollution', which is described as 'externalities' or 'external effects' by Samuelson (1955). In the Pigovian model, land use conflicts are usually conceptualized as a scenario in which one party is assumed blameworthy. The key contribution of Coase is to show that the market can internalize such uncompensated effects, in the absence of transaction costs. Above all, Coase breaks new theoretical grounds by providing an alternative interpretation of rights and harmful activities.[8] As he succinctly puts it:

> We are dealing with a problem of a *reciprocal* nature. To avoid the harm to B would inflict harm on A. The real problem, has to be decided is: Should A be allowed to harm B or should B be allowed to harm A? The problem is to avoid the more serious harm. (Coase 1960: 2) [Italics mine][9]

Coase's theory on the legal front has fostered the development of the field 'Economic Analysis of Law', pioneered by scholars like James R. Atwood and more prominently, G. Calabresi and A.D. Melamed[10] and Professor Judge Richard Posner. This school of thought is labelled as 'utilitarianism' in their confrontation with Professor Ronald Dworkin's 'rights thesis'[11] in the field of jurisprudence. As for land use controls, Coase's theory cumulates in a host of works, notably Robert C. Ellickson's 'Alternatives to Zoning: Covenants, Nuisance Rules and Fines as Land Use Controls' (1973). Allison Dunham's critique of Coase's 1960 paper, 'Promises Respecting The Use of Land', raises the issue of whether the freedom to transfer rights run into conflict with the doctrine in land law that certain obligations or 'promises' run with the land. While Coase could certainly address this issue by transaction cost analysis, Dunham's stress on 'promises', if extended to legislation, would lead one to realize that zoning as a regulatory device could well override or attenuate any such promise.[12] Dunham obviously tries to argue that land law is very much different from contract law as some promises in the former bind all subsequent parties to the object. While Coase does not pay any attention to Atwood's criticism that his analysis of the law of nuisance is static (1969: 298) or Dunham's arguments about promises running with land, he is quite prepared to address the issue raised by Donald H. Regan (1972) about resource allocation sixteen years later in his book *The Firm, the Market and the Law* (1988: 164). Regan and Gerald E. Austen raise the issue that legal rules do affect the outcome of resource allocation. Coase's response is simply that they are wrong because under the assumption of zero transaction costs, 'liability and nonliability are interchangeable at will' (Coase 1988: 164).

Coase's theory in the economic front has fostered the development of transaction cost based property rights analysis, pioneered by scholars like Alchian (1965), Alchian and Demsetz (1973), Cheung (1973, 1974), and Williamson (1975, 1985). As far as zoning is concerned, Coase apparently in his 1960 paper regards it purely as a kind of direct governmental regulation which is to 'confine certain types of business [uses] to certain districts'[13] [brackets mine]. This appreciation of the nature of zoning is of course the ordinary land use planning or how the planners make sense of the word.[14] However, this meeting of minds tends to fixate academic perception of zoning. The same meaning of zoning underlies the critical appraisal of zoning by Crecine (1967), Siegan (1972), Maser, Riker and Rosett (1977), Fischel (1978, 1979, 1980), Mark and Goldberg (1981), Anderson (1982) and Benson (1984).

In their evaluation of zoning, the followers of Coase, or 'Coasians', tend to either present an 'invariance' view of zoning, i.e. zoning does not improve efficiency, or use the property rights theorist's argument of rent-seeking to interpret zoning as a 'zero sum game'. The most sophisticated model is the one presented by William A. Fischel. The Coasian's theoretical views are well received by American real estate researchers.[15]

The Coasian value regression model has a general form which is shown below:

$$V = f (E)$$

In their empirical study of the potency of zoning in tackling externalities, the Coasians generally regress land price or value (V) against some neighbouring uses and/or local amenities (E) within a given locality with land use pattern (X) that allegedly would produce externalities or neighbourhood effects. If the actual regression coefficients (f) are significant in terms of the expected sign and value, then the existence of externalities and hence the relevance of zoning is confirmed. If the externalities are insignificant then the zoning becomes doubtful. Crecine et al. (1967), Reuter (1973), Stull (1975), Maser et al. (1977), Lafferty and Frech III (1978) all adopt this general approach.[16] Crecine et al. conclude that their study on Pittsburgh casts doubt upon the notion that neighbourhood effects abound in the urban property market (Crecine 1967: 95). Reuter suggests in his Pittsburgh study that externality requires no government action, since it is 'controlled efficiently by self-selection in the market' and many zoning restrictions in his study 'could be eliminated without exercising any significant adverse influence in property value' (Reuter 1973: 336–337). Similarly, Stull discovers in his Boston study that value of property is dependent on land use pattern but argues that

> Zoning laws are ineffectual in actually constraining the location of
> economic activities . . . (as) it often appears that land market forces
> are too strong for officials administering a zoning statute to ignore
> . . . zoning regulation is constantly being adjusted to accommodated
> these forces. If this is true, the long run locational equilibrium in a
> zoned community will consist of a configuration of land uses which
> is not very different from which would have occurred had zoning
> never been introduced in the first place. Under such circumstances,
> it may make sense to eliminate zoning laws and save the costs
> associated with their administration. (Stull 1975: 353)

Maser et al. also conclude in their Rochester study that their tests reveal
no price effect attributable to 'zoning' and that

> the externalities which zoning is supposed to prevent could not be
> detected except in one instance where zoning may be associated
> with racial prejudice . . . zoning is ineffective. (Maser et al. 1977: 128)

Mark and Goldberg conclude in their Vancouver Study that

> rezoning does not necessarily lead to changes in land use and land
> value . . . No evidence was found to support the assertion that there
> are significant externalities at work in residential property markets.
> (Mark and Goldberg 1981: 431)

However, most Coasians are aware of the limitations of their study. Crecine
et al. stated in their Pittsburgh Study that the independence of land value
from the 'amenities' should not be interpreted as meaning that there are no
externalities in that market. 'Indeed, the empirical results only indicate that
there was no evidence in support of the externalities of the kind with which
the model was concerned', in other words, chosen by the researcher (Crecine
et al. 1967: 93). Reuter similarly points out that the result of his study

> do *not* demonstrate either that no externalities exist in urban property
> markets or no externalities can exist in urban property markets.
> (Reuter 1973: 336)

The key problem about such regression tests is one of interpretation.
Where externalities (E) under land use pattern (X) are not reflected in land
values (V), the theorists conclude that zoning does not matter. However, does
this confirm the Pigovian thesis that externalities are not 'felt' by the land
market or, indeed, provide a *prima facie* case for even more zoning restrictions?
Where externalities (E) under land use pattern (X) are reflected in land values
(V), the theorists would, according to their way of thinking, conclude that
zoning does matter. Does it mean that zoning has unquestionably achieved

the object of internalizing externalities? A Pigovian theorist would surely affirm this view. Or does it mean contrarily that the market can price 'externalities' so that zoning is redundant. Can we really isolate the influence of 'the market' and 'zoning'? Is it legitimate for the theorists to believe that the 'amenities' they select are really externalities and not internalities? The Coasians themselves are indecisive and always qualify their results with doubts and reservations. This is best illustrated by the conclusion of Lafferty and Frech III when they discover in their Boston Study that their results 'support the conventional position that certain land uses do have an inimical effect on the market-value of neighbouring single family homes and that their results indicate that under zoning, certain configurations of land uses are efficient in maximizing single-family property values.' They assert that

> the finding that neighbouring land uses do matter is not a direct endorsement of zoning. There are alternative means of influencing land uses. Moreover, zoning introduces costs and distortions of its own.' (Lafferty and Frech III 1978: 388–389)

To address these questions, we have to review the Pigovian's arguments and Coase's own writings. The reasons why the Coasians reach conflicting conclusions as given by Hirsch (1979) are quite instructive:

> . . . the reasons why different empirical studies appear to reach opposing conclusions are many. Perhaps the most important is that each study pertains to a particular geographical area and to a particular point in time . . . . (Hirsch 1979: 77)

Unfortunately Hirsch does not suggest a way out of this trap. Mark and Goldberg provide some tentative suggestions like 'continued experiments with performance zoning', mixed use and comprehensive development zoning 'such as that practised in many Canadian cities', and spot zoning. All such suggestions highlight the fact that it is not a simplistic dichotomy between 'zoning' and 'non-zoning' but different forms of zoning. As argued in Chapter 2, zoning is inherent to all exclusive property rights systems. Thus, research focus should better be placed upon the special form of zoning or zoning policies.

The Pigovian tradition

While Coase speaks of the Pigovian tradition as an 'oral tradition',[17] the Pigovian theorization since the publication of the 'Problem of Social Cost' has become less oral and more mathematical.[18]

The proponents of Pigou, notably Baumol (1972), Fisher and Peterson

(1976) and Crone (1983), opt instead to contest Coase's assumption of zero transaction costs, dwell on the philosophical notion of 'time' implied in the assumption or resort to substituting their own assumptions about the nature of some production functions, as in the works of Helpman and Pines (1977). Others simply modify the Coasians test equations to produce test results that are different from the 'invariance' rule.

Others draw attention to the considerations that Coase's theorization about externality is static 'efficiency-based', hence ignoring wealth effects of zoning (Goetz and Wofford 1979).

As Einstein wrote to another Nobel Prize scientist, Werner Heisenberg, 'it is theory which decides what we can observe'.[19] While the choice of the Pigovian or Coasian paradigm dictates how one would perceive the social nature of zoning, there is no reason why ideas from both paradigms cannot be integrated. When referring to Baumol and Oates (1975) and Fisher and Peterson (1976), Bromley points out that as far as policy matter is concerned,

> neo-classical economics now has a body of literature concerned with [Pigovian] environmental policy in the large, rather than solutions for small numbers case in which voluntary [Coasian] solutions seem so compelling. (Bromley 1978: 44)

Limitations of the Coasian paradigm from property rights perspective: Coase v. Coasians

The above literature survey indicates that the Coasian paradigm of zoning, by restricting its attention to the issue of externality in relation to government planning intervention in the land market, could be considered to have overlooked a fundamental character of zoning: it is an institution of exclusive property rights. While Fischel's idea that zoning indicates an 'incomplete assignment of property rights',[20] the alternative view is that zoning denotes an attenuation of rights by the state over the best possible uses of land as decided by the private land users. In terms of planning vocabulary, this governmental process is called 'development control'. Whether zoning as such is more efficient than private solution over land use rights is an empirical matter.

Coase indeed expressly specifies the need for this comparative or 'opportunity cost'[21] (Coase 1960) mode of thinking. In 'The Problem of Social Cost', he states that

> a better approach would seem to start our analysis with a situation approximating that which actually exists (whether there is any prior zoning element), to examine the effects of a proposed (zoning) policy

change, and to attempt to decide whether the new situation (with the inception of zoning) would be, in total, better or worse than the original one. (Coase 1960: 43) [brackets mine]

Coase's comparative thinking is succinctly summarized in Carl J. Dahlman's 'The Problem of Externality', probably the best defence of Coase's theorization about externality:

> The neatness of the Coase analysis lies in the fact that it dispenses completely with what Demsetz has called 'the Nirvana approach' and instead calls for what he labels 'the comparative systems approach' which explicitly attempts to ascertain the economic consequences of alternative ways of organizing the allocation of resources. The analysis thus directs attention to the point that institutions fulfill an economic function by reducing transaction costs and therefore ought to be treated as variables determined inside the economic scheme of things. The question then ultimately becomes: *how can the economic organization be improved upon by endogenous institutional rearrangements?* This is not the outlook of modern welfare theory where the government is seen as a force outside the economic system altogether, which will come to our aid and rectify the havoc wrought by indigenously working market forces, just like the classical *deus ex machina*. Coase opens the door for an economic theory of institutions, whereas modern welfare theory can only gaze into its crystal ball of mathematical abstraction and wisely state that heaven on earth is still far off — which is true, but of no particular consequence either for the correct conduct of economic policy or for the theory of externalities. (Dahlman 1979: 161–162) [Italics mine]

Later, in his book *The Firm, the Market and the Law* (1988), Coase restates his policy view in a more general form:

> Economic policy consists of choosing those legal rules, procedures, and administrative structures which will maximize the value of production. (Coase 1988: 28)

The best view of Coase about zoning, or indeed government regulation, is actually expressed unambiguously in his less well known paper 'The Federal Communications Commission':

> . . . if many people are harmed and there are several sources of pollution, it is more difficult to reach a satisfactory solution through the market. . . . Even the enforcement of rights through the courts may not be easy . . . As a practical matter, the market may become too costly to operate. In these circumstances, it may be preferrable

> to impose special regulations. Thus, the problem of smoke pollution
> may be dealt with by regulations . . . which confine manufacturing
> establishment to certain district by zoning. (Coase 1959: 29)

In other words, zoning as government regulation may be acceptable as
the alternative to free transaction in land market where the transaction costs
of using the unregulated land market become excessive. This must be regarded
as a more appropriate view of Coase's teaching on government intervention.
Zoning policy is not dismissed *a priori* and his view is certainly shared by
Harold Demsetz.[22]

It is true that Coase inclines to consider government as being less efficient.
He argues that 'there is a *prima facie* case against intervention' (Coase 1988:
26) and cites zoning as an example where 'regulation has commonly made
matters worse'. However, this presumption against intervention is rebuttable
and must be read in the light of his caution that

> this belief, even if justified, does not do more than suggest that
> governmental regulation should be curtailed. (Coase 1989: 119)

Besides, Coase in his book reminds economists that markets are often
regulated to promote trade.

> Economists observing the regulations of the exchanges often assume
> that they represent an attempt to exercise monopoly power and aim
> to restrain competition. They ignore or, at any rate, fail to emphasize
> an alternative explanation for these regulations: that they exist in
> order to reduce transaction costs and therefore to *increase the volume
> of trade*. (Coase 1988: 9) [italics mine]

While rights can be attenuated by government, the same government as
the protector of property rights of its subjects[23] must somehow delineate certain rights over land.[24] Coase himself concludes that 'the delimitation of rights
is an essential prelude to market transaction'.[25] From this point of view, Coase's
scenic parable of the wheat field presupposes[26] the existence of a private property rights system. In a land system sense, it presupposes the existence of a fee
simple, or its equivalent. This concept of land law denotes, in the absence of
legislative or policy constraints (like statutory or administrative zoning), the
maximum conceivable freedom over the disposal and use of land. By analogy,
the parable also works for land with a lesser extent of rights, like the old 999-
year unrestricted lease, and the new 75-year restricted lease of Hong Kong.[27]

However, it is also conceivable that there are two possible broader concepts of zoning which are compatible with the parable. The first concept
interprets zoning as a pure forward planning matter assigning, arbitrarily, initial rights to landusers without development control. Thus the subsequent

change in use or transfer of rights is left entirely to the market and application for rezoning to allow subsequent changes and transfer of rights is always costlessly approved by government. Coase seems to have adopted this concept when he discusses the relationship between regulation, including zoning, and property rights:

> [that regulation has disadvantages] does not mean that there should be no such regulation. Nor should it be thought that, because some rights are determined by regulation, there cannot be *others* which can be modified by contract. (Coase 1959: 29–30)[Italics and bracket mine]

However, this 1959 view of Coase would be more in line with his 1960 view or the invariance version of the Coase Theorem if the last sentence in the quotation was interpreted as 'they cannot be *subsequently* modified by the contract'. Instead, he merely accepts the zoned use as being given 'that zoning and other regulations apply to houses does not mean that there should not be private property in houses' (Coase 1959: 30).

The second concept is even more general and predicated on the fact that all categories of land rights have one common attribute: the right to exclude others in the use of land. Such right to exclude is inseparable from the concept of boundary delineation,[28] or zoning understood broadly. 'Non-zoning' in Houston (Siegan 1970) is in fact zoned.[29]

Coase does not seem to appreciate the significance of boundary delineation in land law. In the example of the newly discovered cave given in his 'The Federal Communications Commission' (Coase 1959: 25), cited in the chapter 'Notes on the Problem of Social Cost' in his 1988 work (Coase 1988: 173), he asserts that 'the law merely determines the person with whom it is necessary to make a contract to obtain the use of the cave . . . .' However, what is a cave? 'Extension',[30] an important concept in the philosophy of knowledge, is ignored, although Coase has addressed the criticism about the concept of 'time' in various places.[31]

Zoning is the basic element not only of land law, but also of a theory of the state as a polity with boundaries. The ordinary economic meaning of zoning as a forward planning concept or as a special political entity, like the 'enterprise zones', Shenzhen Special Economic Zone, or Hong Kong Special Administrative Region can be covered by this concept. This concept is also able to cover the conventional but misleading distinction in the planning field between 'planning' and 'market'. As Thomas Sowell argues, echoing Coase's statement about 'planning' within the private firm,[32]

> every economic activity under every conceivable form of society has been planned. What differs are the decision making units that do the planning. (Sowell 1980: 213)

In Coase's terminology, government planning is

> the forcible superseding of other people's plans by government
> officials. (Sowell 1980: 214, also quoted in Kwong 1990: 55)

In other words, it is better to distinguish between 'private planning of firms in the market' and 'public planning by planners in government' than between 'market' and 'planning'.

In the presence of transaction costs, clear delineation of rights over land can indeed establish a market, where one does not exist previously, or enlarge one if one is already in existence. This aspect of zoning raises a serious methodological question for various regression studies about the impact of zoning on externalities. As discussed above, it is ambiguous whether they are actually testing phenomena of 'the market' or rather 'zoning' understood as forward planning or development control. It is also ambiguous whether they are actually testing the Pigovian or property rights propositions because both of them can be mutually consistent. While we may postulate the Pigovian zoning would enhance land value, the same can be said about Coasian zoning, although the reasoning behind it is different. The former is that 'zoning is introduced because the land market fails to internalize externalities' whereas in the latter case, 'zoning is introduced because it reduces some transaction costs in the land market'. It is only where the tests are conducted about *differences* in institutional design or *changes* in right assignment[33] (about land boundary or uses) within a system that they can really measure the costs and benefits of zoning.

It appears that a more appropriate approach, following Coase's comparative cost concept, is to contrast the differences gained from observing land use pattern (X) and another land use pattern (Y), and judge whether these differences in terms of zoning measures are desirable from the point of view of their impacts on land values and externalities. Such differences may be cross-sectional, as in the case of evaluating the variation in values (V) among districts under different degree of zoning restrictions. They may be time-series, by comparing the chronological changes in land values (V) in the same district before and after zoning measures are altered, or cross-sectional, by comparing the values of land under different zoning provisions in the same district. Avrin's cross-sectional and time-series study of changes to the residential zoning of San Franciso in 1960 is an excellent example (Avrin 1977).[34] Where feasible, physical measure of the incidence of externalities (E), like nuisance complaints, may also be used instead of land values (V).[35]

Notes

1. Friedrich von Hayek is a Nobel Prize laureate in Economic Science, 1974. He is "considered a pioneer in monetary theory, the pre-eminent proponent of the libertarian philosophy, and the ideological mentor of the Reagan and Thatcher 'revolution'" by the University of Chicago Press.

2. von Hayek, Friedrich A. 'Housing and Town Planning.' in *The Constitution of Liberty*. London: Routledge, 1960, p. 353.

3. For instance, Hayek, F.A. 1960, op. cit.

4. Pearce's analysis of private property rights and their relations with transaction cost is dubious in the sense that decision criteria are ill-defined regarding the choice of intervention or non-intervention. However, Pearce's notion that land as a good has 'physical attributes' as distinct from a set of legal rights and obligations attached to them (Pearce 1980: 118) is instructive. The notion of 'extension' or boundary delineation used in this book is in agreement with Pearce's concept. Besides, his idea that 'property rights can be created by the settlement of new lands (e.g. through reclamation or colonization) or by increasing the size of the set of rights relating to each land parcel' can well be generalized in the discussion of the initial assignment of exclusive property rights in society. However, Pearce's theorization is vague on the distinction between 'public' and 'private' rights. The concept of 'public leasehold' or 'collective property rights' is inconsistent with the view that leasehold is a lesser private property right (lesser due to limitation in time of enjoyment only). In a M.Sc. dissertation submitted to the University of Wales Institute of Science and Technology 'Zoning control and Property Rights', Wong, Sidney C.C. has applied the notion of 'public leasehold' to discuss the leasehold system of Hong Kong. Nelson's argument that zoning creates 'collective property rights' held by local government may create similiar confusion, unless 'public' or 'collective' refers to Alchian's concept of 'communal property rights'. This is the view of David E. Mills, who argues that 'zoning assigns property rights of landowners and establishes collective right to community environment'. Mills uses the game-theoretic concept of strategic holding out of landowners who are given development rights and comes to the conclusion that neither 'private rights' or 'community rights' are uniformly superior in terms of land market performance. However Mills' study is not empirical. See also Lai (1997e).

5. These two names and Oliver Williamson are cited by Coase in his 1991 paper for the Royal Swedish Academy of Science, op. cit.

6. See for instance, Ronald Dworkin's criticism of Richard Posner's *Economic Analysis of Law* (1972), which adopts Coasian reasoning, in Dworkin, Ronald. *Taking Rights Seriously*. U.K.: Duckworth, 1977, pp. 96–100.

7. Coase is very critical not just of Pigou's analysis but also his manner of working. See Coase, Ronald H. *The Firm, the Market and the Law*. Chicago and London: The University of Chicago Press, 1988, pp. 22–23 and footnote No. 20.

8. See Goldberg Victor P. 1976, op. cit., 877–893.

9. It is not at all odd for Coase and his followers to be called utilitarians. See note 16, Chapter 1, p. 15.

10. For legalist analysis of environmental economics, see Bromley, Daniel W. 'Property Rules, Liability Rules, and Environmental Economics.' *Journal of Economic Issues* XII (March 1978): 43–60.

11. Dworkin, Ronald *Taking Rights Seriously*. London: Duckworth, 1991. See Lai, Lawrence W.C. 'Economic Analysis of Law in English Jurisprudence.' (法律不肯向經濟低頭) in [經濟暢論], Hong Kong: *Hong Kong Economic Journal*, 1992. November 1992, pp. 110–115.

12. In the case of Hong Kong where private land is obtained from the Crown by lease, (a form of contract), planned zoning is a kind of breach of promise. Whether such breach can be justified is another question.

13. Coase, R.H. 1960, op. cit., p. 17, also in Coase, R.H. 1988 op. cit., p. 117.

14. As early as 1921 the British Ministry of Health explained that 'one of the main objectives of a town plan was to fix those areas in which certain types of development should be allowed. This system has become known by the name 'zoning'. It has received much attention in the United States of America, but it has, as yet, been but little studied in this country (UK).' (Bristow 1984, p. 10)

15. See for instance Harris, Jack C. and Moore, William Dunglas 'Debunking the Mythology of Zoning.' *Real Estate Review* 13 (Winter 1984): 94–97.

16. The fact that Lafferty and Frech III apply various levels of the locality to view 'the entire town as a zone' apart from the 'neighbourhood' does not affect the generalization used here.

17. Coase, R.H. 1960, op. cit., p. 39, also in Coase, R.H. 1988, op. cit., p. 149.

18. Coase, R.H. 1988, op. cit., p. 185.

19. As quoted in Chapter 1, 'What is Practice?' in Cole, C.L. *Microeconomics: A Contemporary Approach*. New York: Harcourt Brace Jovanovich, Inc., 1973, p. 10.

20. See Fischel, William A. 'A Property Rights Approach to Municipal Zoning.' *Land Economics* 54 (February 1978): 64–81. This view is strictly speaking correct only if exclusive property rights are assigned by zoning *ab initio*.

21. See Coase, R.H. 1960, op. cit., p. 43, also in Coase, R.H. 1988, op. cit., p. 154.

22. Demsetz, Harold 'The Exchange and Enforcement of Private Property Rights.' (October 1964): 23.

23. Lai, Lawrence W.C., 'Democracy and Political Protection of Property Rights,' unpublished M.Soc.Sc. (Economics) dissertation, Department of Economics, University of Hong Kong, June 1987.

24. Here, Pearce's concept of the creation of property rights by government falls within this category. It is better to use the expression 'delineation' than 'creation', which is more specific.

25. Coase 1959, op. cit., p. 27 also quoted in Cheung, S.N.S. 1990, p. 10.

26. A parallel could be drawn between this view and 'the presupposition of the grundnorm' in Kelsen's jurisprudential reasoning.

27. Leasehold, as derivates of freehold, is a lesser kind of private property rights.

28. This point is in agreement with B.J. Pearce's point that land as a good has 'physical attributes' or alternatively, spatial dimension. See Pearce, B.J. (1980), op. cit. See note 9, Chapter 2.

29. The concept of 'the entire town as a zone' adopted in the empirical study of

Lafferey and Frech III (1978) is in line within this concept.

30. 'Extension' is a better expression than 'physical attributes' because it is more general and encompassing in philosophical terms. In Runes' *Dictionary of Philosophy*, it reads : Physical space, considered as a single concrete, continuum as contrasted with the abstract conceptual space of mathematics. The distinction between extension and 'space' in the abstract sense is clearly drawn by Descartes (1596– 1650) in *The Principles of Philosophy*, part II, Princ. IV-XV. See Runes, Dagobert D. ed., *Dictionary of Philosophy*. Totowa, New Jersey: Littlefield, Adams & Co., 1960, p. 105.

31. See Coase, Ronald H. 1988, op. cit., p. 15.

32. See note 10, Chapter 1.

33. See Bromley, Daniel W. 1978, op. cit. and 'Entitlements, Missing Markets, and Environmental Uncertainty.' *Journal of Environmental Economics and Management* 17 (1989): 181–194.

34. This approach is attempted in Hypotheses 2, 3, 4, 5, 7 and 8 in Chapter 5.

35. This approach is attempted in Hypotheses 1 and 6 in Chapter 5.

Chapter Four

Initial Assignment of Exclusive Property Rights: The Fish Story

In my youth it was said that what was too silly to be said may be
sung. In modern economics it may be put into mathematics. (Coase
1988: 185)

Introduction

Marine and riparian fish are often evaluated in economic literature as a common
or non-exclusive property allocated on a 'first-come-first-served' basis. However, there exists ways to transform marine fish into a private property by
means akin to commercial riparian or fresh water fish culture in private lakes,
artificial ponds or even paddy fields,[1] as in the case of many Asian countries.
In the rural bays and coves of Hong Kong, government has designated since
1982 a number of 'Marine Fish Culture Zones' (abbreviated hereinafter MFCZ)
which can be regarded as measures to establish private property rights over
marine water by zoning, as it is an offence to culture fish outside the MFCZ.[2]
Any person can obtain the rights to utilize such MFCZ by applying for a
licence from the Argiculture and Fisheries Department (officially abbreviated
AFD) and paying an annual licence fee. The AFD currently allocates MFCZ
area largely by rationing or waiting, as a matter of policy, for the purpose
of fish culture. The licence fee is at present proportional to the culture area
irrespective of MFCZ location. While there are no regulations stipulating the
cultivation method and species of fish reared, the common practice of fish
culture is to capture fry from the coastal waters or buy them in the open
market[3] and rear them in cages suspended by rafts within the MFCZ. The
licence of the MFCZ is renewed on an annual basis and is non-transferrable.
Public protection against theft of fish is offered by the Marine Police and

the common self-help measures are keeping dogs and watchmen in floating guard houses in the vicinity.

This chapter (Lai 1992, 1993A, 1993B)[4] seeks to:

(a) describe the establishment of private property rights over marine fish in Hong Kong;

(b) test empirically Cheung's thesis that the formation of private property rights constrains rent dissipation in a case where water pollution is alleged to have affected fish yield in public coastal waters; and

(c) test the environmentalist's Pigovian argument that the price mechanism has failed to reflect the impact of water pollution on cultured fish in the consumer and factor markets.

Objective (b) arises from the assertion made in Chapters 2 and 3 that zoning could be a way to assign exclusive property rights and hence constrain rent dissipation. Objective (c), as a subsidiary task, tests the Coasian belief that the price mechanism should not be assumed to be unable to reflect social costs.

Although the establishment of private property rights over marine fish is nothing new and has been extensively adopted in countries like Norway, Thailand, the Philippines, Taiwan and Japan, the case of Hong Kong is more interesting on a number of grounds. Firstly, unlike other countries, government subsidy to fish farmers is virtually zero. The fish farmers can hardly carry out off-shore fish farming in rough seas and can only farm in sheltered coastal waters. Secondly, the small size of the territory renders mutual avoidance between high density urban (residential and industrial) development and fish farming virtually impossible. These two factors make a study of private property rights and pollution less fettered by regulations.

In the property rights literature on marine fishing, the received theory is that overfishing, a form of rent dissipation, is due to unrestrained competition among fishermen in the absence of exclusive property rights. The theoretical analysis described in Chapter 2 about common property is directly relevant.[5] In the environmentalist perception, however, the fall in fish yield in coastal waters is often ascribed to an increase in the level of water pollution. An interesting question therefore arises where the same phenomenon, a fall in coastal fish yield, can be explained by two factors: overfishing (an economic explanation), and water pollution (an environmental explanation). While these two explanations are not necessarily mutually exclusive, by comparing the productivity of Hong Kong's coastal fish culture areas, which is subject to pollution of different degrees, with the productivity of fish harvest provides a unique opportunity for assessing the relevance of these explanations. If coastal cultured fish yield increases notwithstanding an increase in water pollution, then the observed fall in coastal fish harvest cannot be concluded as a result of pollution but the absence of exclusive property rights which protect cultured fish. The corollary is that exclusive property rights, which is a result of marine zoning, constrain rent dissipation. Besides, a comparison between the prices of potentially polluted fish in coastal culture areas (cultured fish) and those of clean off-shore ocean fish (captured fish), and also derived comparisons among coastal culture areas with different levels of water pollution, can provide an opportunity to verify if the price mechanism is able to reflect the impact of the externality of water pollution. Thus, the Pigovian notion about the need for public intervention other than a clear delineation of private property rights (the most important version of the Coase Theorem[6]) will then be suspect if: a) there are price differentials between cultured and captured fish, b) pollution resistant fish are reared in more polluted culture zones and c) the demand for higher yield culture zones is greater than lower yield zones.

The findings of the empirical tests would throw light on the significance of zoning, which is understood as a means of assigning initial private property rights, not only in stimulating production but also in internalizing certain external effects.

Formation of private property rights by squatting and zoning

Private mariculture using rafts first appeared in Hong Kong waters in the late 1960s. It originated when some fishermen found that their practice of keeping surplus captured live fish in cages for private consumption could be adapted for commercial purpose. The success of the pioneers led to extensive imitation and many fishermen ceased operating their in-shore or off-shore fishing vessels and switched to coastal fish culture (Photograph 8). Such activities infringe upon the Crown's marine rights and can be regarded as a form of squatting.[7] The squatters' civil rights were defended by their own might.[8] The culturist's illegal use of floating cages for fish farming is conceivably a way to reduce high policing costs for illegal net impoundment or embankment of bays without Crown permission.[9] Using cages, the investment return to buying fry and feeding could be protected more easily from human thieves. Furthermore, natural predators such as seagulls, jelly fish, octopus, dolphins, sharks and also typhoons can be kept at bay as cages can be towed to havens when necessary. Besides, the transaction costs involved in selling one's cage business or in making contracts with a bulk or 'permanent' wholesale buyer of fish are conceivably lower than those in the situation where impoundment or embankment is used. The reason is that cage culture would make it easier to assess the capital value of the fish if their species, number and size are readily observable — especially under conditions where squatter's property rights are hard to enforce in civil law.

Photograph 8   Marine Fish Culture Rafts in 1977 (Courtesy of the Hong Kong Government)

The photograph shows the congested arrangement of culture rafts before the Marine Fish Culture Ordinance was introduced.

Competition in the industry became so hectic that it led to disputes among culturists and infiltration of underground societies involving violence. Illegal culture activities ran into direct conflict with public activities viz coastal development projects (reclamation, dredging, dumping of marine spoils, extraction of sand) and the use of coastal resources for purposes such as water recreation, fairways and typhoon shelters.[10] In response, the government passed the Marine Fish Culture Ordinance in 1980 to regulate the industry. In May 1982, a survey was carried out. The survey identified 1789 culturists operating 2,745 culture rafts scattered in 50 areas and occupying 25 ha of coastal waters.[11] Non-transferrable culture licences were then granted under the Ordinance to the surveyed culturists and subsequent application for fish culture rights have since then been processed on a first-come-first-serve basis. The distribution of marine fish culture zone is shown in Figure 4.1. Fish culture without a licence would be an offence.[12] The government in effect assigned exclusive rights though apparently non-transferrable to marine squatters by direct grant and the extent of rights within the culture zones is defined by the terms in the licence (Photograph 9). Since 1982, only one more MFCZ has been designated and the total culture area has not been increased. On the contrary, the government sought to reduce congestion in some zones by not reallocating the licences given up by the farmers who had abandoned the business.

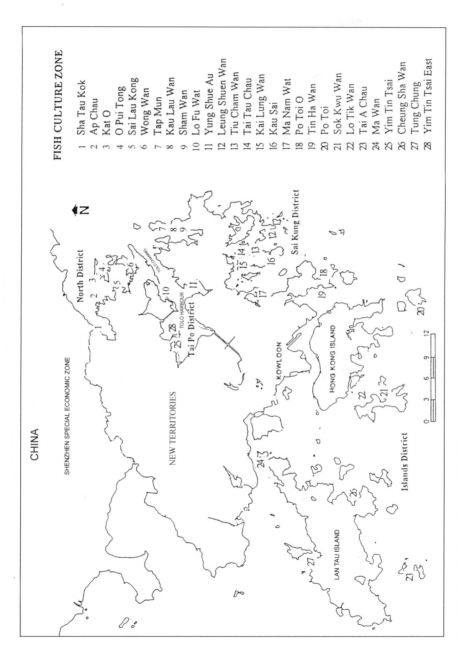

FISH CULTURE ZONE

1　Sha Tau Kok
2　Ap Chau
3　Kat O
4　O Pui Tong
5　Sai Lau Kong
6　Wong Wan
7　Tap Mun
8　Kau Lau Wan
9　Sham Wan
10　Lo Fu Wat
11　Yung Shue Au
12　Leung Shuen Wan
13　Tiu Cham Wan
14　Tai Tau Chau
15　Kai Lung Wan
16　Kau Sai
17　Ma Nam Wat
18　Po Toi O
19　Tin Ha Wan
20　Po Toi
21　Sok Kwu Wan
22　Lo Tik Wan
23　Tai A Chau
24　Ma Wan
25　Yim Tin Tsai
26　Cheung Sha Wan
27　Tung Chung
28　Yim Tin Tsai East

Fig. 4.1　Distribution of Marine Fish Culture Zones

Photograph 9   Marine Fish Culture Rafts in 1982 (Courtesy of the Hong Kong Government)
It shows a culture zone near Lamma Island.

Government allocation of commercial, residential and industrial land rights and marine (seabed) rights for the purpose of container port development in Hong Kong is carried out by either public auction or closed tender. There is little restriction on subsequent transfer of such property titles. On the contrary, government allocation of marine rights in the case of MFCZ is carried out initially by direct grant and subsequently by queueing, i.e. waiting (Barzel 1974) on payment in either case of a flat-rate fee for a licence which is non-transferrable. As for the initial assignment of exclusive property rights by means of grant, the government has forgone a huge part of her monopoly rights over marine rent which could be maximized by auction or tender. Under the maximization postulate, however, the government's choice for non-price allocation of initial MFCZ rights is definitely non-random and must be interpreted as maximization behaviour subject to the constraints of transaction costs. Such transaction costs will inevitably involve the political costs of choosing the alternative. Direct grant of marine rights by licensing saves the costs in using the Marine Police to enforce formal Crown rights by evicting the illegal culture activities. It also helps save the resulting costs involved in political confrontation between the fish farmers and the government.[13] The Marine police were heavily involved in controlling illegal immigration from China and Vietnamese refugees in the early 1980's.[14] Besides, AFD has a long tradition of providing assistance to primary producers via different types of subsidies, although none is provided for fish farmers except emergency relief for fish kill due to red tides.[15]

However, the policy of subsequent allocation by waiting and the legal prohibition against licence transfer is not immediately intelligible. The transaction costs involved in acquiring MFCZ rights by non-price allocation (i.e. waiting) must be higher than those acquired by auction or tender. At present there are about one thousand outstanding MFCZ applications.[16] This policy and the legislative intent behind the legal constraint of non-transferrability might be based on some equity considerations. The policy maker and the legislator might think that non-transferrability would prevent the culturist who has acquired initial rights at near zero price from earning windfall gain by selling his licence.[17] However, this is not true in reality. The non-transferrability rule could not prevent the culturists who were granted the initial rights from transferring their rights to someone else through employment or joint-venture contracts, as there is no legal limitation on the form of commercial enterprise the licencee may choose to adopt. A licencee could well be an employee of a company which controls both an MFCZ and a seafood restaurant. In the application form for a licence, the applicant has to state his or her employment status, if any. Similar contractual arrangement occurs where a law clerk with good connections in the real estate business 'employs' junior solicitors, who have monopoly rights created by law to process conveyancing but few business contacts. Alternatively, the licencee could form a joint-venture company with other individuals who do not possess a licence but other inputs. In either case, the rights to the licence, though not the licence itself, are transferred from the licencee to a third party who come to have some possessory rights of the MFCZ. Inevitably, the transaction costs involved in such contracting will be higher than those in the situation where the licence itself is transferrable, as the licence could only be renewable for the life of the licencee and could not be inherited. Costs need to be borne by the third party to assess and insure against the life risk of the licencee. The economic explanation the AFD have for not allocating transferrable licences on a price competitive basis after the initial grant is not easily intelligible, although the licensed culturists would welcome the current practice of licence renewal based on non-price competitions. In the absence of a theory to explain legislative actions, judgement on the wisdom of this policy is suspended. In any case, the system has worked well.

The initial establishment of exclusive possessory rights and freedom of contract is a significant innovation, in spite of the above comments on the method of subsequent assignment of marine rights and the non-transferability rule. Such exclusive rights should substantially reduce the transaction costs involved in commercial marine fish culture and the dissipation of ocean rent (fish yield) under common or unclearly defined property rights. These would be discussed in the following sections.

▧ Market response to pollution under exclusive property rights

When compared to commercial fresh water fish culture in private ponds, where carefully selected species of fish adapted to different water layers can grow and reproduce themselves in relatively controlled water conditions, the MFCZ method has an inherent physical limitation. The MFCZ farmer cannot easily control the quality of the ocean water and there is no private right to prevent competing users of the water from polluting the water, who easily escape the water pollution control and de-pollution measures[18] of the government. To resort to criminal action is either too costly or ineffective as it does not lead to civil remedies. The water quality problem is twofold. Firstly, the system depends on the sustained supply of fry, as it has not yet been possible to reproduce fish in floating cages. At present, most of the fry are caught in local waters, notably Victoria Harbour which is one of the busiest ports on earth and the world's number one container port in terms of cargo throughput. Victoria Harbour and many other water systems such as Tolo Harbour, are also used effectively as domestic and industrial sewers for 5.6 million people. A hectic manufacturing industry is established in the new towns which include the Tai Po Industrial Estate. Besides, gigantic urban reclamation projects are always on the move. The local source of fry is thus subject to a great ecological threat. However, this problem is not considered insurmountable as the MFCZ enterprises are commercially viable and can afford imported fry.[19] Actually, the fact that marine fish can be commercially domesticated has created a market value for fry and off-shore fishermen would seek to conserve them for the coastal fish farmers.[20]

The second problem is more difficult and has captured the attention and efforts of local environmentalists. Given the peculiar geographical constraints of the territory the fish inside the cages in designated MFCZ are liable to become occasional preys of anoxicity and poisoning due to pollution.[21] The fish may simply die or their health deteriorates. The environmentalists' views are in accord with the topical technical reports of the Environmental Protection Department (officially abbreviated EPD) which reveal that the water quality in Victoria Harbour and the fish culture areas notably Tolo Harbour is rapidly deteriorating. EPD's water quality indicators or standards are largely physical and defined in terms of (a) the incidence of red tides; (b) the level of dissolved oxygen; and (c) the density of biological/chemical pollutants and heavy metals. However, the economic relationship between pollution thus measured and marine fish culture is hitherto an unexplored area. We may define pollution as changes in the attributes of water due to human activities. It would appear from the comments of the environmentalists that (i) the consumer is quite ignorant of the health implications of eating MFCZ fish and (ii) the MFCZ industry takes no account of the deterioration in the quality of marine water. Indeed, the environmentalists and EPD once alleged that the primitive methods[22] of feeding would itself contribute to water pollution due to the decomposition of food debris on the sea bed. In economic terms within the Pigovian tradition, this view asserts that the social costs of pollution are not internalized in consumption and production activities. Such assertions have never been satisfactorily tested against facts.[23]

To carry out such tests, an analytical model developed on the basis of the received property rights analysis of ocean fishing is first constructed. Some theoretical assertions are built in the model so that they are tested against facts subsequently.

Analytically, although it cannot eliminate the presence of pollution, the MFCZ could constrain the rent dissipation of ocean fish due to competition in fish harvesting. Following the Knight-Gordon-Cheung tradition,[24] A and B in Figure 4.2 represent respectively the equilibrium of ocean fish yield under a private property rights regime and a common property rights regime subject to full dissipation. The MFCZ is a possible means to attain A by delineation of private property rights other than (i) collusion or (ii) central regulation.[25] Conceptually the impact of pollution does not affect the analysis at all. We may postulate that the set of values of the marginal and average product curves is some function of the ocean water quality. Hence we may characterize the equilibria of alternative property rights regimes (i.e. common and private property rights) at a lower quality of ocean water caused by pollution

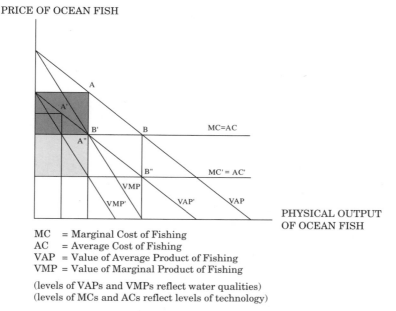

PRICE OF OCEAN FISH

PHYSICAL OUTPUT OF OCEAN FISH

MC   = Marginal Cost of Fishing
AC   = Average Cost of Fishing
VAP = Value of Average Product of Fishing
VMP = Value of Marginal Product of Fishing

(levels of VAPs and VMPs reflect water qualities)
(levels of MCs and ACs reflect levels of technology)

Fig. 4.2   Fish Productivity and Pollution Under Common Property Rights and Private Property Rights

by A' and B' which lie on a lower set of values of the marginal and average cost curve, assuming that the quality of fish reared in polluted water is reflected in their prices. If it is assumed that the polluted fish do not die and their growth is not retarded, their marginal physical product will not be affected. However, in the absence of transaction costs, their lower quality is observed perfectly by the consumer and hence attracts a lower price. An increase in the level of pollution would lead to a parallel downward shift of the values of the marginal and average product curves. The parallel shift can be fully explained by a change in price. As long as the set of the values of the marginal and average curves is above marginal or average costs, rent is captured by the MFCZ fish farmer at different ocean water quality or pollution levels. The problem of water pollution confronting the fish farmer in the real situation of positive transaction costs is therefore conceptually the same as air pollution confronting a farmer growing crops in fields beside a factory emitting aerial pollutants or a railway track where train sparks affect wheat harvest. In either case, the rights to pollute are unclearly defined or transaction costs are so high that mutual agreement of the optimal level of pollution is not worthwhile to enter.

Environmental scientists have frequently ascribed the decline in fish yield in coastal waters under common ownership to an increase in the level of pollution caused by agricultural, domestic and industrial discharges. However,

Photograph 10   Typical Hong Kong Fishing Boats (Courtesy of the Hong Kong Government)

The photograph shows two typical ocean going fishing vessels in Hong Kong.

according to Cheung's rent dissipation model, the same decline would be predicted to occur even if the sea water has been undisturbed by human activities so long as there is competition. In short, pollution and competition would both drive the virgin rental value of the ocean down to zero towards the same direction. The establishment of exclusive property rights over the ocean, therefore, would constrain competition irrespective of the attributes of water pollution. On the grounds that under private ownership, there would be an incentive to invest, we may further postulate that the establishment of exclusive property rights would also lead to investment in anti-pollution measures like artificial aeration and improved feeding inputs. The effect of such measures can be isolated when the changes in fish yield in the coastal waters are compared to those in the MFCZ. We may assert, accordingly, that the fall in yield in the common waters must be faster than that, if any, in the MFCZ.

According to the maximization postulate, regardless of the transaction costs, it also makes sense for the fish farmers to seek to minimize the impact of pollution and the corresponding fall in rent of his private property. In addition, they will also tend to reduce investment in coping with pollution. They may employ the following strategies: (a) paying a lower tender price for MFCZ if they were allocated by competitive auction or tender and/or (b) rearing pollution-resistant species[26] in more polluted MFCZ if the alternative of concealing the lower quality of fish is assumed away. In the limiting case, the tender price or the cost of rearing pollution-resistant fish falls by the same amount as the drop in fish price, and hence rent earned at equilibrium A' is same as that at A. Then the rent of more polluted and less polluted MFCZ would be the same. This would not be the case if the fish were common property because there would be little incentive to invest in the habitat of the fish or on the fish themselves. As MFCZ is not allocated by competitive auction or tender but by direct grant, method (a) apparently is not relevant. However, this can be approximated by the length of the queue for licences.[27] For a more polluted zone, the queue must be shorter, *ceteris paribus*.

While the above model is reasonable in theory, it must be tested against facts. Within the analytical framework discussed above, the following testable propositions can be derived:
(1) the fall in fish output as a result of deteriorating water quality in MFCZ is less than that in in-shore fishing grounds due to dissipation in the latter;
(2) the fish reared in more polluted MFCZ are lower in price than those reared in less polluted MFCZ or those captured in off-shore fishing grounds;
(3) the queues for licences for the more polluted MFCZ are shorter than those for less polluted MFCZ; and
(4) more pollution-resistant fish are kept in the more polluted MFCZ than in the less polluted ones.

Failure to reject proposition (1) would reveal the significance of the establishment of private property rights in constraining dissipation and pollution. The proposition is falsified if the fall in output is identical to or if the fall is greater in MFCZ than in coastal fishing grounds. If other propositions are not refuted by facts, not only would the benefits of exclusive rights be demonstrated, the allegation of market failure would also be negated. Proposition (2) is rejected if (a) the prices of fish reared in more polluted MFCZ are the same as or higher than those in less polluted MFCZ or those captured in off-shore fishing grounds and if (b) the prices of fish captured in polluted coastal fishing grounds are the same as or higher than those captured in off-shore fishing grounds. Proposition (3) is negated if the queue for licences for the more polluted MFCZ is equal to or longer than that for the less polluted MFCZ. Proposition (4) is falsified if there is no systematic pattern in the fish mix for different MFCZ. Furthermore, confirmation of (2) and/or (3) would imply that attempts to conceal fish quality are absent or not effective.

For the purpose of empirical investigation, the data of Tolo Harbour in Tai Po District and Sha Tau Kok in North District are compared. Both are located in the eastern part of the New Territories in Hong Kong and are not affected by the brackish water from the Pearl River System to the west of the Colony. While in general terms, the eastern coastal waters, including Sai Kung, are clean mainly because of good dispersion rates and a low level of urbanization, Tolo Harbour is an exception because it is a large embayment with a narrow entrance, Tolo Channel. In the Sung Dynasty, Tolo Harbour was a royal enclosure for pearl culture. Such culture by modern firms was discontinued only in the early eighties when an MFCZ in Tolo Channel was gazetted. Into the Harbour is now discharged daily domestic and industrial sewage of Sha Tin and Tai Po New Towns which have a brief urban development history of less than two decades. The towns have a total population of 710,000 and ninety hectares of intensive industrial area, including Tai Po Industrial Estate for high-tech industries.

This empirical study differs significantly from the study of Angello and Donelley (1975) in terms of test design and results. In comparing wild and cultured oysters, they found that:
(1) wild oysters are harvested earlier in the season, baecause there is less incentive to conserve the oysters;
(2) markets served purely by culturists command higher prices since they have the ability to respond to market conditions, whereas common property harvesters are driven by competition to catch and sell as many oysters as possible; and
(3) wild oyster harvesters earn substantially lower income than culturists as potential profits are dissipated for reasons stated above.

Without questioning the statistical methodology of Angello and Donnelley (1975), it is odd from a Chinese consumer's point of view that cultured oysters are more expensive. This may be the case where dissipation in wild oysters has been so extreme that the natural replenishing cycle of wild oysters is breaking down. Thus in terms of quality control, probably oyster size or weight, cultured oysters are more satisfactory and fetch higher prices. However, this surely requires the calibrating of the statistical tests with biological parameters and also quality differences, which are absent from their study. The income thesis also requires some specification of the extent of dissipation in wild oysters because, unless their reproduction and growth cycle degenerates, income receivable by these two markets should be equal in competition through entry and exit. We are ignorant, however, not only of the biology of the oysters and quality preferences of the market, but also of the institutional details of the two markets.

The present study specifies and controls biological quality and institutional aspects of the marine and cultured fish market. Instead of evaluating dissipation versus private property in terms of price variances *per se*, the physical productivity of fish under different property rights regimes are tested directly, using pollution as a dummy variable.

Empirical findings and interpretation

The pollution and MFCZ fishery data for two local water systems (hereinafter referred to as 'study areas'), Tolo Harbour (Tai Po District) and Sha Tau Kok (the North District) and other two systems (Sai Kung and Island Districts) are presented in Tables 4.1, 4.2 and 4.3. Obviously, Tolo Harbour is consistently more polluted in terms of the commonly used physical pollution indicators. It is indeed the most polluted culture area in the territory.

From Tables 4.1 and 4.2, the followings are observed:
(a) output levels of fish culture increased in both study areas (Table 4.2) in spite of increases in the level of pollution (Table 4.1); and
(b) output shares of fish culture increased in both study areas (Table 4.3) in spite of increases in the level of pollution (Table 4.1).

The level of pollution is shown in Table 4.1 in terms of seven indicators, namely the annual frequency of red tide occurrence; annual mean chlorophylla concentration; annual mean 5-day biochemical oxygen demand (BOD); annual dissolved oxygen (% saturation); surface, annual mean dissolved oxygen (% saturation); bottom, annual geometric mean E. Coli; and heavy metal (lead) contents in bottom sediments. Except annual mean dissolved oxygen, all indicators are positive measures of water pollution. Tai Po District is systematically more polluted than the North District. The absolute output levels (in tonnes) and relative output shares (output of one district as a percentage of the output of all districts) are shown in Table 4.2. In absolute terms,

Table 4.1 Times Series Comparison of Pollution Levels in Local Waters

Pollution Indicators	Year	North District (Sha Tau Kok Area)		Tai Po District (Tolo Harbour Area)		Rest of Hong Kong	
1. Annual frequency of Red Tide Occurrence	1977	0		2		1	
	1978	0		1		1	
	1979	0		1		0	
	1980	2		4		3	
	1981	0	(Mirs Bay	3	(Tolo	1	(Including
	1982	0	and	3	Harbour	8	Victoria
	1983	2	Eastern	9	and Tolo	12	Harbour)
	1984	6	Waters)	15	Channel)	18	
	1985	3		16		6	
	1986	4		17		4	
	1987	3		17		13	
	1988	14		39		32	
	1989	4		12		5	
	1990	2		19		6	
	1991	3		5		7	
2. Annual Mean Chlorophyll-a concentration *Chl-a(mg/l)*	1984	1.5		11			
	1985	1.25	(Port	14	Centre		
	1986	1.1	Island)	15	Island)		
	1987	2.5		20			
	1988	3.25		25			
	1989	2.9		30			
	1990	3.2		28			
	1991	3.1		27			
3. Annual Mean 5-day Biochemical Oxygen Demand *BOD(mg/l)*	1986	1.0	(Port	2.6	(Centre		
	1987	0.5	Island)	2.5	Island)		
	1988	1.1		2.3			
	1989	1.0		3.4			
	1990	0.9		2.9			
	1991	1.0		2.7			
	1992	1.7		3.4			
4. Annual Mean Dissolved Oxygen *(%saturation), Surface*	1986	95.6	(Port	103.4	(Centre		
	1987	95.5	Island)	110.8	Island)		
	1988	102.3		112.2			
	1989	100.6		113.3			
	1990	105.5		90.4			
	1991	109.3		96.3			
	1992	104.9		93.5			
5. Annual Mean Dissolved Oxygen *(%saturation), Bottom*	1986	80.9	(Port	62.3	(Centre		
	1987	85.0	Island)	62.5	Island)		
	1988	61.6		50.7			
	1989	69.1		57.0			
	1990	88.6		84.1			
	1991	101.2		82.7			
	1992	80.8		72.2			
6. Annual Geometric Mean E. Coli *(No./100ml)*	1986	0	(Port	107	(Centre		
	1987	1	Island)	123	Island)		
	1988	11		26			
	1989	8		42			
	1990	5		34			
	1991	4		28			

Table 4.1   (Cont.)

Pollution Indicators	Year	North District (Sha Tau Kok Area)		Tai Po District (Tolo Harbour Area)		Rest of Hong Kong
7. Heavy Metal (Lead)	1986	32	(Port	59	(Centre	
Contents in Bottom	1987	32	Island)	59	Island)	
Sediments	1988	22		84		
Pb (mg/Kg d.s.)	1989	19		67		
	1990	21		62		
	1991	18		65		

Sources: (1) Hong Kong Government, *Environment Hong Kong* 1986 to1992 editions. Hong Kong: Environmental Protection Department, 1990.
(2) Hong Kong Government, *Marine Water Quality in Hong Kong.* Hong Kong: Environmental Protection Department, 1987 to 1990 editions.

Notes: 1. The major cause of fish kill in MFCZ due to eutrophication and anoxicity.
2. A positive measure of the propensity of algal blooms and the resulting eutrophication and anoxicity.
3. A positive measure of pollution due to organic matters.
4. Same as 2. above.
5. A negative measure of pollution due to organic matters.
6. A positive measure of pollution due to domestic (faecal) sewage.
7. A positive measure of pollution due to industrial sewage.
8. Data for 1992 covers the period January to July 1992 only.

Table 4.2   Physical Output of Coastal Cultured Fish by Weight by District 1979–1989

Year	North District	Tai Po District	Sai Kung District	Islands District	All Districts
Output (metric tonnes)					
1979	58	57	407	198	720
1980	104	75	396	185	760
1981	119	111	417	315	962
1982	134	182	484	355	1,155
1983	112	151	403	294	960
1984	149	202	538	394	1,283
1985	185	250	666	488	1,589
1986	400	428	779	491	2,098
1987	483	653	1,011	723	2,870
1988	604	790	1,063	824	3,281
1989	525	719	993	782	3,019
Output as % of all districts					
1979	8%	8%	57%	27%	100%
1980	14%	10%	52%	24%	100%
1981	12%	12%	43%	33%	100%
1982	11%	16%	42%	31%	100%
1983	11%	16%	42%	31%	100%
1984	11%	16%	42%	31%	100%
1985	11%	16%	42%	31%	100%
1986	19%	20%	37%	24%	100%
1987	17%	23%	35%	25%	100%
1988	18%	24%	33%	25%	100%
1989	17%	24%	33%	26%	100%

Source: Agriculture and Fisheries Department, Hong Kong Government, 1990

Table 4.3 Physical Output of Coastal Captured and Cultured Fish by Weight by District 1979–1984

| | North District (Sha Tau Kok and Mirs Bay) | | Tai Po District (Tolo Harbour and Tolo Channel) | | |
| | | | Captured | | |
Year	Captured	Cultured	Tolo Harbour	Tolo Channel	Cultured
Metric Tonnes					
1979	1,312	58	935	1,034	57
1980	998	104	902	962	75
1981	852	119	787	828	111
1982	975	134	773	802	182
1983	978	112	586	880	151
1984	1,179	149	606	786	202
% annual increase					
1979–80	-24%	+79%	-4%	-7%	-32%
1980–81	-15%	+14%	-13%	-14%	+48%
1981–82	-14%	+13%	-2%	-3%	+64%
1982–83	0%	-16%	-24%	+10%	-17%
1983–84	+21%	+33%	+3%	-11%	+34%
1979–84	-10%	+157%	-35%	-24%	+254%

Sources: (1) Coastal Captured Fish — Richards, J. *Fisheries Production in Hong Kong Waters*, internal report, Agriculture and Fisheries Department, Hong Kong Government, 1985.
(2) Coastal Cultured Fish — Agriculture and Fisheries Department, Hong Kong Government, 1990.

the physical output of cultured fish in the North District and Tai Po District increases from 58 metric tonnes and 57 metric tonnes to 525 metric tonnes and 719 metric tonnes respectively between 1979 and 1989. In relative terms, these two districts witness increases from 8% and 8% to respectively 17% and 24% between 1979 and 1989.

From Tables 4.1 and 4.3, the followings are observed:
(c) As water pollution is becoming more and more serious (Table 4.1 and the explanation above),
   (i)   in both study areas, output levels of in-shore fishing (coastal captured fish) outside MFCZ, fell over the years (Table 4.3); and
   (ii) in the study area of Tai Po District, output levels of in-shore fishing, outside MFCZ, in Tolo Harbour (which is more polluted) fell faster than those in Tolo Channel (which is less polluted) by 9% between 1979–1984.

This observation in isolation bears witness to the environmentalist claim that water pollution affects fish production.

From interviews with operators in the trade and a review of local newspapers,[28] it is learnt that
(d) Tolo Harbour is a more popular culture area than Sha Tau Kok with the reason given being 'convenient transport', and this is consistent with official information presented in Table 4.4.

Table 4.4 Licence Queues for Different Marine Fish Culture Zones in the Eastern Sector of Hong Kong Waters (1986)

Districts	Number of Applications Allocated Sites	Number of Applications Waitlisted		
		Number	Applied Area (m²)	Average Applied Area (m²)
North District	114	5(83)	1,040(13,720)	167
Sai Kung District	266	42	7,134	170
Tai Po District	420	132	24,522	186
Total	800	179(83)	32,696(13,720)	182

Source: Agriculture and Fisheries Department, Hong Kong Government, 1986.
Note: The Eastern Sector is oceanic and includes all culture districts other than the Islands District which is estaurine. Numbers in brackets are application pending for decision on the issue of licences.The cultured zones in Tai Po District, which is more accessible due to the presence of Route 2 Highway and the Kowloon-Canton Railway, and is the most populated district, are the most popular in terms of actual allocation, waitlisted application and area under application.

(e) each culture area has specialized in rearing particular species of fish and the culture cycle for Tolo Harbour, except Yung Shue Au, needs to start with larger fry.[29]

The distribution of species by MFCZ is shown in Table 4.5. The North District specializes in the culture of gold-lined seabream and yellow grouper, the Sai Kung District brown-dotted grouper and red grouper, and the Islands District red grouper and yellow seabream. Tai Po District, which is the most polluted, has more varieties of cultured fish, including gold-lined seabream, brown-dotted grouper, various species of seabreams, Russell's snapper, red pargo, sea perch, and green grouper.

The average wholesale prices of fish from 1988 to July 1992 are collected[30] from the Agriculture and Fisheries Department. The followings are observed:
(f) the prices for a given species of a given weight at a given year are consistently lower for those cultured in coastal MFCZ than those captured in offshore fishing grounds.

The greatest discount in cultured fish price is given to red grouper (with a range of 40% to 85%). The lowest ones are given to red snapper and red pargo (with a range of 83% to 100% and 84% to 100% respectively), and they are among the dominant species in the most polluted Tai Po District.

This conclusion is highly reliable as both government officials and traders interviewed said that MFCZ fish have always been cheaper than live fish captured in off-shore fishing grounds. The same opinion is reached in Lai and Yu's study (Lai and Yu 1992, 1995).

The correlation between the two variables, price of captured fish (X) and the price of cultured fish (Y), is estimated by linear regression using the formula

Table 4.5   Fish Species by Marine Fish Culture Zone Area

District	Dominant Species
North District	
Sha Tau Kok	gold-lined seabream, yellow grouper
Ap Chau	gold-lined seabream, yellow grouper
Kat O	gold-lined seabream, yellow grouper
O Pui Tong	gold-lined seabream, yellow grouper
Sai Lau Kong	gold-lined seabream, yellow grouper
Wong Wan	gold-lined seabream, yellow grouper
Tai Po District	
Tap Mun	gold-lined seabream
Kau Lau Wan	gold-lined seabream
Sham Wan	gold-lined seabream
Lo Fu Wat (Tolo Harbour)	brown-dotted grouper
Yung Shue Au (Tolo Harbour)	seabreams, Russell's Snapper, red pargo, sea perch
Yim Tin Tsai (Tolo Harbour)	green grouper
Yim Tin Tsai East (Tolo Harbour)	green grouper
Sai Kung District	
Leung Shuen Wan	brown-dotted grouper, red grouper
Tiu Cham Wan	brown-dotted grouper, red grouper
Tai Tau Chau	brown-dotted grouper, red grouper
Kai Lung Wan	brown-dotted grouper, red grouper
Kau Sai	brown-dotted grouper, red grouper
Ma Nam Wat	brown-dotted grouper, red grouper
Po Toi O	(no cultured fish, wholesale storage only)
Tin Ha Wan	brown-dotted grouper, red grouper
Islands District	
Po Toi	red grouper
Sok Kwu Wan	red grouper
Lo Tik Wan	red grouper
Tai A Chau	red grouper
Cheung Sha Wan	red grouper
Ma Wan	yellow seabream
Tung Chung	yellow seabream

$Y = a + bX$. In a perfect correlation, the result is exactly predicted by using the above formula. However in the practical situation, there is an error from the result using the above formula which is defined as the standard error of coefficient. If the error is 1, there is absolutely no correlation. If the error is 0, there is absolutely no error (i.e. the result is exactly predicted by the above formula). Errors less than 5% are considered acceptable.

The results are shown in Table 4.6. The results show that the standard errors are very low (all less than 2% and most 0.85%) implying that prices of cultured fish can be predicted very accurately if captured fish prices are given.

Observations (a) and (b) when considered against (c) reveal the significance of private property rights in constraining competition and pollution, as they fail to falsify proposition (1). Observation (c), as mentioned, is the standard environmentalist evidence that a fall in coastal fish capture is correlated with a rise in the level of pollution. However, the causal relationship, is negated

Table 4.6   Regression of the Average Wholesale Price of Live Off-shore Captured and
Coastal Cultured Fish by Species 1988-1992

Common Name of Fish Species	Regression Coefficient	Standard Error of Coefficient
Gold-lined Seabream	93.98%	0.67%
Sea Perch	93.82%	0.51%
Red Snapper	92.51%	0.81%
Red Pargo	90.09%	0.84%
Yellow Grouper	87.89%	0.48%
Black Seabream	85.62%	0.42%
White Seabream	85.03%	0.40%
Yellow-finned Seabream	84.06%	0.45%
Russell's Snapper	79.97%	0.61%
Green Grouper	78.94%	0.83%
Mangrove Snapper	78.75%	0.76%
Black-tipped Rudder Fish	72.06%	0.76%
Red Grouper	63.23%	1.81%

by observations (a) and (b) which reveal that fish yield in the culture areas in the same water bodies are increasing over time.

Observation (d) in respect of tender queue falsifies proposition (3) because the more polluted zones are actually in greater demand. However, this must be interpreted jointly with the above conclusion based on observations (a), (b) and (c), i.e. this phenomenon must be regarded as the possibility of investment which is made possible by the establishment of private property rights over the ocean or else the MFCZ must have some advantages, like location as claimed, which offset the adverse effect of pollution.

Proposition (4) also fails to be falsified by observation (f). More varieties of fish are reared in the most polluted Tai Po District and two species cultured there have the least pollution discount. This also lends support to the argument that private property rights would induce investment in fighting pollution. Although different culture areas rear different species and thus it is hard to tell whether differences in species are a result of conscious coping with pollution or the inherent attributes of culture water, the more polluted zones need to start with larger fry than the less polluted zones in the culture cycle. The selection of fry of the appropriate size reflects that water quality is taken into account by fish farmers. Would it be possible that pollution leads to higher productivity, *ceteris paribus*? In privately owned rural commercial fresh water fish ponds in Hong Kong, farmers would by modern urban standard 'pollute' the pond by dumping in night soil and agricultural wastes. The level of such pollution must be optimal under the maximization postulate. The same could be said of 'overfeeding' in MFCZ. However, the same could not be said of the source of pollution which is exogenous (and hence uncontrollable) in the case of marine fish culture and pollution.

The adverse impacts of pollution on fish quality are reflected by obser-vation (f). Pollution does lead to price differentials for MFCZ and off-shore fish, when fish species and size are controlled. The possible complication resulted from 'taste difference' of domesticated fish and 'natural grown' fish could in theory be controlled by comparing the fish prices of two MFCZ with different levels of pollutions. However, as each MFCZ area has specialized in rearing a particular species and prices of fish by zone are not readily available, this comparison cannot be made in practice. Observations (f) itself fails to falsify proposition (2), i.e. the fishmongers conceal such price differentials in the retail market by mixing MFCZ and off-shore fish? Theoretically, this is not possible as, under competition, the prices paid by the fishmongers should be proportional to those paid by the consumer. It is the consumer who can tell the differences between 'polluted' and 'clean' live fish. The Chinese gourmets who place great emphasis on freshness can tell differences in the degree of 'freshness' and 'taste'. MFCZ fish, although alive before cooking, typically have a 'kerosene' taste. The same logic applies to apples or oranges of different qualities. In the local market, whether they are sold in super-markets, fresh food markets or street hawker stalls, it is seldom observed that they are sold in a deliberate mix.

Indeed, the distribution channels of MFCZ and offshore fish are actually separate. The institutional details of the evolution and separation of the two markets is documented in a paper written by Lai and Yu (1992, 1995 forthcoming). Most offshore fish go to the fresh food market for domestic consumption via the fish wholesale market run by the Fish Marketing Organization under regulation. Some of the live ones will be sent to res-taurants and served for important occasions such as weddings and other celebration parties. The live MFCZ fish, on the other hand, would be sold to restaurants via a wholesale and retail chain and appear in 'packaged' meals which represent a kind of tie-in sale in mass production.[31] The explanation of the integration of fish culture and packaged meals lies in the technology of cage culture which, as mentioned above, reduces the transaction costs of measurement as well as searching.[32] The commercial viability of economical lunches depends on a steady supply of live and fresh fish of standardized quality, which can be offered by MFCZ fish. If MFCZ fish living in waters polluted by some environmental standards had health implications (although no medical evidence had been found[33]), the consumer could still make the choice based on prices or 'taste'. The consumer is still sovereign so long as 'polluted fish' is cheaper, and that they do not taste as good as clean fish. The facts examined indicate the significance of private property rights in con-straining dissipation and pollution. They also suggest that the argument from consumer or producer ignorance is problematic.

The significance of establishing private property rights by zoning over an otherwise non-exclusive asset is demonstrated in this chapter in terms of the constraining of rent dissipation and the potency of market mechanism in reflecting and tackling 'social costs'. From the producer's point of view, private property rights induce investment, as reflected in fry size and species selection. From the consumer's point of view, eating polluted fish is a choice which could be based on price differentials if not on 'taste'. Current research efforts on fishing have leaned towards the identification of theoretical 'efficient solutions' in the absence of private property rights.[34] The empirical content in such analysis is, disappointingly, virtually zero.

The implication of this empirical study on marine zoning can be generalized to discuss a whole array of zoning matters on land. This can be illustrated by examining the history of the countryside in Hong Kong.[35]

Notes

1. See Cheung, Steven N.S. 'Mobile Assets' [會走動的資產] in *Thus Spake the Tangerine Seller* [賣桔者言] [Chinese] 11th edition. Hong Kong: Hong Kong Economic Journal, November 1987, pp. 21–24. Some statistics on local fresh water fish culture can be found in C.T. Wong, 'Urbanization and Agriculture: the Impact of Agricultural and Town Development on the Rural Environment in Hong Kong' in Hill R.D. and Bray, Jennifer M. eds. *Geography and the Environment in Southeast Asia*. Proceedings of the Department of Geography and Geology Jubilee Symposium, University of Hong Kong, 21–25 June 1976, Hong Kong: Hong Kong University Press, pp. 166–167.

2. Except for the purpose of 'scientific research' and the 'maintenance of fish in captivity for purposes other than the propagation or promotion of growth' of fish, 'no one shall engage in fish culture within the waters of Hong Kong outside a fish culture zone', s.7, *Marine Fish Culture Ordinance* (1980), Chapter 353, *Laws of Hong Kong* (1983). Any person who contravenes this section commits an offence under the Ordinance.

3. The source of fry is both local (seabreams) and overseas, including Taiwan (groupers and black-tipped rudder fish), Thailand (red and green groupers) and China (seaperch).

4. For an in-depth account of the institutional details of the fish culture zones, the technology of culture and the market structure of the industry, see Lai, Lawrence W.C. and Yu, Ben, T, 'The Hong Kong Solution to the Overfishing Problem: A Study of the Cultured Fish Industry in Hong Kong', *Managerial and Decision Economics,* Vol. 16 (March, 1995), pp. 525–535. For a case study of fresh water pond culture of fish, see Lai, Lawrence W.C. and Lam, Ken, 'A Guide to the Culture of *Ophiocephalus maculatus,*' *Fish Farming International,* September 1996: 54–55 and Lai, Lawrence W.C. and Lam, Ken, 'Pond Culture of Snakehead in Hong Kong: A Case Study of an Economic Solution to Common Property Resources,' *Aquaculture International,* December 1998, forthcoming.

5. See section on 'Common Property Rights', Chapter 2, ante.

6. See note 26, Chapter 1, ante.

7. Administratively, a squatter may refer to a person who occupies land without lawful authority or without consent in 'a derelict boat or by the foreshore or in a typhoon shelter' — p.S.6, *Town Planning Glossary* u.d. Hong Kong: Hong Kong Government.

8. Umbeck's 'Might Makes Rights: A Theory of the Formation and Initial Distribution of Property Rights,' *Economic Inquiry*, January 1981, is surely applicable here.

9. These methods are conceived of by Cheung, Steven N.S., see note 132, ante.

10. See Wu, Rudolf, S.S. 'Marine Fish Culture in Hong Kong: Problems and Some Possible Solutions,' in *Fish Farming International*, Vol. 12, 1985, pp. 12–13.

11. Op. cit.

12. S.6, *Marine Fish Culture Ordinance (1980)*, op. cit.

13. The government of Hong Kong has always been very benevolent to squatters. Hillside squatters have the privilege under a housing policy to queue for public housing at sub-market rent irrespective of their income or wealth status. At present, about 48% of the 5.6 million population are living in public housing of one kind or another, although the maximum salary or profit tax rate is 15%. From this perspective, might really makes rights. The government's lenient policy towards marine squatters are not inconsistent with the stance for land squatters. However, while the lands released by squatter rehousing could yield more profitable land revenue for the government which leases them to developers, the conferrment of rights to marine squatters yield little revenue gain for the administration. For a reference to the financial logic of the government in respect of land squatters, see the author's criticism of Keung in the last section of 'The Formation of Squatters and Slums in Hong Kong: From Slump Market to Boom Market,' *Habitat International* Vol. 9, 1985, No. 3/4 pp. 251–260.

14. Under the 'touch-base' policy, which permitted any illegal immigrant to become a citizen of Hong Kong on successful reach of the urban areas, about 400,000 Chinese illegal immigrants arrived in Hong Kong in the late seventies and early eighties. The policy was cancelled in 1981. The annual number of the Vietnamese refugees entering Hong Kong and waiting to be accepted by other host countries has ranged from a few thousands to twenty thousands.

15. The relief is meant to compensate for the cost of the fry only.

16. Discussion with officials of the Agriculture and Fisheries Department, see also p. 34 *Sing Tao Daily News* 27 August, 1989 and Table 4 for applications in the Eastern Sector of Hong Kong Waters.

17. 'A licence shall not be transferable.' S.8(5), *Marine Fish Culture Ordinance (1980)*, op. cit.

18. Water treatment by the Environmental Protection Department depends on the sewage system. However, many industrialists connect without authority their sewage reticulation system with the storm water drains and hence foul effluence enters the sea untreated. It is very difficult to trace the responsibilities of the offender as all drains in Hong Kong are covered and the density of development is extremely high. In any case, the water treatment plants in Hong Kong only provide 'primary' (i.e. screening), and at most 'secondary' treatment. A Territorial Sewage Strategy

will be implemented to discharge sewage into the South China Sea via submarine tunnels after primary and secondary treatment.

19. See note 3.
20. A complicated price system has been well-established for fry. Some, like red grouper, are sold by weight, and some, like green grouper, by number. The most expensive fry is red pargo, which costs about HK$3 each, as the live mature fish is in heavy demand in Japan.
21. See for instance the controversy recorded in the October 1989 issues of the *Hong Kong Economic Journal*, especially those on 10.10.89 and 11.10.89.
22. See Lam, Catherine W.Y. 'Pollution Effects of Marine Fish Culture in Hong Kong.' *Asian Marine Biology 7* (1990): 1–7.
23. Knight, Frank H. 'Some Fallacies in the Interpretation of Social Cost,' *Quarterly Journal of Economics* 91924), pp. 160–179, reprinted in *Readings on Price Theory*, (Stigler, George J. and Boulding, Kenneth eds. 1952)., Gordon, H. Scott 'The Economic Theory of a Common Property Resource: The Fishery,' 62 *Journal of Political Economy* 124 (1954), pp. 124–142, reprinted in *Economics of the Environment: Selected Readings*, 2nd ed., (Dorfman, Robert and Dorfman, Nancy S. eds, 1977); and Cheung, Steven N.S. op. cit.
24. See Note 23, ante.
25. See Cheung, Steven N.S. 1970, op. cit., pp. 50–58.
26. For instance, from interview with culturists, the red grouper is less heat-tolerant than the green grouper, which is more adaptive to the changes in water temperature resulted from industrial dischargers. The red grouper is not as popular as the green grouper in Tolo Harbour, which is a big outfall for domestic and industrial sewage.
27. Barzel, Yoram 'A Theory of Rationing by Waiting,' *Journal of Law and Economics* 17 (April 1974):73–95.
28. See note 16.
29. This is especially true of groupers and seabreams, as informed by the officials and culturists interviewed.
30. For raw data, see Lai and Yu (1992, 1995).
31. Burstein, Myer L. 'The Economics of Tie-In Sales,' *Review of Economics and Statistics* (February 1960).
32. See George J. Stigler, 'The Economics of Information,' *Journal of Political Economy*, June 1961 and Yoram Barzel, 'Measurement Cost and the Organisation of Markets,' *Journal of Law and Economics.* Vol. XXV (April 1982), pp. 27–48.
33. The medical professionals of the Urban Council and the Medical and Health Department (now Hospital Authority), who are responsible for the public health in connection with food, have never identified any evidence that the fish cultured locally have adverse health implications.
34. A brief survey of the literature establishes that the academic interest in fish lies mainly in the identification of axiomatic 'efficient' solution of commercial fish harvest in the absence of private property rights in the public ocean within a stock and flow framework, as exemplified by Lee G. Anderson, 'The Relationship Between Firm and Fishery in Common Property Fisheries,' *Land Economics* 52(2) May

1976 pp. 179–191, which follows the tradition of Vernon L. Smith's 'Economics of Production Natural Resources', *American Economic Review*, Vol. 58, 1968, pp. 409–431 and 'On Models of Commercial Fishing', *Journal of Political Economy* Vol. 77, 1969, pp. 181–198. Private property rights are briefly discussed without empirical evidence in Anthony Scott, 'The Fishery: The Objectives of Sole Ownership,' in the *Journal of Political Economy* Vol. LXIII, 1955, pp. 116–124. As regards 'texts' on 'fisheries economics', marine fish culture is seldomly mentioned and private property rights are usually peripherally discussed, stopping short of Scott Gordon's exposition on rent dissipation (see note 20). See for instance Rowena Lawson, *Economics of Fisheries Development*. London: Frances Printer (Publishers) 1984, pp. 32–58. For property rights analysis of fishes as common resources, see Ostrom, Elinor, *Governing the Commons*. US: Cambridge University Press, 1990 (6th printing, 1995), pp. 149–157, 238; and Lai and Lam (1998 forthcoming).

35. When the British colonialists first came to Hong Kong, they found a territory which was more barren : the original subtropical forest had been removed by unrestrained lumbering and burning for agriculture. Trees existed largely as *fung shui* woods as a result of customary rules — some indigenous property rights relating to that helped conserve the environment. The British implanted their own system of land law which allowed the government to implement a successful programme of afforestation, having delineated the citizens' duties to protect Crown land. This success was reversed during the latter part of the Japanese Occupation that conservation needs, recognized even by the invaders, gave way to the more urgent need of power generation. The government forests were decimated as common property by both the Japanese and local residents for fuel. The return of British rule and law and order brought with it the successful re-afforestation by the then Forestry Department. The present Country Park designation as a kind of statutory zoning has also contributed significantly to the protection of artificial tree covers which are so vulnerable to exploitation in the absence of protection by clear rules relating to property rights. Even where there is a developed land law system based on contract, there may be a need to supplement this with zoning legislation. The rapid deterioration of village environment in the New Territories, in spite of customary and common law rules, bears witness to this additional requirement. The government is now in the process of choosing an appropriate rural zoning system for the rural areas. Zoning reduces the costs of competition among landusers by indicating exactly what can be developed, what may be developed and what cannot be developed. For a good account of the economics of forestry in Hong Kong, see Chow, Shuk Fun, Bessie 'Forestry in the New Coasian Institutional Economics,' unpublished B.Sc. (Surveying) dissertation, Department of Surveying, the University of Hong Kong, June 1994.

Chapter Five

Subsequent Attenuation of Exclusive Property Rights: Some Empirical Tests

Introduction

Zoning by contract (as in the case of leaseholds) or legislation (as in the case of Marine Fish Culture Zone) can be a means to establish private property rights and hence constrain rent dissipation in a situation where initial property rights are common or ill-defined. Town planning (zoning) legislation, however, may also attenuate private property rights that are already in existence. The impact of such attenuation depends on the nature of the planning system and specific policies in question. No general analytical conclusion is possible, as argued in Chapters 2 and 3. Using simple statistical techniques, this chapter examines empirically several key aspects of the town planning zoning legislation of Hong Kong which attenuates the rights of the landowners to use, derive income from and alienate land acquired by civil contract[1] which are stipulated in the lease conditions. As discussed in Chapter 3, whether such legislation is justified is an empirical cost-benefit analysis question.[2] Some generalizations are made about the findings within the property rights framework presented in Chapter 3. Under two conditions, zoning legislation can be considered desirable, beneficial, or efficient:

(1) the benefits of the zoning legislation exceeds its costs; and
(2) superior (in terms of greater net benefits) alternative legislative or policy measures are not available.

The costs of zoning legislation include not only the private costs of loss in value of land due to use, development or development boundary restrictions, and downzoning (i.e. specifying a use of lower value or reducing the intensity of use), but also the social costs of the rise in the transaction costs in the land and development market due to the attenuation of private property rights conferred by lease conditions, notably rent dissipation in the planning application process.

The benefits of zoning legislation include the benefits of:
(a) achieving more developable space (or in the high-rise built environment of Hong Kong, more Gross Floor Area);
(b) enhancing land value by improving the environment through various zoning techniques, like plot ratio reduction, in areas generating 'negative externalities';
(c) control of layout design quality and public goods provision; and
(d) enlarging the land market.

The hypotheses presented in this chapter are summarized below, and they will be explained in detail in the following sections.
(1) comprehensive development areas (CDA) have less (smaller percentages of) environmental complaints than areas outside CDA (*testing impact of zoning on externalities*);
(2) CDA have smaller price variances than areas outsides CDA (*testing impact of zoning on externalities*);
(3) Property prices of CDA are higher than areas outsides CDA (*testing impact of zoning on intangible benefits*);
(4) CDA development under unitary ownership is more efficient than under multiple ownership (*testing impact of zoning on transaction costs*);
(5) Downzoning (reduction in plot ratios) in Tsuen Wan industrial areas has created a significant rise in the expected value of residential development (*testing impact of zoning on externalities*);
(6) Planning Areas with more (greater percentages of) building plans (numbers/G.F.A.) vetted under the development control (statutory planning application) process tend to have less (smaller percentages of) environmental complaints than districts with less (*testing impact of zoning on externalities*);
(7) The urban-rural rent gradients have become more elastic (less steep) with the inception of statutory planning in the New Territories (*testing impact of zoning on market enlargement*); and
(8) In the New Territories, the volume of land transactions have significantly increased with the inception of statutory planning in the New Territories (*testing impact of zoning on market enlargement*).

The level of sophistication of the tests are limited by the level of data detail released by or obtainable from the government. In many instances, judgement needs to be made. Such judgement is placed within the theoretical framework, elucidated in Chapter 2, to highlight some general property rights implications. The objectives of the tests simply seek to examine whether different forms of zoning are *prima facie* beneficial. This level of analysis is sufficient to either confirm or cast doubts upon Pigovian interventionist reasoning, which asserts that the existence of externalities always provides a *prima facie* case for regulation.

▦ Restrictions on the rights to alter the boundary of development: requirement of joint development under the comprehensive development area concept

Under the 'contractual zoning' system as described in Chapter 2, the tenants of leasehold land can always subdivide their property (or combine their property with the property of others) for the purpose of the most profitable development or redevelopment as permitted by the lease. Typically, the leasehold land was first allocated by competitive auction or tender in the form of a full 'street block', which is a land parcel delineated by public roads and is the lowest unit of census in the urban area. In time, the street block was subdivided into smaller lots and assigned to sub-tenants who erected on them 3-storey Chinese-style tenements. With the relaxation of plot ratio control in the 1950s and 1960s, the tenements gave way to high rise housing blocks in order to cope with huge influx of Chinese refugees. The height of these blocks range from 6 to 30 or more storeys, depending on the plot ratio permissible. Plot ratios, under the Buildings Ordinance, in turn vary according to the size and location of the land lots. This can be illustrated by the development of Wan Chai. Wan Chai was first developed in the 1840s.[3] The layout of Wan Chai before major reclamation is shown in Figure 5.1. After reclamation, the new land created was subdivided into street blocks. Each street block was later sold, usually to a single owner which was a large firm, as shown in Figure 5.2. The street block was subsequently further subdivided into smaller lots. Figure 5.3 shows the present layout of the same district as in Figure 5.2. Although the area has experienced intensive postwar redevelopment by recombining the tenements, remnants of the old tenements are still identifiable, particularly the two street blocks bounded by Johnston Road, Mallory Street, Wan Chai Road and Burrows Street.

The maximum achievable plot ratios for 'Class C' residential and commercial sites are 15 and 10 respectively and for industrial sites 15. The exact height of a building depends largely on the site coverage which the 'Authorized Person' would like to adopt. A Class C residential block with 100% site coverage can be built to 10 storeys, 50% to 20 storeys, and so forth. As plot ratios are not uniformly applied to individual land lots, highly irregular building profiles dominate the city scape of Hong Kong, except areas under the flight path of the Hong Kong International (Kai Tak) Airport. In that zone, there are specified building height limits which are often more restrictive

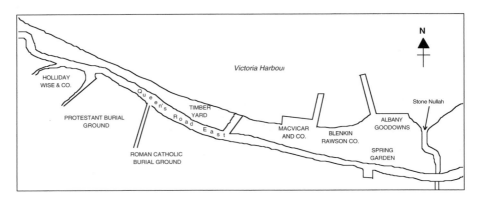

Fig. 5.1 Wan Chai in 1843

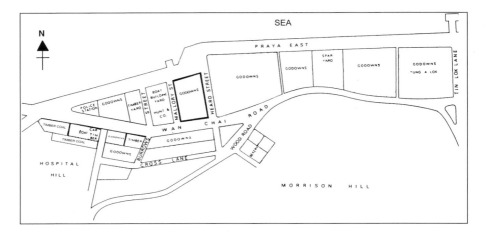

Fig. 5.2 Street Blocks in Wan Chai Road Area in 1864

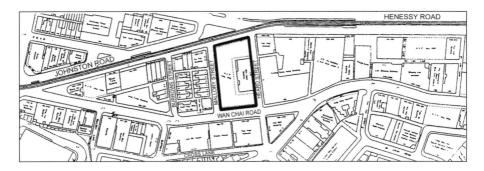

Fig. 5.3 Layout of Wan Chai Road Area in the 1990s

(Modified extract from 1:1000 Survey Sheet 11-SW-15A, courtesy of the Lands Department, Hong Kong Government.)

than plot ratios. This encourages the adoption of a greater site coverage percentage and a uniform roof line. Public facilities and open space are developed on government reserves within or outside these street blocks.

With the inception of government zoning legislation, land use zones were imposed on the developed street blocks and future development area not yet allocated by government. Planning standards, which are largely population-based, are formulated to serve as yardsticks for government reservation of zoned land for public purpose.

The concept of 'Comprehensive Development Area' (CDA) in statutory zoning plans was first introduced in the 1970s as 'Comprehensive Redevelopment Area' (CRA) to existing street blocks with the intention to ensure redevelopment on a comprehensive basis and avoid the hazard 'piecemeal redevelopment' when subdivision and combination were unrestricted. When a street block is zoned CDA, an individual tenant or sub-tenant can no longer redevelop his or her land through subdivision or in situ, and must get an agreement with each and every other tenant and sub-tenant for a planning scheme, namely a Master Layout Plan, for the whole street block. If this scheme is approved by the Town Planning Board, the proposed redevelopment may proceed. Imposing CDA zoning on existing leasehold land attenuates the rights of landowners to freely subdivide or combine property for the most profitable purpose. Transaction costs would be expended by landowners in their attempts to negate or comply with the CDA zoning.

In new development areas, especially in new towns, the same is achieved by prior restriction on subdivision of street blocks via lease conditions when they are allocated. In this situation, the administrative restriction of subdivision is part of the civil contract between the government and the property owners and does not constitute an infringement of rights.

The concept of comprehensive development (referred to below as CDA), whether achieved through statutory CDA zoning or by lease conditions, has three major benefits from the planner's point of view. Firstly, CDA sites (usually being Class C sites) can achieve the maximal plot ratios. This is further elaborated below. Secondly, it should achieve a better designed layout and block disposition and provide adequate communal facilities for the development. Thirdly, the CDA concept allows substantial economies of scale in property and environmental management governed by the deed of mutual convenant.

The Central Business District of Hong Kong, i.e. Central, is the hub of the third largest financial centre in the world. It has an existing office GFA of 1,688,200 m^2.[4] If the street blocks were all developed according to the CDA concept as Class C sites, the achievable office GFA would be 2,881,500 m^2.[5] In other words, piecemeal redevelopment, under the existing plot ratio regulations, can only achieve 59% of the legal maximum. Given the average 1992 monthly office rental of HK\$ 483.6 per square metre,[6] this entails a loss of HK$ 577 million per month. Many would argue that this indicates economic waste.

While its higher economic (GFA) yield can be easily assessed numerically and design better adjudged in qualitative terms, the CDA's planning benefits in comparison with ad hoc or piecemeal development are more difficult to measure quantitatively. Three empirical tests, however, are available. They are:

(i)   comprehensive development areas (CDA) have less (smaller percentages of) environmental complaints than areas outside CDA (testing impact of zoning on externalities) [Hypothesis 1];

(ii) Property sales price variances in CDAs are smaller than those in areas outside CDAs (testing impact of zoning on externalities) [Hypothesis 2]; and

(iii) Property sales prices in CDAs are higher than those in areas outside CDAs (testing impact of zoning on intangible benefits) [Hypothesis 3].

If the empirical results lead to a positive answer, then it could be concluded that the zoning intervention of CDA designation is *prima facie* beneficial. If the answer is negative, it can be concluded that there is no *prima facie* evidence from the land valuation point of view that zoning is beneficial. There is no claim, however, that zoning makes things worse.

Hypothesis 1 involves a direct measurement of the impact of zoning regulation upon externalities. If CDA zoning really achieves the purpose of avoiding negative externalities and integrating positive externalities, then there should be a lower incidence of environmental complaints within CDAs than in areas without. Hypothesis 1 will be refuted if areas outside CDA have even lower or same incidence of environmental complaints. Hypothesis 2 about rent variances is an indirect test. It is intended to test the assertion that area with zoning regulations, such as those relating to CDA zoning and restriction on sub-division in modern leases, are able to protect private property rights better in terms of use than areas without such regulations. The intuitive reason is that the old Crown lease conditions leave unspecified the type, form and nature of uses and their architectural manifestations. Examples are the erection of advertisement signs and choice of external finishes. As such, each owner would seek to capture the rental value of such unclearly specified rights, notably those concerning orientation, view (which is convertible into rental for advertisement sign boards) and sunlight, which is particularly scarce in the high-rise context of Hong Kong. The result is rent dissipation under intense competition, a situation like ocean fish or wild oyster examined in chapter 4. By contrast, CDAs, being comprehensively planned, would be able to constrain such competition and enable an orderly allocation of rights to aspect, view and sunlight, etc. As a result, the variances in rental level and capital value of non-CDA development would generally be greater than those for CDA development. The price variance approach adopted here has been used in a more sophisticated form by Angello and Donnelley for comparing the value of wild and cultured oysters.[7] Hypothesis 2 will be rejected if the price variances of CDA development are even greater or the same as those of non-CDA development. Hypothesis 3 about sales price premium is also an indirect test, which is similar in purpose and reasoning to hypothesis 2. Hypothesis 3 is falsified if the sales prices of housing units outside CDAs have similar or even greater premium in comparison with those inside CDAs. To reiterate, CDAs include statutory CDA zones and estate type housing development.

To test Hypothesis 1, the environmental complaint data for each urban district are examined. Data on environmental complaints by districts are available since 1986 and are shown in Table 5.1. As the environmental complaint data have no exact address codification, the test can only be carried out on a probability basis. Moreover, districts vary in terms of areas and population. Therefore the test is weighed by population through calibrating complaints on a per capita basis. The hypothesis is modified as follows:

Table 5.1 Environmental Complaints for Each Urban District, 1986–1991

Districts	1986	1987	1988	1989	1990	1991	Total
Tsuen Wan	127	215	230	212	395	298	1,477
Kwai Tsing	154	349	322	467	1,020	459	2,771
Central & Western	128	209	212	245	416	459	1,669
Wan Chai	101	145	142	276	635	346	1,645
Eastern	139	247	236	319	527	334	1,802
Southern	31	74	91	121	127	117	561
Kowloon City	137	238	218	317	574	493	1,977
Kwun Tong	121	253	219	310	410	329	1,642
Mong Kok	79	141	125	246	500	229	1,320
Sham Shui Po	111	136	154	389	550	227	1,567
Wong Tai Sin	48	77	74	89	281	206	775
Yau Tsim	52	100	86	175	345	330	1,088

Sources: *Environment Hong Kong*, Environmental Protection Department, Hong Kong Government, 1986 to 1992 editions.
Note: The Central Administration of Complaints of the Environmental Protection Department commenced on 2 June 1986. Therefore the Environmental Complaints of 1986 covers the period from June to December only.

Residential districts with greater percentages of street blocks for residential use (in terms of areas) developed under Comprehensive Development concept have less (smaller percentages of) environmental complaints per person than residential districts with lower percentages [Hypothesis 1^A]

As the population figures for each district are only available in the census and by-census years, the census data of the year 1991 are used to calculate the number of environmental complaints per person. The number of environmental complaints per person for each urban district in 1991 is tabulated in Table 5.2.

Table 5.2 Environmental Complaints per Person for Each Urban District in 1991

Districts	Environmental Complaints in 1991	Population at 1991 Census	Environmental Complaints per thousand people
Tsuen Wan	298	271,576	1.10
Kwai Tsing	459	440,807	1.04
Central & Western	459	253,383	1.81
Wan Chai	346	180,309	1.92
Eastern	334	560,200	0.60
Southern	117	257,101	0.46
Kowloon City	493	402,934	1.22
Kwun Tong	329	578,502	0.57
Mong Kok	229	170,368	1.34
Sham Shui Po	227	380,615	0.60
Wong Tai Sin	206	386,572	0.53
Yau Tsim	330	111,692	2.95

Sources: (1) *Environment Hong Kong*, op. cit., 1986 to 1992 editions.
             (2) *Hong Kong 1991 Census*, Census and Statistics Department, Hong Kong Government, 1992.
Note: The Central Administration of Complaints of the Environmental Protection Department commenced on 2 June 1986. Therefore the Environmental Complaints of 1986 covers the period from June to December only.

The test results are shown in Table 5.3 and Figure 5.4. From Table 5.3 and Figure 5.4, it can be seen that the above hypothesis is not falsified. Districts with more CDAs (mainly public or private housing estates) such as Southern, Wong Tai Sin, Kwun Tong and Eastern Districts have the lowest number of complaints. Yau Tsim, Wan Chai, Central and Western, and Mong Kok Districts with no developed CDAs, have the largest numbers.

The correlation between the two variables, percentage of land developed under CDA concept (X) and number of environmental complaints per capita (Y), is estimated by linear regression using the formula $Y = a + bX$. The results are as follows:

Regression constant a =   1.8668983
Regression coefficient b =   -1.761787
Standard Error of Coefficient = 0.3791939

The negative sign of the regression coefficient b shows an inverse relationship between the number of environmental complaints per capita and the percentage of land developed under CDA concept. The magnitude of the standard error of coefficient (closer to 0 than 1) shows that the result

Table 5.3 Percentage of Residential Land Developed Under the Comprehensive Development Concept and the Number of Environmental Complaints per Person for Each Urban District, 1991

Districts	Environmental Complaints per thousand people	Percentage of Residential land developed under the Comprehensive Development concept
Yau Tsim	2.95	0%
Wan Chai	1.92	0%
Central & Western	1.81	2%
Mong Kok	1.34	5%
Kowloon City	1.22	8%
Tsuen Wan	1.10	42%
Kwai Tsing	1.04	51%
Sham Shui Po	0.60	43%
Eastern	0.60	69%
Kwun Tong	0.57	78%
Wong Tai Sin	0.53	82%
Southern	0.46	89%

Notes: 1. Residential land include land for public housing, private housing but excluding village type development. Mixed Commercial-Residential land is considered as residential land if it is predominantly used for residential purposes.
2. In addition to the land designated as CDA in Outline Zoning Plan, Comprehensive development also include all public and private housing estates with master layout plan design.

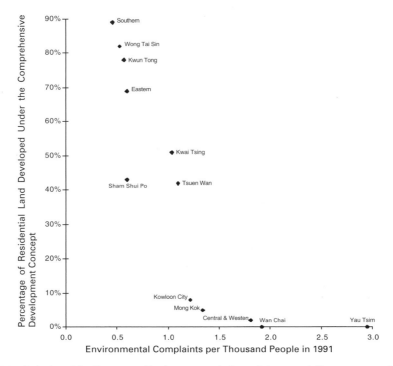

Fig. 5.4 Relationship Between Environmental Complaints and Percentage of Land Developed Under the Comprehensive Development Concept

can be predicted with fairly high degree of accuracy. Hypothesis 1A therefore can be said to be statistically valid and hence not rejected.

The sceptic may argue that the above methodology is unconvincing because there are indeed many other variables which jointly produce the results. However, what is attempted here is not to explain the causes of the complaints or to show that there is a simple one-to-one relationship between zoning control and environmental complaints. What is established is merely that the hypothesis claiming CDAs have less complaints is not falsified.

To test hypothesis 2, the sales prices of the residential units in developed CDAs are compared with others in the district. Seven large CDAs of private housing estates are selected for the test and their sales prices are compared with their respective districts (see table below).

Comprehensive Development Estates	Districts where the Estates are located
Taikoo Shing (Photographs 11, 12)	Shau Kei Wan
Kornhill (Photographs 13, 14)	Shau Kei Wan
Heng Fa Chuen	Chai Wan
Whampoa Garden	Hung Hom
Mei Foo Sun Chuen	Cheung Sha Wan
Belvedere Garden	Tsuen Wan
Luk Yeung Sun Tsuen	Tsuen Wan

The sales prices of the housing units within each CDA and their corresponding district are illustrated graphically in Figures 5.5–5.9. The price variances of each CDA and its corresponding district are also evaluated in Table 5.4. With the exception of Kornhill and Belvedere Gardens, the statistical variances of sales prices of all other CDAs are higher than those in the corresponding districts. Thus the hypothesis is rejected. To give the CDA zoning the benefit of a doubt, the influence of exogenous political shocks[8] which might have significant impacts on property rights is controlled by dividing the time series into 'politically stable' and 'politically unstable' periods. The watershed is the Tiananmen Square or the June 4 Incident in 1989. Hypothesis 2 is therefore refined as:

> Property sales price variances in CDAs are smaller than those in areas outsides CDAs in a politically stable investment environment [Hypothesis 2A]

The politically unstable period may be said as commencing from April 1989, the prelude to the June 4 incident, and ending in December 1991 just before the economy in China regained its growth momentum in the early 1992. The result is presented in Table 5.5. It can be seen from this

Photograph 11   Taikoo Dockyard in 1976 (Courtesy of the Hong Kong Government)

Photograph 12   Taikoo Shing in 1985 (Courtesy of the Hong Kong Government)

These photographs show the conversion of a dockyard into a 'comprehensively development area' which is built according to modern Hong Kong planning standards.

Photograph 13   Kornhill Under Construction (Courtesy of the Hong Kong Government)

Photograph 14   Kornhill Development (Courtesy of the Hong Kong Government)

These photographs show another 'comprehensive development area'. It was developed in connection with the construction of the Mass Transit Railway Island Line.

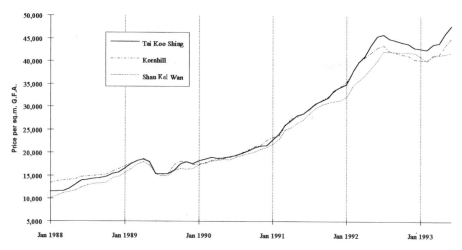

Fig. 5.5   Sales Prices of Private Domestic Units in Shau Kei Wan

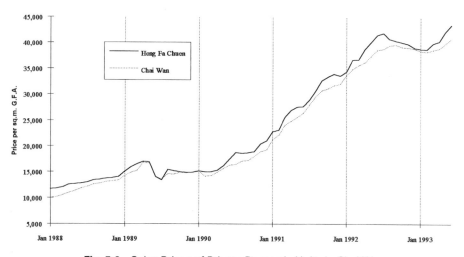

Fig. 5.6   Sales Prices of Private Domestic Units in Chai Wan

table that in the two politically stable periods (January 1988 to March 1989 and January 1992 to March 1993), the price variances of the housing units in CDAs are generally smaller than the variances of those in their corresponding districts (the exceptions are Whampoa Garden, Belvedere Garden, and Luk Yeung Sun Tsuen in the period from January 1988 to March 1989 and Heng Fa Chuen in the period from January 1992 to March 1993). Hypothesis 2 is hence not conclusively rejected, given a stable political environment. The introduction of 'political factors' may be objectionable because

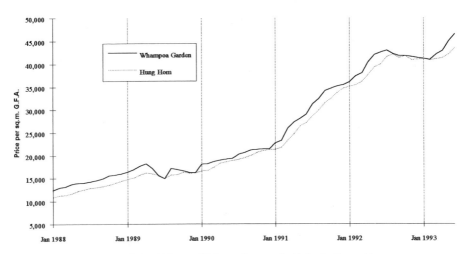

Fig. 5.7   Sales Prices of Private Domestic Units in Hung Hom

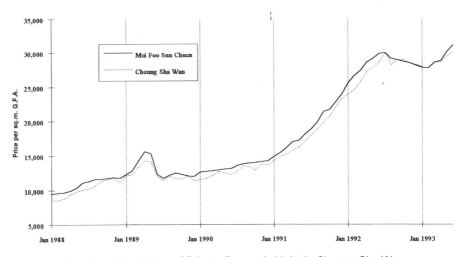

Fig. 5.8   Sales Prices of Private Domestic Units in Cheung Sha Wan

they tend to bring in too many variables not directly explicable in planning terms.

To test hypothesis 3, the prices of CDA housing are compared with the district averages. Figures 5.5–5.9 show that the prices of all CDA housing units are higher than the district averages. In other words, the prices of all CDA housing units are at a premium to those in their corresponding districts. The premium of housing in each CDA are plotted by month and compared with the percentage of price change. Figures 5.10–5.16 show the results. Two

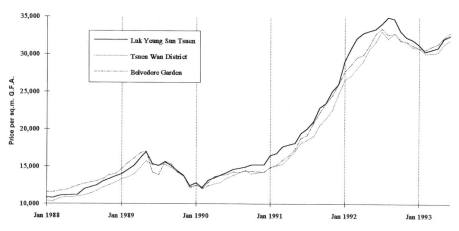

Fig. 5.9   Sales Prices of Private Domestic Units in Tsuen Wan

Table 5.4   Price Variances of Developed Comprehensive Development Areas and Their Corresponding Districts

Name of Comprehensive Development Areas/Districts	Variance (thousand)			Standard Deviation		
	Statistical Variance (variance from the means)	Variance of the actual from the quarterly moving average	Variance of the actual from the half-yearly moving average	Statistical Standard Deviation (deviation from the means)	Deviation of the actual from the quarterly moving average	Deviation of the actual from the half-yearly moving average
Taikoo Shing	140,037	56,959	264,639	11,834	7,547	16,268
Kornhill	115,745	47,116	211,116	10,758	6,864	14,530
Shau Kei Wan District	117,206	39,895	189,740	10,826	6,316	13,775
Heng Fa Chuen	121,474	51,474	212,894	11,022	7,175	14,591
Chai Wan District	114,175	37,423	172,635	10,685	6,117	13,139
Whampoa Garden	123,481	48,300	206,932	11,112	6,950	14,385
Hung Hom District	121,850	32,397	168,136	11,039	5,692	12,967
Mei Foo Sun Chuen	51,562	29,808	122,523	7,181	5,460	11,069
Cheung Sha Wan District	51,656	25,069	106,248	7,187	5,007	10,308
Belvedere Garden	60,833	35,854	158,099	7,800	5,988	12,574
Luk Yeung Sun Tsuen	67,915	37,690	180,971	8,241	6,139	13,453
Tsuen Wan District	60,893	29,323	149,037	7,803	5,415	12,208

observations from these figures, which lend further support to the above general conclusion, are as follows:

(a) Housing units in CDAs in their infancy stages (i.e. newer CDAs) have higher premium relative to non-CDA units. There is a very high premium

Table 5.5 Price Variances of Developed Comprehensive Development Areas and Their Corresponding Districts by Period

Name of Comprehensive Development Areas/ Districts	Statistical Variance (thousand)			Statistical Standard Deviation		
	Jan 88 – Mar 89	Jan 92 – Mar 93	Apr 89 – Dec 91	Jan 88 – Mar 89	Jan 92 – Mar 93	Apr 89 – Dec 91
Taikoo Shing	4,482	9,231	33,110	2,117	3,038	5,754
Kornhill	2,119	4,168	33,044	1,456	2,042	5,748
Shau Kei Wan District	4,560	10,456	28,470	2,135	3,234	5,336
Heng Fa Chuen	2,033	3,949	44,889	1,426	1,987	6,700
Chai Wan District	2,686	3,278	38,000	1,639	1,810	6,164
Whampoa Garden	2,351	4,127	41,245	1,533	2,031	6,422
Hung Hom District	2,161	5,780	35,057	1,470	2,404	5,921
Mei Foo Sun Chuen	1,742	1,353	11,605	1,320	1,163	3,407
Cheung Sha Wan District	2,128	2,742	10,583	1,459	1,656	3,253
Belvedere Garden	1,985	2,560	12,947	1,409	1,600	3,598
Luk Yeung Sun Tsuen	2,041	2,794	12,988	1,429	1,672	3,604
Tsuen Wan District	1,447	3,797	9,547	1,203	1,949	3,090

in 1988 for Kornhill, Heng Fa Chuen, Whampoa Garden and Belvedere Garden (the newer CDAs) but a lower premium for Taikoo Shing, Mei Foo Sun Chuen and Luk Yeung Sun Tsuen (the older CDAs) in the earlier years.

(b) When the general housing price is rising, the CDA premium tends to rise faster. However, when the general housing price is falling, the CDA premium tends to be smaller. This seems to indicate that when the society is more affluent, buyers are willing to pay more for the intangible benefits of the CDA concept but not so when the economy does not perform as well.

It can therefore be said that the results fail to refute hypotheses 2 and 3 and hence *prima facie* CDA zoning is beneficial in land value terms, subject to the strong assumption about political stability. The results of the three tests above, and the point about GFA yield could of course provide the planner with convenient environmental and economic justifications for CDA imposition. However, the benefits of CDA zoning must be discounted not only by the reliance on 'political factors' as mentioned above, but also the opportunity costs, notably the transaction costs, involved in implementation. For existing land holdings or newly formed land with lease restrictions on subdivision and requirement for planning schemes, implementation poses little problem. However, for street blocks which are already subdivided, the transaction costs

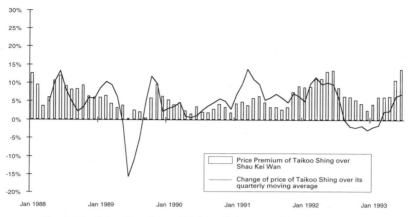

Fig. 5.10   Price Premium of Taikoo Shing over Shau Kei Wan

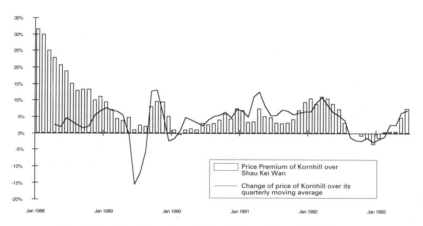

Fig. 5.11   Price Premium of Kornhill over Shau Kei Wan

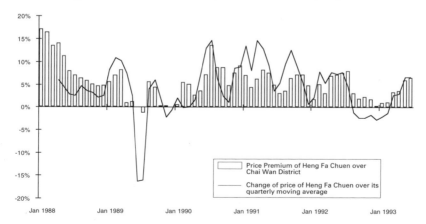

Fig. 5.12   Price Premium of Heng Fa Chuen over Chai Wan

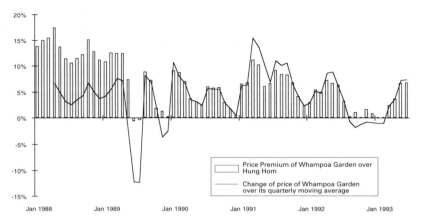

Fig. 5.13   Price Premium of Whampoa Garden over Hung Hom

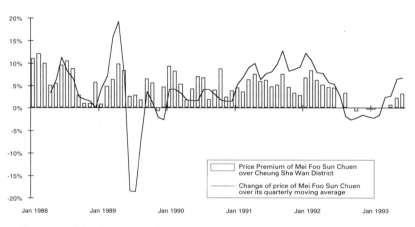

Fig. 5.14   Price Premium of Mei Foo Sun Chuen over Cheung Sha Wan

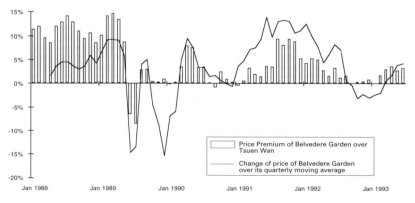

Fig. 5.15   Price Premium of Belvedere Garden over Tsuen Wan

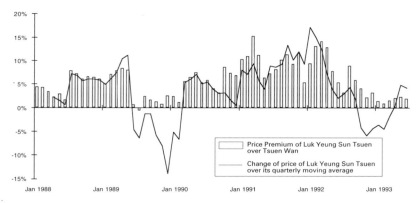

Fig. 5.16 Price Premium of Luk Yeung Sun Tsuen over Tsuen Wan

involved in land assembly could be prohibitive. In the case of Hong Kong's CBD, one should ask a fundamental question: why would the market be so irrational to allow an uncaptured rental value of HK$ 577 million per month?[9] The answer is that the costs of land assembly must be more expensive than the status quo. The value of 'wasted' plot ratio is a measure of the transaction costs involved. Hypothesis 4 is intended to test the significance of the underlying ownership pattern and its transaction costs implications of CDA development:

> Comprehensive Development Area (CDA) development of sites under unitary ownership is more efficient than under multiple ownership [Hypothesis 4].

'Efficiency' in hypothesis 4 broadly means less costly: in terms of time, and/or money involved in development. A corollary of Hypothesis 4 is:

> CDA development on sites under multiple ownership is extremely costly or even unattainable [Hypothesis 4[A]].

The reason is that the time and money involved to realize the CDA schemes under multiple ownership may approach infinity.

Again as a word of caution, a positive answer to the proposition raised in the hypothesis, which is commonly accepted, leads to the modest conclusion that single ownership is *prima facie* beneficial. A negative answer would falsify the intuitive reasoning about the significance of landownership in constraining redevelopment.

This hypothesis can be tested by examining the landownership pattern of developed CDAs in the urban areas (Table 5.6) and the case history of proposed statutory CDAs under multiple ownership (Table 5.7). From

Table 5.6 (a)   Comprehensive Development on Land Under Private Unitary Ownership

Estates	Developer	Year of completion	Owner before completion	Use before completion	Area (ha)
Hong Kong Island					
City Garden	International (Cheung Kong Group)	83 – 86	Hong Kong Electric Group	The north portion (north of Wharf road) was seabed. The south portion (south of Wharf road) was used for electricity generation plant.	3.1
Nam Fung Sun Chuen	Nam Fung	77 – 78	Nam Fung	North portion was a service reservoir. South portion is industrial.	3.2
Taikoo Shing	Swire Properties	76 – 87	Swire Group	Dockyard (Taikoo dock)	21.4
Heng Fa Chuen	Mass Transit Railway Corporation	86 – 89	Mass Transit Railway Corporation	Mass Transit Railway construction site (prior to which was partly undeveloped land (hill) and partly seabed)	19.2
Harbour Height	Cheung Kong	88	Watson Group	Wharf	0.9
Park Vale	Swire Properties	89	Swire Group	Reservoir	0.6
Chi Fu Fa Yuen & Pok Fu Lam	Hong Kong Land (Chi Fu Fa Yuen), Sun Hung Kai Properties (Pok Fu Lam Gardens)	78 – 81	Dairy Farms Group	Dairy Farm	9.1
South Horizons	Cheung Kong & Hitchison Whampoa	91 – 95	Hong Kong Electric Group	Electricity generation plant	15.5
				Sub-total	73.0
Kowloon					
Mei Foo Sun Chuen	New World Development	68 – 78	Texaco Group	Oil Depot	9.5
Cosmopolitan Estate	Hitchison Whampoa	74 – 76	Whampoa Group	Dockyard (Tai Tung Dockyard)	2.2
Beverly Villa	Cheung Kong	81 – 82	Hong Kong Catholic Church	School (La Salle College)	1.3
Wai Heng Chong Sun Chuen	Tai Cheong	76 – 77	Hong Kong & China Gas Co. Ltd.	Gas plant	2.0
Whampoa Garden & Whampoa Sun Tsuen	Hutchison	85 – 90	Whampoa Group	Dockyard (Whampoa Dock)	22.2

Table 5.6 (a)   *(Cont.)*

Estates	Developer	Year of completion	Owner before completion	Use before completion	Area (ha)
Amoy Gardens & Tak Bo Gardens	Hang Lung and Amoy Group	81 – 87	Amoy Group	Factory	4.0
Telford Gardens	Mass Transit Railway Corporation	80 – 82	Mass Transit Railway Corporation	Mass Transit Railway construction site (prior to which is the military land and seabed)	10.0
Laguna City	Cheung Kong	91 – 95	Shell Group (Cheung Kong Holding later purchased the land for development)	Oil Depot	8.8
Sceneway Garden	Cheung Kong	91 – 93	Mass Transit Railway Corporation	Mass Transit Railway Corporation construction site (prior to which is undeveloped land (hill))	4.7
				Sub-total	*74.7*

Tsuen Wan

Estates	Developer	Year of completion	Owner before completion	Use before completion	Area (ha)
Allway Garden	Hopewell	78 – 80	New Territories Development Co. Ltd. (Hopewell purchased the land from this company for development)	Undeveloped land (hill)	2.8
Bayview Garden	Hang Lung	91 – 92	Amoy	Canning Factory	1.4
Belvedere Garden	Cheung Kong	87 – 91	Nam Fung Textile Group	Spinning Factory	4.8
Luk Yeung Sun Chuen	Mass Transit Railway Corporation	83 – 84	Mass Transit Railway Corporation	Mass Transit Railway Corporation Construction site (prior to which is a village)	6.0
Riviera Garden & Waterside Plaza	Tsuen Wan Property Co. Ltd.	87 – 88	Texaco Group	Oil Depot	6.7
Tsuen King Garden	Sun Hung Kai Properties	86 – 88	China Dyeing Group	Police station adjoining undeveloped land	3.2
Tsuen Wan Garden	Far East Group	80 – 82	Far East	Amusement Park	0.2
				Sub-total	*25.1*

Grand Total					**172.8**

Table 5.6 (b)   Comprehensive Development on Land Under Public Unitary Ownership

Estates	Present use	Owner before development	Use before development
Hong Kong Island			
Admiralty	Commercial & Park	H.M. Army	Military land (Victoria Barrack & Wellington Barrack)
Wan Chai north of Gloucester Road	Commercial	Government (by reclamation)	Seabed
Taikoo Trading Estate	Industrial	Swire Group	Manufacturing and service industries
Siu Sai Wan	Public housing, HOS & industrial	Government (by reclamation)	Seabed
Lai Tak Tsuen	Hong Kong Housing Society Estate	Government	Undeveloped land (hill)
Provident Centre	Private housing	Government (by reclamation)	Seabed
Kornhill	Private housing	Mostly owned by the Government and a small portion is owned by the Mass Transit Railway Corporation	Undeveloped land (hill) in which the north portion have been used temporily for Mass Transit Railway construction site
Braemar Hill Mansion	Private housing	Government	Service Reservoir (Braemar Reservoir)
Pacific Palisades	Private housing	Government	Undeveloped land (hill)
Lei King Wan	Private housing	Government (by reclamation)	Seabed
Island Gardens	Private housing	Government	Undeveloped land (hill)
Shan Tsui Court & Hing Man Estate	Public housing HOS	Government	Undeveloped land (hill)
Baguio Villa	Private housing	Government	Partly undeveloped land (hill) and partly seabed
Wah Kwai	Public housing	Government (by reclamation)	Seabed
Aberdeen Centre	Private housing	Government (by reclamation)	Seabed
Ap Lei Chau Estate	Public housing	Government	Public burial ground
Lei Tung Estate & Yuen On Court	Public housing & HOS	Government	Undeveloped land (hill)
Shouson Hill	Private housing	Government	Undeveloped land (hill)
Parkview	Private housing	Government	Undeveloped land (hill)
Red Hill Peninsula	Private housing	Government	Undeveloped land (hill)
Kowloon			
Tsim Sha Tsui East	Commercial	Government (by reclamation)	Seabed
Kowloon Park & Parkway	Public Open space and Retailing	H.M. Army	Military land (Whitefield Barracks)
Parc Oasis	Private housing	Government	Undeveloped land (hill)
King's Park	Government Quarter	Government	Undeveloped land (hill)
So Uk	Hong Kong Housing Society Estate	Government	Undeveloped land (hill)

Table 5.6 (b)   *(Cont.)*

Estates	Present use	Owner before development	Use before development
Lei Cheung Uk (redevelopment)	Public housing	Hong Kong Housing Authority	Public Housing (Prior to which is undeveloped land (hill))
Chak On	Public housing	Government	Undeveloped land (hill)
Pak Tin (redevelopment)	Public housing	Hong Kong Housing Authority	Public Housing (Prior to which is occupied by illegal structures)
Shek Kip Mei (redevelopment)	Public housing	Hong Kong Housing Authority	Public Housing (Prior to which is occupied by illegal structures)
Lai Kok	Public housing	H.M. Army	Military use
Lai On Estate & Yee Ching Court	Public housing & HOS	H.M. Army	Military use
Nam Cheong	Public housing	Government (by reclamation)	Seabed
Nam Shan & Tai Hang Tung (redevelopment)	Public housing	Hong Kong Housing Authority	Public Housing (Prior to which is occupied by illegal structures)
Sunderlands	High class private housing	H.M. Army	Military land (Osborn Barracks)
Wang Tau Hom (redevelopment)	Public housing	Hong Kong Housing Authority	Public Housing (Prior to which is undeveloped land (hill))
Lok Fu (redevelopment)	Public housing	Hong Kong Housing Authority	Public Housing (Prior to which is burial ground)
Tsui Chuk Garden, Tin Ma Court, Tin Wang Court & Pang Ching Court	HOS	Government	Undeveloped land (hill)
Chuk Yuen North Estate & Chuk Yuen South Estate	Public housing	Government	Illegal structures
Upper & Lower Wong Tai Sin Estates (redevelopment)	Public housing	Hong Kong Housing Authority	Public Housing (Prior to which is burial grounds)
Tsz Oi, Tsz Ching, Tsz Lok, Tsz Man & Tsz On Estates (redevelopment)	Public housing	Hong Kong Housing Authority	Public Housing (Prior to which is undeveloped land (hill))
Fung Tak Estate	Public housing	Government	Undeveloped land (hill)
Lung Poon Court	HOS	Government	Illegal structures (Tai Hom Village)
Fu Shan Estate, King Shan Court & King Lai Court	Public housing & HOS	Government	Undeveloped land (hill occupied by graveyard)
Tung Tau (redevelopment)	Public housing	Hong Kong Housing Authority	Public Housing (Prior to which is occupied by villages (Sha Po Village & Nga Tsin Wai Village)
Ho Man Tin & Oi Man	Public housing	Government	Burial grounds (Wah Yan cemetery)
Choi Wan	Public housing	Government & a private organization	Partly undeveloped land (hill) and partly occupied by a home for the aged

Table 5.6 (b)　　*(Cont.)*

Estates	Present use	Owner before development	Use before development
Choi Ha	Public housing	Government	Undeveloped land (hill occupied by some illegal structures)
Kowloon Bay Industrial Area	Industrial and Warehouses	Government & H.M. Army	Partly military land and partly seabed
Belcher Gardens	Private housing	H.M. Army	Military land
Lok Wah	Public housing	Government	Undeveloped land (hill)
Kai Yip Estate & Richland Gardens	Public housing & HOS	Government & H.M. Air Force	Partly military land and partly seabed
Shun Lee, Shun On, Shun Tin Estates & Shun Chi Court	Public housing & HOS	Government	Undeveloped land (hill)
Hing Tin Estate & Hong Wah Court	Public housing & HOS	Government	Undeveloped land (hill)
Tsuen Wan			
Tsuen Wan Centre	Private housing	Government	Undeveloped land (hill)
Clague Garden Estate	Hong Kong Housing Society Estate	Government (by reclamation)	Seabed
Fuk Loi Estate	Public housing	Government (by reclamation)	Seabed
Cheung Shan	Public housing	Government	Undeveloped land (hill)
Kwai Tsing			
Wonderland Villas	High class private housing	Government	Undeveloped land (hill)
Wah Yuen Estate	Civil Servant Private housing	Government	Undeveloped land (hill)
Greenfield Garden	Private housing	Government (by reclamation)	Seabed
Mayfair Garden	Private housing	Government	Undeveloped land (hill)
Tai Wo Hau (redevelopment)	Re-developed Public housing	Hong Kong Housing Authority	Public Housing (Prior to which is undeveloped land)
Shek Yam	Public housing	Government	Undeveloped land (hill)
Shek Li (redevelopment)	Re-developed Public housing	Hong Kong Housing Authority	Public Housing (Prior to which is undeveloped land)
On Yam	Public housing	Government	Undeveloped land (hill)
Kwai Shing East & Kwai Shing West	Public housing	Government	Undeveloped land (hill)
Kwai Hing (redevelopment)	Public housing	Hong Kong Housing Authority	Public Housing (Prior to which is seabed)
Kwai Fong (redevelopment)	Public housing	Hong Kong Housing Authority	Public Housing (Prior to which is seabed)
Lai Yiu	Public housing	Government	Undeveloped land (hill)
Cho Yiu	Hong Kong Housing Society Estate	Government	Undeveloped land (hill)
Lai King & Ching Lai Court	Public housing & HOS	Government	Undeveloped land (hill)
Ching Wah Court	HOS	Government	Undeveloped land (hill)

Table 5.6 (c)   Comprehensive Development on Land Under Private Multiple Ownership

Estates	Present use	Owner before development	Use before development
Hong Kong Island			
Sheung Wan Urban Renewal Pilot Scheme	Commercial and Residential	Multiple Ownership	Mixed Commercial and Residential
Kowloon			
Beacon Heights	High class private housing	Resumption from the villagers by the government who sold to private developer after land formation	Village (Tai Wo Ping Village)
Tsuen Wan & Kwai Tsing			
Shek Wai Kok	Public housing	Resumption from the villagers by the government	Village (Shek Wai Kok Village)
Lei Muk Shue	Public housing	Resumption from the villagers by the government	Village (Lei Muk Chue Village)
Broadview Garden	Private housing	Resumption from the villagers by the government who sold to private developer after land formation	Village (Saint Paul Village)
Tsing Yi Garden	Private housing	Resumption from the villagers by the government who sold to private developer after land formation	Village (Lam Tin village)
Cheung On & Cheung Fat Estates	Public housing	Resumption from the villagers by the government	Village (Cheung Shue Tau Village)
Tsing Yi Estate	Public housing	Resumption from the villagers by the government	Village (Fung Shui Wo Village)
Cheung Hang Estate	Public housing	Resumption from the villagers by the government	Village (Sun Uk Village)
Cheung Ching Estate	Public housing	Mostly owned by the government (undeveloped land). Land occupied by the village were resumed by the government.	Part of the land is village (Ha Ko Tan Village) and part of the land is undeveloped land (hill).
Cheung Hong Estate	Public housing	Mostly owned by the government (undeveloped land). Land occupied by the village were resumed by the government.	Part of the land is village (Chung Mei Village) and part of the land is undeveloped land (hill).

Table 5.7 Abandoned and Proposed Statutory Comprehensive Development Areas

Name of the CDA projects	Ownership	Status
Tsim Sha Tsui Four Street	Multiple	Abandoned
Yau Ma Tei Six Street	Multiple	Under Development
Ma Tau Kok, Kowloon City	Multiple	Not yet developed
Jubilee Street, Central	Multiple	Not yet developed
Wing Lok Street, Central	Multiple	Not yet developed
Queen Street, Central	Multiple	Not yet developed
Argyle Street/Shanghai Street, Mong Kok	Multiple	Not yet developed
Shamchun Street, Mong Kok	Multiple	Abandoned
Yee Man Square, Kwun Tong	Multiple	Not yet developed
Tsuen Wan Town Centre (bounded by Tai Ho Road, Sha Tsui Road, Yeung Uk Road and Wo Tik Street)	Multiple	Not yet developed

Table 5.6, we can see that all implemented residential CDAs, developed according to Master Layout Plans, were all redeveloped from lower value uses (notably dockyards, power stations, oil depots) under unitary landownership. A few cases involve village land holdings under fragmented private ownership were resumed by government under the Crown Lands Resumption Ordinance.[10]

As for the proposed statutory CDAs, the history of the urban renewal scheme in Tsim Sha Tsui is illuminative. With the intention to stimulate comprehensive renewal of the old commercial hub of Tsim Sha Tsui, the scheme was met by hostile objections of property owners right from the outset and did not materialize as expected because of land assembly difficulties. This outcome is not inconsistent with Hypothesis 4A. It is noteworthy that this CDA scheme, unlike the recent Land Development Corporation (LDC) schemes, was imposed at a time when the land leases were coming to expiry. The success of the Tsim Sha Tsui East comprehensively developed commercial centre in the vicinity by contrast illustrates once again the cost implications of landownership. Part of the new centre site is reclaimed land whereas the rest is the former Chatham Road military camp and terminus of the Kowloon Canton Railway. In other words, the site is under the unitary proprietorship of the Crown. The fate of the Tsim Sha Tsui CDA (designated as 'Comprehensive Redevelopment Area') has apparently convinced the government that CDA concept for land under multiple ownership must be backed by the government compulsion. Thus, the Land Development Corporation with statutory power to use the Crown Lands Resumption Ordinance was established in 1987 to carry out urban renewal schemes. The above analysis of successful and unsuccessful CDAs reveals the significance of the transaction costs of land assembly. The economic benefits and costs of CDA zoning cannot be fully assessed without reference to such costs.

Taxation on the rights to use land for a given use: downzoning and land value

Following the Pigovian line of thought, a tax on externality would reduce pollution. The planning equivalent of this 'Pigovian tax' is reduction in plot ratios. A local example is the case of the downzoning of industrial plot ratio from 15 to 9.5 in Tsuen Wan Industrial Area (Photograph 15).[11] This amounts in value terms a 37% cut in the long term stream of rental value. The reason is that any redevelopment could not exceed the now reduced plot ratio of 9.5, entailing a potential loss of 5.5. This could be regarded as taxation in kind, attenuating the rights of landowners to derive the maximum amount of income from their property. The transaction costs involved are quantifiable cardinally in terms of the value of the lost GFA. Transaction costs would also be incurred by the owners in their attempts to upturn the plot ratio restriction in objecting to the draft statutory plan and subsequent proposals for rezoning. The planner's intention is to reduce the intensity of industrial activities and, hence, the level of externalities in terms of pollution and traffic congestion. If this Pigovian theory is valid, the expected value of housing near the industrial area will rise as a result of this statutory intervention. This leads to Hypothesis 5:

Photograph 15   Tsuen Wan Industrial Areas (Courtesy of the Hong Kong Government)

It is the relocation of manufacturing processes to China rather than the lowering of industrial plot ratios which leads to immediate improvement in air and water pollution in this densely populated new town. (Riviera Garden to the left)

Downzoning (reduction in plot ratio) in Tsuen Wan industrial areas has created a significant rise in the expected value
of residential development (G.F.A.) [Hypothesis 5].

Three private housing estates in Tsuen Wan are selected to test this
hypothesis. Belvedere Garden and Riviera Garden are adjacent to the industrial
area. Luk Yeung Sun Tsuen is a private housing estate in Tsuen Wan further
away from the industrial areas. The location of each estate and the downzoned
area is shown in Figure 5.17. The sales prices of units in these three private
housing estates are compared with the average private domestic price of units
in the New Territories. Should hypothesis 5 be valid, these private housing
estates will outperform the New Territories averages. In addition, the performance of housing estates adjacent to the industrial areas would be better
than the housing estates further away from the industrial areas in terms of
price increase. The prices of the three private housing estates and the average
prices in the whole New Territories for the period 1988 to 1992 are shown

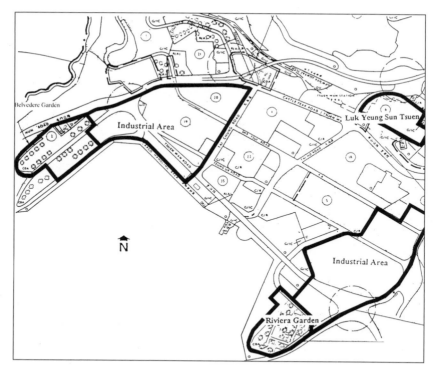

Fig. 5.17 Location of Industrial Downzoning Areas and Three Selected Comprehensively
Developed Estates in Tsuen Wan OZP Area.

(Modified extract of Outline Zoning Plan S/TW/5, courtesy of the Planning Department,
Hong Kong Government.)

in Figure 5.18. Figure 5.19 shows the price trend of performance of these private housing estates relative to the general trend of private housing prices in the New Territories. From Figure 5.19, there is no conclusive evidence that either of the price trends has changed abruptly after the inception of the plot ratio reduction. Belvedere Garden and Riveria Garden, the two private housing estates adjacent to the industrial areas, are deteriorating in price performance relative to the New Territories averages after the reduction of industrial plot ratio in Tsuen Wan. On the contrary, Luk Yeung Sun Tsuen experienced a small rise in performance relative to the New Territories averages in the year after the reduction of industrial plot ratio in Tsuen Wan.

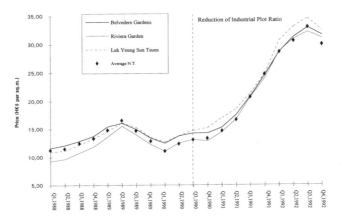

Fig 5.18   Price Movements of Selected Private Housing Estates in Tsuen Wan

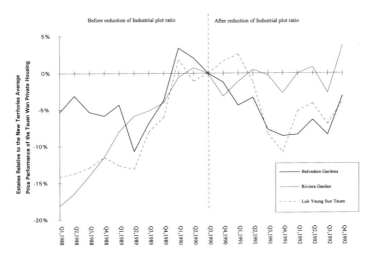

Fig 5.19   Price Performance of Selected Private Housing Estates in Tsuen Wan Relative to New Territories Averages

While one might argue that perhaps residential property will (a) only benefit from actual improvement in the environment in the long run, (b) become adversely affected if there is no downzoning, one could equally speculate that the environmental benefits of downzoning from the stance of professional planners are only imaginary. In any case, there is no evidence of immediate neighbourhood benefits in economic terms. Again, it is not attempted here to quantify the relative influence of variables affecting property value. What is revealed is that land value is not apparently sensitive to downzoning and it is *not sure* whether downzoning can be really useful in improving the environment in a short period of time, presuming that a cleaner environment attracts a premium and that market information is costless.

Public interference with private decisions about putting land under the most valuable uses: planning applications and environmental complaints

The institution of planning application entails that private planning decisions are superseded by public planning decisions.[12] This constitutes an attenuation of the rights of landowners to use land for the most profitable use. In addition, it creates an environment for rent-seeking activities. The planning machinery as a development rights rationing mechanism, which exerts its real effect on new land supply via the planning application system, has adopted a negative stance towards development. The success rate of planning applications and reviews in recent years has been less than 60% and 35% respectively, entailing enormous transaction costs (Figures 5.20 and 5.21).

Scholars and practitioners have criticized the existing planning permission system as such for being too slow and hence resulting in huge cost of delay. The official view about delays in the planning system is that the statutory period for processing planning applications, reviews and appeals is short enough.

> Procedures for planning applications, appeals and objections are bound by time limits laid down in the law. For example, s.16 applications are required to be submitted to the Town Planning Board (TPB) for consideration within two months, and applications for review have to be considered by TPB within three months. It is more difficult to control the time for processing objections to draft, or amendments to, statutory plans, as the number and complexity of the objections can vary considerably. (Hong Kong Government 1994: 24)

The government's account however does not reveal the fact that many rejected s.16 applications or s.17(1) reviews/s.17B appeals have been followed

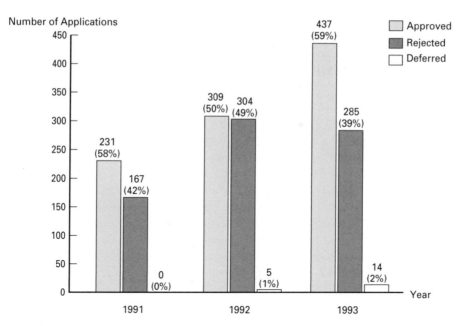

Fig. 5.20 A Comparison of Planning Applications Considered by The Town Planning Board in 1991–1993

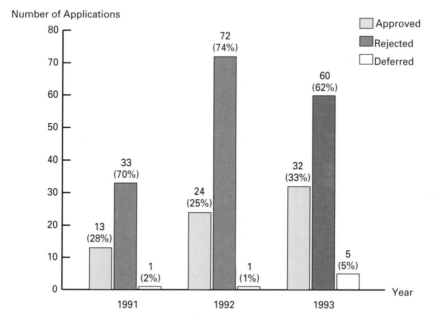

Fig. 5.21 A Comparison of Review Applications Considered by The Town Planning Board in 1991–1993

modified resubmissions and lobbying activities which eventually allow the original proposal to get through the planning system. It is hard to tell whether the rejected projects are any better than the successful ones. The planning system from this point of view operates as a system of *development rights rationing*. Staley (1994) has worked out the cost of delay for typical development projects in Hong Kong. Upon the completion of his Hong Kong planning research in 1992, he found that 'if development were delayed for one year, *added costs per project* on Hong Kong Island could range from HK$241 million for a 500,000 square feet commercial office building to HK$603 million for a 1 million square feet office building, depending on prevailing interest rates. If all new office spaces added on Hong Kong Island in 1991 were subject to a one-year delay, the added costs for financing new developments would exceed HK$1 billion. A one-year delay could add between HK$480 per square foot to HK$603 per square foot to the cost of commercial development, depending on prevailing interest rates. Similarly, a one-year delay in the construction of new residential units could add HK$1.1 billion to the cost of developing a 5 million square feet residential estate. Overall, the added costs to residential construction could vary from HK$250 per square foot to HK$300 per square foot, depending on prevailing interest rates.

Another area where a major reform is necessary is the uncertainty created by the arbitrary use of discretion in planning. Unlike the statutory building application procedure, the existing planning procedure with its review and appeal process is extremely discretionary.

Any s.16 planning application a s.17 review or appeal may be refused on the grounds that the use under application is incompatible with the environment in general or specific development in the vicinity. The standard reason given is that the use under application is inconsistent with 'the planning intention' for the zone (Table 5.8). This appears to be irrational to the extent that the use itself is entered into 'Column 2' and this indicates it is by nature compatible with the adjoining uses, or the use should not appear in the plan in the first place. A more appropriate view is that discretionary power in the planning application should be restricted to determine the intensity and design aspects of the use rather than the use *per se*. This would greatly reduce uncertainty about the use of land and channel resources to deal with technical and design matters only.

Besides, the Town Planning Board's discretion is often fettered with by sub-delegating authority to another authority when imposing planning conditions for approved development proposals.

If one holds that the cost of zoning by legislation is worth expending, one must be able to give evidence of its greater benefits, notably the tackling of externalities and public goods issues. As the intent of zoning is largely safeguarded by the planning application process, the relevance of this process in addressing externalities and public goods is of greater importance. As discussed

Table 5.8 Reasons for Dismissing Planning Appeals

Appeal Cases	Type of Reasons									
	A	B	C	D	E	F	G	H	I	J
01/91										√
01/92								√		
02/92				√				√		
03/92	√			√				√		
04/92			√							
05/92								√		
07/92		√		√		√				
08/92				√			√			
09/92				√			√			
12/92	√								√	
13/92		√		√						
14/92	√			√						
15/92		√							√	
18/92	√	√		√	√					
19/92	√	√		√	√					
02/93		√								
04/93	√			√						
05/93	√			√						
11/93	√			√						
12/93			√					√		
17/93	√	√		√		√				
19/93		√		√		√				

Note: √ denotes the reasons given
Key for types of reasons: A - Traffic
B - Environment and/or pollution
C - Comprehensive Development Area
D - Planning intention
E - Precedent
F - Compatibility with neighbouring development
G - Cumulative effect
H - Development control
I - Site constraints
J - Development Intensity

in Chapter 2, the planning application process deals with these two aspects of 'market failure' by screening 'incompatible uses', and controlling the quality of layout and building design. It also takes care of the provision of public goods, including infrastructure, in accordance with planning standards and judgements of planners, which may be purely intuitive at one end or predicated on very detailed and sophisticated planning studies at the other.

As discussed in Chapter 3, the Coasian analysis of zoning adopts an indirect approach to measure the impacts of zoning upon externalities by examining changes in land values upon introduction of zoning regulation. Externalities can indeed be directly measured by the actual incidence of nuisance, as revealed by court cases or resident complaints. The transaction costs of using the court is much greater than making complaints to government departments. Hence, the latter should be more 'democratic' in reflecting public opinion about the environment. The Environmental Protection Department has since 1986 maintained a public service of environmental complaints, which is very accessible and does not cost as much as litigation. We may postulate that if the planning application mechanism is able to tackle externality issues with development control on the basis of relevant zoning plans, a district which has more development schemes that go through the s.16 (and s.17) planning application (review) procedure[13] should witness less environmental complaints. The hypothesis, ideally, is:

> Planning Areas with more (greater percentages of) building plans (numbers/G.F.A.) vetted under the development control (statutory planning application) process tend to have less (smaller percentages of) environmental complaints than districts with less (testing of zoning on externalities) [Hypothesis 6].

Attempts have been made to obtain the number of approved building plans which have planning approval by district. Unfortunately, neither the Buildings Ordinance Office (now Buildings Department) nor the Planning Department registers information as systematically as such. Therefore, a revised hypothesis is adopted:

> Planning areas with more approved planning schemes tend to have less environmental complaints over time [Hypothesis 6^A].

Again, as a word of caution, a positive answer to the proposition raised in the hypothesis will establish that *prima facie*, the Hong Kong planning application system is beneficial to nuisance mitigation. A negative answer does not suggest that the system is necessarily counter-productive. However, it does suggest there is no *prima facie* grounds from the point of nuisance control that the system is effective.

Development will need to go through the s.16 process if it is a 'Column 2' use, which may be a CDA use. An unsuccessful application may be re-examined under the review (s.17(1)) and appeal (s.17B(1)) (s.17 and s.17B) procedures. Usually a successful application would need 3 years to complete building development. Hence, there is a need to allow for lags when comparing the incidence of planning application and that of complaints. Figures 5.22–5.24 show the number of planning applications and complaints by region from 1986 to 1992, allowing a lag period of 3 years. From Figures 5.22–5.24, there is no evidence that regions with more successful applications are necessarily better off in terms of environmental complaints. On Hong Kong Island, Kowloon and in the New Territories, a rising incidence of complaints

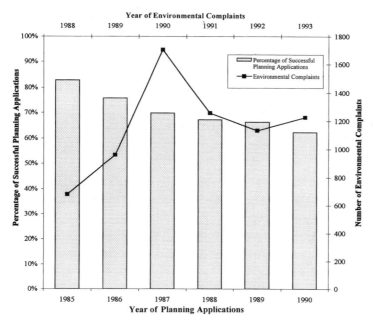

Fig. 5.22 Number of Environmental Complaints After 3 Years of Successful Planning Applications (Hong Kong Island)

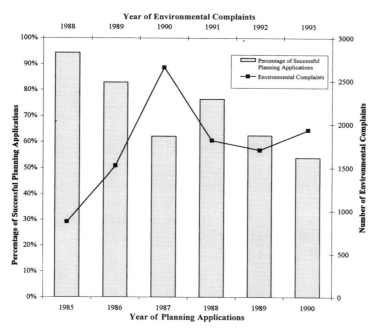

Fig. 5.23 Number of Environmental Complaints After 3 Years of Successful Planning Applications (Kowloon)

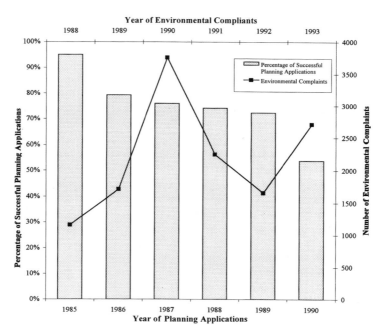

Fig. 5.24 Number of Environmental Complaints After 3 Years of Successful Planning Applications (New Territories)

is matched by a falling rate of success of planning applications, as reflected in the ratios of complaints to successful applications in Column (D) and the very low t values (three places of decimal) between successful planning applications and complaint statistics of Table 5.9 suggests that Hypothesis 6^A is falsified. One could argue that the incidence of environmental complaint depend on residents' awareness of the importance of the quality of the environment. However, we may still hold that it at least reflects the subjective assessment of externalities by individuals. This is as good as the 'dollar vote' as expressed by property value, which indicates the willingness of the people to pay for a certain environmental quality.

Unclear delineation of statutory development rights: rural zoning and land transaction

As argued by Coase, regulation in general may be conducive to enlarging the market.[14] Where zoning legislation enlarges the land market by reducing certain transaction costs (such as uncertainty about the nature of land uses), the volume of land transaction would increase. In 1991, the government extends statutory zoning to the agricultural leaseholds in the rural New Territories,

Table 5.9   Number of Environmental Complaints After 3 Years of Planning Application

Year	Total number of planning applications (A)	Number of successful planning applications (B)	Environmental complaints after 3 years (C)	Complaint ratio (C)/(B) (D)	Student t test of (B) and (C) t values
Hong Kong					+0.004
1985	64	53	681	12,85	
1986	66	50	961	19.22	
1987	63	44	1,705	38.75	
1988	76	51	1,256	24.63	
1989	98	65	1,135	17.46	
1990	93	58	1,227	21.16	
Kowloon					+0.004
1985	53	50	876	17.52	
1986	35	29	1,526	52.62	
1987	95	59	2,660	45.08	
1988	114	87	1,814	20.85	
1989	165	103	1,704	16.54	
1990	141	76	1,935	25.46	
New Territories					+0.001
1985	61	58	1,157	19.95	
1986	53	42	1,710	40.71	
1987	54	41	3,758	91.66	
1988	58	43	2,250	52.33	
1989	65	47	1,654	35.19	
1990	78	42	2,710	64.52	
Total					+0.001
1985	178	161	2,714	16.86	
1986	154	121	4,197	34.69	
1987	212	144	8,123	56.41	
1988	248	181	5,320	29.39	
1989	328	215	4,493	20.90	
1990	312	176	5,872	33.36	

requiring planning application for all except a few specified uses. The hypotheses are as follows:

(i)   the urban-rural rent gradients have become more elastic (less steep) with the inception of statutory planning in the New Territories (testing impact of zoning on market enlargement) [Hypothesis 7]; and

(ii) in the New Territories, the volume of land transactions have significantly increased with the inception of statutory planning in the New Territories (testing impact of zoning on market enlargement) [Hypothesis 8].

If the answer to the propositions raised in the hypotheses is positive, it could be said that *prima facie* statutory rural zoning is beneficial. A negative answer only establishes that there is no *prima facie* evidence that rural zoning is beneficial in terms of land value enhancement but not that it is useless or counterproductive.

Hypothesis 7 is rejected if the urban-rural rent gradient is becoming steeper, constant or eratic through time and is not falsified if the gradient is becoming less steep continuously. A similar approach has been used by Lai[15] to test the impact of transport improvement upon rent parity between CBD and off-CBD office nodes. As records of land transaction of land property in the New Territories have not yet been computerized, Hypothesis 8 is modified as:

> In the New Territories, the number of planning applications
> for large sites have significantly increased with the inception
> of statutory planning (testing impact on market enlargement)
> [Hypothesis 8^A].

The average rentals of private domestic units of different class sizes in urban areas (Hong Kong Island) and in rural areas (the New Territories) from 1982 to 1992 are examined. The urban-rural rent gradients of different class of housing by year are illustrated in Figures 5.25–5.29. Figure 5.30 shows the rentals of private domestic units of each class size in the New Territories (the rural extreme of the urban-rural gradient) as percentages of the rentals of the same class of units on the Hong Kong Island (the urban extreme of the urban-rural gradient). The percentage measures are relative measures and are used to control the impact of inflation, which would affect the absolute levels of rentals over time. Such relative measures avoid the difficulties concerning deflating absolute rentals. There is no evidence that the gradients of all types of housing have become less steep. Different grades of units have different performance over time on a point-to-point (1982–1992) basis. As shown in Figure 5.30, the rental parity between urban and rural areas widened (with negative regression gradient coefficients ranging from −0.4% to −0.7%) for domestic units of size under 100 square metres by comparing the observations of the end years of 1982 and 1992. However the rental gaps for domestic units of size over 160 square metres were reduced (with positive regression gradient coefficients of +0.5% to +1.8%). (This is probably because enhanced mobility as a result of improved transport benefits the higher income groups more. This is significant in the light that there is statistical evidence that contemporaneous improvement in rail transport reduced rent differentials for urbanized housing land along the Kowloon-Canton Railway.[16]) Hypothesis 7 is thus rejected.

The statistics of planning applications for land of more than 3,000 square metres, which may indirectly reflect the incidence of land assembly, are examined. Here, there is evidence that the land market is quite hectic and hypothesis 8A is not rejected. From the facts shown in Table 5.10 and Figure 5.31, we may speculate that the high cost of transactions involved in the

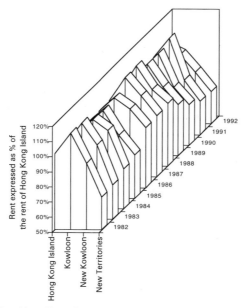

Source: *Property Review*, Hong Kong Government Rating and Valuation Department.

Fig. 5.25 Rental Gradient of the New Territories *vis-à-vis* the Urban Area for Private Domestic Units Under 40 Square Metres

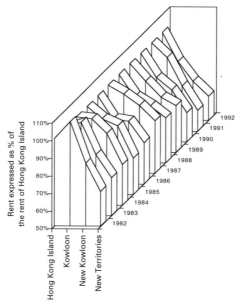

Source: *Property Review*, Hong Kong Government Rating and Valuation Department.

Fig. 5.26 Rental Gradient of the New Territories *vis-à-vis* the Urban Area for Private Domestic Units 40–69.9 Square Metres

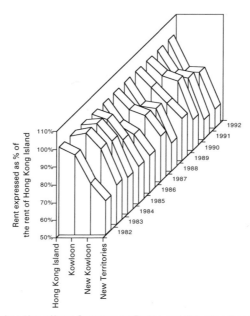

Source: *Property Review*, Hong Kong Government Rating and Valuation Department.

Fig. 5.27   Rental Gradient of the New Territories *vis-à-vis* the Urban Area for Private Domestic Units 70–99.9 Square Metres

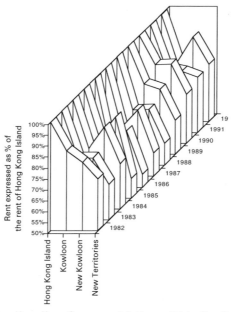

Source: *Property Review*, Hong Kong Government Rating and Valuation Department.

Fig. 5.28   Rental Gradient of the New Territories *vis-à-vis* the Urban Area for Private Domestic Units 100-159.9 Square Metres

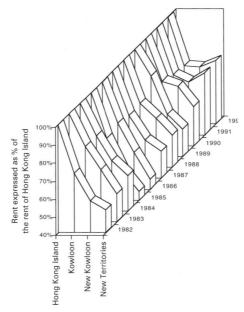

Source: *Property Review*, Hong Kong Government Rating and Valuation Department.

Fig. 5.29 Rental Gradient of the New Territories *vis-à-vis* the Urban Area for Private Domestic Units over 160 Square Metres

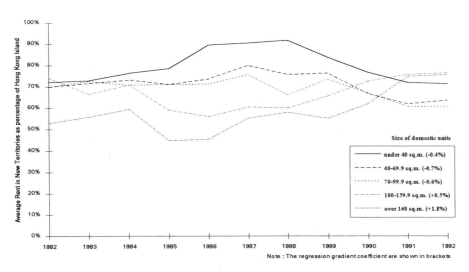

Fig. 5.30 Rent in the New Territories compared With the Urban Area by Sizes of the Private Domestic Units

Table 5.10   Planning Applications on Site Over 3000 Square Metres in North West New
Territories

Locations	Zoning	Site Area (sq.m.)	Uses applied for	Dated first considered by Town Planning Board
Ha Tsuen	UNSP	5,845	Warehouse	Nov 91
Ha Tsuen	UNSP	5,506	Container Related	Mar 92
Ha Tsuen	UNSP	27,200	Open Storage	Feb 93
Ha Tsuen	UNSP	13,250	Container Storage	Jan 93
Kam Tin North	UNSP	15,514	Residential	Feb 92
Kam Tin North	UNSP	10,481	Industrial	Sep 92
Kam Tin North	UNSP	10,481	Industrial	Oct 92
Kam Tin South	V, UNSP	4,220	Village Type Housing	Feb 92
Kam Tin South	V, UNSP	4,848	Village Type Housing	Feb 92
Kam Tin South	UNSP, V	17,299	Residential, Club	Mar 92
Kam Tin South	V, UNSP	14,369	Residential	Mar 92
Kam Tin South	UNSP	6,300	Residential	May 92
Lau Fau Shan	UNSP	800,000	Residential	Oct 92
Mai Po	UNSP, V	6,500	Residential	Oct 91
Mai Po	UNSP	130,000	Residential	Jan 92
Mai Po	UNSP	5,924	Residential	May 92
Mai Po	UNSP	3,717	Container Park	Jul 92
Mai Po	UNSP	315,600	Residential	Jul 92
Mai Po	UNSP	260,000	Residential	Aug 92
Mai Po	UNSP, R(C)	7,068	Residential	Jan 93
Nam Sang Wai	UNSP	13,430	Driving School	Oct 91
Nam Sang Wai	UNSP	3,338	Residential	Feb 92
Nam Sang Wai	UNSP	3,724	Warehouse, Open Storage	Sep 92
Nam Sang Wai	UNSP	20,035	Garage	Sep 92
Nam Sang Wai	R(C), UNSP, SSSI	1,369,000	Residential, Commercial Centre, Club	Sep 92
Nam Sang Wai	UNSP	3,327	Residential	Dec 92
Ngau Tam Mei	UNSP	11,325	Residential, Club	Jul 92
Ngau Tam Mei	UNSP	10,000	Village Type Housing	Nov 92
Pat Heung	UNSP, V	3,035	Industrial	Dec 91
Pat Heung	UNSP	4,200	Residential	Jul 92
Pat Heung	UNSP	4,036	Film Studio	Aug 92
Pat Heung	UNSP	7,415	Residential	Aug 92
Pat Heung	UNSP	7,415	Riding School	Dec 92
Pat Heung	UNSP	4,200	Residential	Feb 93
Shek Kong	UNSP	3,561	Village Type Housing	Nov 91
Shek Kong	UNSP	5,500	Columbarium	Dec 91
Shek Kong	UNSP	22,370	Columbarium	Dec 91
Shek Kong	UNSP	5,500	Columbarium	Jul 92
Shek Kong	UNSP	21,800	Columbarium	Jul 92
San Tin	UNSP	3,000	Industrial (Offensive), Open Storage	Jan 92
San Tin	UNSP	5,100	G/IC	Mar 92
San Tin	UNSP	340,000	Residential, Club	Sep 92
Tai Tong	UNSP	3,652	Industrial	Nov 91
Tai Tong	UNSP	3,652	Open Storage	Nov 91

Abbreviation used for zoning categories: UNSP = Unspecified Use
V   = Village Type Development
R(C)   = Residential (Group C)
SSSI   = Site of Special Scientific Interest

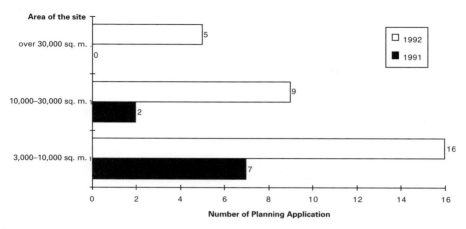

Fig. 5.31 Volume of Planning Applications for Land of More Than 3000 Square Metres in North West New Territories

present planning application system, which is reminiscent of the British 'non-zoning' regime, renders development by small landowners extremely difficult. Therefore, they tend to sell their land to large development companies which have a comparative advantage in rent-seeking or lobbying in the planning process. This is further illustrated in Table 5.11 by the high proportion of

Table 5.11 Planning Applications on Site Over 3000 Square Metres in Mai Po and Fairview Park Areas

Locations	Zoning	Site Area (sq.m.)	Uses applied for	Dated first considered by Town Planning Board
Mai Po	UNSP, V	6,500	Residential	Oct 91
Mai Po	UNSP	130,000	Residential	Jan 92
Mai Po	UNSP	5,924	Residential	May 92
Mai Po	UNSP	3,717	Container Park	Jul 92
Mai Po	UNSP	315,600	Residential	Jul 92
Mai Po	UNSP	260,000	Residential	Aug 92
Mai Po	UNSP, R(C)	7,068	Residential	Jan 93
Nam Sang Wai	UNSP	13,430	Driving School	Oct 91
Nam Sang Wai	UNSP	3,338	Residential	Feb 92
Nam Sang Wai	UNSP	3,724	Warehouse, Open Storage	Sep 92
Nam Sang Wai	UNSP	20,035	Garage	Sep 92
Nam Sang Wai	R(C), UNSP, SSSI	1,369,000	Residential, Commercial Centre, Club	Sep 92
Nam Sang Wai	UNSP	3,327	Residential	Dec 92

Abbreviation used for zoning categories: UNSP = Unspecified Use
V = Village Type Development
R(C) = Residential (Group C)
SSSI = Site of Special Scientific Interest

large site planning applications in the Mai Po and Fairview Park Development Permission Area (DPA) in comparison with the neighbouring DPAs in the Northwestern New Territories. In the Yuen Long DPAs, only three applications are related to large sites. The reason, on investigation is that the properties in the Mai Po and Fairview Park Area are fish ponds. The size of these ponds are much greater and shape more regular than farm lots which have been intensively subdivided. This reflects the impact of transaction costs of land assembly. However, as data on the volume of land transaction are not readily available due to the slow progress of computerization in land registration and the practice of developers in concealing their identity by shell companies, the conclusion remains only speculative.

Photograph 16   Fish Ponds in Yuen Long (Courtesy of the Hong Kong Government)

Compare the pattern of the ponds shown in this photograph and the pattern of land parcels in Figure 2.3(C). The more rectilinear and larger ponds attract developers to risk buying extensive areas of ponds controlled by zoning against development. The economic value of such pond areas implies that much resources will be expended on planning consultancies, lawyers and experts.

Notes

1.   Inheritance, adverse possession and other means to acquire private land rights should not alter the propositions in this chapter, if Coase theorem is applicable.

2. See Chapter 3, p. 64, reference to Coase (1960: 43) and Chapter 2, p. 38, section on 'Attenuation of Private Property Rights by Zoning'.

3. Smith, Carl T. 'Wanchai — In Search of An Identity' in Sinn, Elizabeth ed. *Between East and West : Aspects of Social and Political Development in Hong Kong.* pp. 47–93, 1992.

4. *Hong Kong Property Review 1993*. Rating and Valuation Department, Hong Kong Government, Table 17.

5. Central District Outline Zoning Plan No. S/H4/3.

6. *Hong Kong Property Review 1993*, ibid, Table 23.

7. Agnello, Richard J. and Donnelley, Lawrence P. 'Property Rights and Efficiency in the US Oyster Industry.' *Journal of Law and Economics* 18 (October 1975): 253–262.

8. For a rigorous approach to assess political risks, see Chau, Kwong Wing, Lai, Wai Chung Lawrence and Ho, Chi Wing Daniel, 'Political Risk, Rental Yield and the Methods of Development/Investment Appraisal and Valuation Techniques Used in Hong Kong', PRRES Conference, Melbourne: RMIT, pp. 929–937.

9. See reference to Staley (1994), note 49, Chapter 2 and discussion in p. 98, ante.

10. Crown Lands Resumption Ordinance, *Laws of Hong Kong* Chapter 124.

11. Tsuen Wan Outline Zoning Plan No. S/TW/5, October 1990 p. 5 states that 'On land designated "Industrial", any new building and any addition, alternation and/or modification to the existing building should not result in a total development or redevelopment in excess of the maximum plot ratio of the existing building whichever is the greater.'

12. See reference to Thomas Sowell in Chapter 3, p. 67 and note 10, Chapter 1, ante.

13. These cover Column 2 uses only. See description of the planning control system of Hong Kong in Chapter 2, p. 46–49, ante.

14. See reference to Coase (1988: 9) in Chapter 3, p. 66.

15. Lai, Lawrence W.C. 'The Effect of MRT on Land Values Rekindled — An Empirical Survey of the Impact of Mass Transit Railway on Office Rental Structures and Locations in Hong Kong.' *Journal of Property Valuation and Investment* 9 No. 2 (February 1991): 123–136. 'Evaluating Office Decentralization of a Financial Centre', *Australian Land Economic Review* 3 (No. 1, 1997a): 13–24.

16. Ip, Ying Yee. 'Effect of Transportation Improvement on Land Rent Gradient: An Empirical Study of KCR Electrification: Impact on Shatin — Tai Po Residential Gradient,' unpublished B.Sc. (Surveying) dissertation, Department of Surveying, University of Hong Kong, June 1992; and Han, Zhi. 'The Impact of Transportation Improvement on the Gradient of Residential Property Prices: A Study on Tolo Highway,' unpublished B.Sc. (Surveying) dissertation, Department of Surveying, University of Hong Kong, June 1994.

Chapter Six

Conclusion

Research directions, key arguments and findings

Research directions

In tackling the stated research objectives, the present study described in the previous chapters has sought to adopt different approaches of theoretical and professional interest. Firstly, zoning as a key planning tool is interpreted in a property rights framework. Unlike conventional economic analysis of zoning, which is restricted to the property rights attenuation aspects of zoning, the theoretical framework adopted here also incorporates the property rights delineation and establishment aspects of zoning. The framework should introduce academics and practitioners in the Commonwealth planning regimes to research focus and vocabulary for the socio-economic analysis of zoning they have hitherto ignored. In the context of Hong Kong, the framework proposed should be particularly important for two reasons. To begin with, it represents a systematic inception of Coasian property rights ideas into a practical and growing professional realm. In addition to that, Hong Kong will soon be subject to a critical constitutional experiment for a 'One Country — Two Systems' mode of economic-political governance. This system involves the co-existence of capitalist and socialist modes of economic orders. As a planning system operates within a broader socio-political context, there is an imminent need for local planning researchers and practitioners to be able to articulate in terms of concepts that are fundamental to debates about the economic nature of their practice. This is desirable as a way to keep abreast of and influence social developments. The property rights paradigm, by now a well received branch of economics should be able to offer a powerful set of analytical and operational concepts.

Secondly, the present study deals with some research limitations in respect of zoning. As discussed in Chapter 3, it is argued that (a) the property rights delineation of planning intervention cannot be ignored and (b) whether a zoning policy is justifiable is an empirical cost-benefit question rather than an *a priori* one. The rights delineation aspect of zoning is empirically evaluated in Chapter 4 with reference to marine zoning in Hong Kong. The test itself is an original contribution to property rights research on fisheries as an aspect of natural resources economics. It is also an attempt to test empirically the Knight-Gordon-Cheung analytical model. The results are consistent with standard property rights predictions. The cost-benefit view of zoning, asserted to be the proper interpretation of Coase's thinking, is applied in Chapter 5 to examine several aspects of zoning regulations in Hong Kong. Theoretically, the hypotheses present alternatives to the hedonic pricing and land values regression models. Practically, they should provide local researchers new directions for empirical district planning research. While at the strategic, sub-regional and sectoral levels, socio-economic planning studies and research in Hong Kong have attained a high level of sophistication, research on district issues like impact of zoning regulations, has hitherto been rare. The hypotheses set out here should be of both theoretical and practical interest to local researchers who are keen on the economic consequences of zoning. The issues raised in the present study about Comprehensive Development Areas, for instance, are crucial because they pertain to comprehensive urban renewal which would be the major vehicle for achieving a number of strategic and sub-regional planning objectives, such as thinning out urban population and restructuring obsolete urban areas.

Key arguments and findings

Chapter 2 presents a property rights view of the evolution of zoning and its nature. Three main arguments emerge from the discussion:
(1) Zoning in its broadest sense can be regarded as a means to establish exclusive property rights by the state so as to constrain the costs of competition over land in a state of anarchy.
(2) Zoning in the technical sense can be regarded as a means to provide an initial delineation of rights (and obligations). This could be provided by civil contract, as in the English freehold system and the leasehold system of Hong Kong, or by government design via forward planning, as normally understood by planners.
(3) Zoning in its technical sense is also commonly regarded as a form of land use regulation to attenuate any initial assignment of rights via the government forward planning or development control process.

Generally, Coase holds that market transactions can internalize social costs, thereby providing an alternative to regulation. However, it is shown in Chapter 3 that the Coasian-Pigovian debate cannot establish whether or not *zoning* as a land use regulation specifically is definitely effective in terms of internalizing externalities. The proper construction of Coase's view is that it really depends on the concrete policies involved and no *a priori* judgement can be made.

Although Coase does not pay much attention to the implicit significance of boundary delineation in exclusive rights assignment, three main arguments emerge from Coase's transaction costs analysis, which are consistent with the framework presented in Chapter 2:

(1) Zoning can be interpreted as the substitute for voluntary transactions of rights and liabilities in the unregulated land market due to its huge transaction costs.

(2) Whether such attenuation is justifiable is an empirical cost-benefit analysis rather than an *a priori* question.

(3) Zoning can also be regarded as a pure forward planning instrument assigning initial rights, thereby constraining rent dissipation in a state of common property.

The first argument provides a *prima facie* property rights economic justification for planning, which is further investigated in the study. The second argument, the archetypal Coasian view, is adopted in Chapter 5 to examine empirically some aspects of zoning in Hong Kong. The third argument, often ignored even by Coasian economists, is empirically tested in Chapter 4 with reference to marine fish culture zoning in Hong Kong. This incidentally provides an opportunity to test the most general Pigovian thesis that the price mechanism fails to reflect social costs.

In Chapter 4, marine zoning, as a means to establish initial property rights is examined. It is shown that in spite of deterioration in water quality, the productivity of fish in the marine fish culture zones of Hong Kong increased. This falsifies the environmentalist assertion that the fall in fish harvest in public water is due to pollution and establishes the property rights hypothesis that over-fishing is an explanation to the fall in fish harvest. By contrasting the opposing trends in productivity of private marine fish culture zones and public water bodies, the theoretical contribution of exclusive property rights delineation in constraining rent dissipation is verified in terms of a modified Knight-Gordon-Cheung model.

It is also shown that the fish farmers do attempt to enhance productivity by selecting the appropriate species and size of fry in the production cycle instead of growing them at random. This investment behaviour is not expected in a common property situation.

Above all, it is discovered that prices of the potentially more polluted cultured fish are at a statistically significant discount of ocean fish. This rejects the assertion that the price mechanism fails to reflect pollution and hence, by extension, lends support to the Coasian theory that market transactions can internalize externalities.

In Chapter 5, several forms of statutory zoning regulation which override property rights assigned initially by contract (lease) are examined. It is established that generally the impacts of such regulations are not necessarily beneficial, as Pigovians might think, nor adverse, as suggested by the Coasians. Different forms of regulations have different results.

The alleged positive aspects of zoning attenuating private property rights through requirement of joint development within the CDA concept are empirically not rejected. It is discovered that the extent of CDA zoning has a significant negative correlation with the environmental complaints. However, as far as land values are concerned, the effects of these regulations are dubious. The alleged benefits of zoning in the form of, (a) Pigovian tax through downzoning, (b) supersedure of freedom of land use for the highest possible private use by the planning application system or through supersedure of agricultural leases, are rejected. These findings are supported by correlation analysis which produce statistically significant results.

The above apparently inconsistent results are of course subject to data limitation and interpretation problems. However, a number of general property rights conclusions are discernable.

Firstly, the constraints of transaction costs are decisive. The positive gains of CDA zoning are obtainable only because one pre-condition tested in this study is satisfied : the issue of land assembly is avoided due to unitary ownership. This lends support to the Coasian emphasis of transaction costs. Where such costs are too high, government resumption may be necessary. As argued in Chapter 2, the existing LDC resumption practice is not immune to criticism. The rights of landowners of not joining a redevelopment scheme are derived from the terms of their leases which are based on reciprocal promises between the government and citizens. Thus the attenuation of such rights before the expiry of the lease by urban renewal legislation merits due compensation to uphold the spirit of freedom and privity of contract. Respect for contracts has been regarded as one of the key factors behind the economic success of Hong Kong. To keep a blind eye to the issue of compensation and its implications could bring about econ-political costs and repercussions which exceed the financial and environmental benefits of individual urban renewal projects.

Secondly, regulatory zoning, albeit attenuating private property rights, does not always 'fail'. They could enhance land value, as in the case of CDA development, although it appears to have failed in relation to downzoning. A pollution tax in cash payable to residents in Tsuen Wan (or alternatively, rebates in rates) may be more effective in internalizing the costs of pollution. Planning application involves an institutional arrangement conductive to rent-seeking activities, which could be constrained by clearer delineation of rights. Reforms of the planning application system by constraining 'as a matter of principle' decisions or the 'planning intention' argument against Column 2 applications have already been mentioned in Chapter 2. It is not unusual that one of the reasons given for Town Planning Board's decisions against a Column 2 planning application is that it is categorically inconsistent with the planning intention for a specific area. This is illogical. If this should be the case, the use would not be considered as acceptable in the first place. The argument, as mentioned,[1] is that the discretion of the Board should be restricted to the scale, intensity and design of the specific development and that it should not question the use generally. More detailed guidelines on these aspects should be made public.

Thirdly, the negative results about rural zoning which supersedes agricultural leases can be explained by the absence of clear assignment of rights. The reasoning here is analogous to that for the 'non-zoning' in the United Kingdom, which allows for a wide scope of rent dissipation. What remains to be seen is whether the maturity of the rural zoning system would significantly alter the relationship between planning application and nuisance for the New Territories. At present, the rural leases are overridden by statutory DPA plans. Such plans impose on vast areas the need for planning application for virtually all forms of development and changes in use. Thus, uncertainty in land use rights is great and the scope for rent-seeking is extensive. The new system will introduce Columns 1 and 2 uses, thereby reducing the costs of rent-seeking.

Methodological issues

General

The property rights model, which is presented in Chapter 2 and applied in Chapters 4 and 5, is built upon received property rights concepts favoured by the so-called Chicago School economists. Such concepts are claimed to have a high degree of generality. What is said about wheat farming and cattle raising (as in Coase's 1960 article) in an imaginary world of zero transaction costs can be extended to analyze what actually happens in the case of Hong Kong, with industrial-residential land use incompatibility. What is said about lighthouses (as in Coase's 1974 paper) and apples and bees (as in Cheung's 1973 paper) can similarly be said about fish. What is said about fish within marine zoning can be generalized to deal with land property value under zoning regulation. Many economists support such claims of generalization by insisting that theories must be subject to real life observation and empirical tests. The test methodology is one of Popperian 'falsification'. This approach is broadly adopted in the tests discussed in Chapters 4 and 5. Some basic features of the falsification approach need reiteration. There is no attempt to confirm a hypothesis. Instead, the attempt is to reject it. If it is falsified, it will then be rejected as a *prima facie* correct theory. Where a hypothesis is not falsified by facts, it is not regarded as being verified as a true or exclusive theory. It is simply considered to be *prima facie* acceptable. In either case, there is no claim that alternative explanation is not possible. Thus, for instance, one may assert that the price differentials found between cultured and captured fish are due to 'taste' differences but not pollution, and that the apparent insensitivity of residential property value to reduction in industrial plot ratio in Tsuen Wan may be due to time lag or lack of public knowledge.

Issues of the theoretical framework

The present study adopts a very broad definition of zoning, i.e. boundary delineation, which implies an almost universal presence of zoning for all political entities. This broad concept of zoning is adopted to focus on the significance of property rights delineation and attenuation. It also helps derive empirical hypotheses, as applied respectively to marine zoning and CDA concept of Hong Kong. This broad concept is potentially highly controversial. One possible objection is that this will stretch the concept of zoning far too much. However, a broad definition could be meaningful and operational in developing new ideas. The broad concept of transaction costs adopted by the property rights theorists is a case in point. In this study, the broad definition of zoning facilitates theorization and evaluation of different *forms* of zoning, thus avoiding the Pigovian and Coasian concept of zoning as necessarily a rights attenuation instrument. Apart from the example of marine fish culture zones, the distinction between 'zoning by contract' of the Hong Kong leasehold system and 'obligatory zoning', the conventional meaning of zoning as understood by planner and economists would not be amenable to property rights interpretation, had the broad definition been discarded.

The property rights model established in Chapter 2 is predicated on received property rights concepts. The model presents an idealized account of the transition of society from anarchy to a polity with government planning. Model construction as such has been adopted by scholars of different persuasions: Karl Marx on economic history, Max Weber on sociology and H.L. Hart on the evolution of law. There is no claim that the zoning modes of all societies would undergo the same process of evolution. What is intended instead is that different forms of zoning involve different transaction cost implications. The phases in the model show an ideal gradation of transaction cost minimization arrangement. Anarchy involves the greatest transaction costs of competition whereas the developed government zoning system stands for the attempted minimization of the transaction costs of using the unregulated market.

Limitations of empirical tests

While the results of the empirical tests in Chapter 4 are in general consistent
with the predictions of the framework presented in Chapter 2 and, in particular,
the results of the test of correlation between captured and cultured fish prices
are 'statistically significant', one must only take the findings as being tentative
to the extent that (a) the time series for data in Table 4.3 (relating output
of captured and cultured fish) obtained are restricted to 6 years from 1979
to 1984; and (b) the prices of each species of cultured fish by zone are not
readily available. It would have been useful if a fall in fish yield, unrelated
to the level of pollution, were shown in comparing the two fish harvest areas
with different water quality (albeit under common property). This would
establish that, *prima facie*, overfishing would be the explanation. Furthermore,
whether the price differentials between cultured and captured fish reflect 'taste
difference' or actual pollution is worth further inquiry. To this end, there
is a need to compare the actual level or extent of intoxication of various
species of the captured and cultured fish examined in Chapter 4.

The tests in Chapter 5 are constrained not only by data availability but
also problems of interpretation. While the former may be overcome in time,
the latter is inevitable in empiricism[2] in social sciences. While the results
of the correlation test between the extent of CDA development and environmental complaints is statistically significant, the test results regarding the
impact of CDA zoning *vis-à-vis* land value and industrial downzoning upon
land values in Chapter 5 are rather disappointing from the planning point
of view. The hypotheses about the price variances of CDA units could be
better tested if price and rental data of specific piecemeal building development could be obtained to replace the coarse district averages used in the
tests. The prerequisite of this approach is that Rating and Valuation Department would release their data on a building-by-building basis. As far as
the impact of industrial downzoning is concerned, an opinion survey on
perceived effects of downzoning can be carried out among residents of the
three selected estates. By comparing various environmental complaints arising
from the residents before and after the downzoning can also provide direct
information about externalities. As argued in Chapter 3, land values are only
indirect measures of externalities. Such efforts require institutional support.
For instance, address codification of complaints in EPD's district environmental complaint registry is essential. Therefore, the hypotheses and their
analysis cannot be considered as conclusive of all respects of zoning in Hong
Kong. They should, however, provide meaningful insights into some crucial
aspects of Hong Kong's planning system within the property rights framework
established in Chapter 2.

To reiterate, the objective of the tests are to show whether there are
prima facie economic grounds to justify zoning regulations and whether they

are beneficial or not. Negative results do not entail that they serve no useful purpose or are necessarily counter-productive.

The question of methodology for multi-disciplinary research

A problem was revealed in the course of preparing this book, which is the lack of a commonly accepted methodological stance for cross-disciplinary research. The standard 'Popperian falsification' approach may not be welcome by all researchers, especially those who are fond of dynamic model testing, and would be considered as being far too restrictive by planners. Planning research normally involves not only inductive causal reasoning but also a host of normative considerations, *a priori* principles, assertions and teleological arguments. The hypotheses in Chapter 5, for instance, would not be regarded as being decisive or sufficient for a planning policy review even if their methodological issues were ironed out and data limitations fully overcome. Conversely, planning explanations would be rejected by economists as empiricists for being ad hoc and value-laiden. This book adopts the empiricist position in order to tackle the Coase-Pigou economics debate and to demonstrate the observable economic consequences of right delineation and attenuation aspects of zoning within the transaction cost paradigm. A shortcoming of this approach is that the usual planning propositions and arguments for and against various forms of zoning cannot be utilized. Another significant methodological issue is that the nature of the tests presented in Chapter 5 are not only simplistic but also purely 'micro' or district planning related. Zoning in the planning hierarchy of Hong Kong is only one of the implementation tools at the lowest tier of a strategic-regional-district planning hierarchy. District planning is officially represented as the arena where 'the plan' and 'the market' interface, via the planning application mechanism. However, the author feels that the real economic 'transmission mechanism' of planning works like this: strategic and regional planning provides strong investment guides and constraints for developers, who then reveal their preferences through the district planning system. District planning is therefore largely the result of market-driven forces rather than rigid constraints for the market. However, modelling the economic consequences and property rights implications of strategic and regional planning is not as easy as for individual zoning policies; especially because the relevant objectives and constraints are markedly different.

CDA zoning backed by compulsory resumption, for instance, is a district planning tool violating private property rights as much as a strategic solution for urban restructuring under constraints of the transaction costs of land assembly and negotiation. The question that needs to be addressed is how should economic benefits and costs at different levels of planning be compared and articulated. Attempts to deal with this question, however, could lead to a costly digression from the objectives of the present study, which is to clarify the economic nature of zoning as a district planning tool. It is not to say that the attempts made towards this objective would lead to a clarification of the economic nature of zoning as a strategic urban policy tool. Nor is there any pretence that the empiricist methodology adopted is adequate in evaluating the effectiveness or appropriateness of planning intervention. Sound professional judgement backed by consultation for specific incidents some-times are more cost-effective, if not being the only feasible recourse, than running statistical tests which demand gathering an enormous amount of data over a long period of time. However, the author believes that it is beneficial for the planning profession to balance their sense of self-righteousness in their quest for more discretionary power, so as to intervene with refutable factual evidence and not mere good intention.

Policy and research implications

Policy implications

From the above analysis, the most important policy implications are:

(1) zoning as a means to assign exclusive property rights can effectively constrain rent dissipation, as illustrated by the study on marine fish culture. However, if the rights assigned by zoning are unclearly delineated, the land market may be retarded. In the light that rural areas are subject to pressures for urbanization or sub-urbanization and that the uses in DPA plans are unclearly specified, it is proposed that more resources should be devoted to prepare rural OZPs as quickly as possible to constrain rent dissipation and enlarge the land market. In the rural OZPs, the unspecified use areas in DPA Plans would be delineated into specific land use zones, hence reducing uncertainty for both the market and public sector.

(2) The fact that zoning overrides Crown leases and infringes on private property rights allocated by contract must be acknowledged in policy formulation and every possible precaution taken to constrain rent dissipation. In particular, (i) Column 2 uses should always be permitted and discretion should apply only to their intensity and design and (ii) the Pointe Gourde rule should be abandoned for LDC profit-seeking schemes and replaced by a development gain sharing method of compensation or the concept of trust in favour of the landowners for profits reaped from redevelopment.

(3) As the number of planning applications does not appear to correlate with the incidence of nuisance, the externality issue is *prima facie* suspect as a justification for planning regulation. However, as the test is inconclusive and subject to a number of limitations, it is worthwhile to establish an

internal monitoring system within the government which correlates planning applications, planning conditions, building applications and value and nuisance generation. Thus direct assessment of the performance of the planning system can be implemented continuously.

(4) Marine fish culture appears to be the only viable primary production for a number of reasons. To begin with, commercial agriculture in Hong Kong has experienced an apparently irreversible structural decline due to keen overseas competition. Rising opportunity costs of land and labour in the absence of government subsidy, and demise of poultry and pig farming have also helped foster the marine fish culture industry. Marine fish culture, however, has been criticized by scientists as a source of water pollution. It is revealed in Chapter 4 that although the fish culture industry is likely to be the victim of pollution, (as the existence of price differentials between cultured and captured fish suggest), it can effectively conserve fish species which could be dissipated by over-fishing. Apart from introducing urban fringe parks as advocated by the planners, properly regulated mariculture could well become an area of major policy innovations for the Agriculture and Fisheries Department (AFD), which appears to have been rather passive or ignored in the past decade.

(5) The Environmental Protection Department (EPD) may wish to adopt, in addition to purely physical environmental indicators, economic proxies of pollution to supplement their environmental auditing apparatus which also receives public complaints. The price differentials between cultured and captured fish may be used as proxies for water pollution. Liaision between AFD and EPD in this respect may produce fruitful results. Finally, one should not forget that billions of dollars has been paid as compensation to coastal fishermen who have allegedly been affected by marine dredging of sand and dumping of sludge for reclamation projects.

Research implications

The most significant research implications of the book are:

(1) The property rights framework and empirical tests on marine fish culture would contribute further to theoretical development of the economic modelling of natural resources in general (for instance, similar empirical tests can be carried out on forestry), and fishery in particular. It would also lead to further research about the ability of the price mechanism in measuring pollution (as exemplified by the price discount for cultured fish) and the explanation of the specific model of land allocation practice in developing areas. As for the pricing of pollution, an attempt has been made by Lai and Yu (1992, 1995) to construct an empirical model of the demand for and supply of water pollution. As regards land allocation, a possible research

area is the American homesteading under the 1862 Homestead Act. Yoram Barzel (1989) has expressed curiosity about the non-price allocation arrangement.[3] The granting to Hong Kong marine squatters of exclusive property rights may throw light on the homesteading system, which could be regarded as an initial assignment of exclusive property rights in a context where settlers occupied land in an anarchic situation.

(2) As mentioned in the section on methodological issues above, the tests on fish culture are subject to limitations. It is however apparent that there exists a systematic pattern of price discount for cultured fish. This phenomenon should not be ignored for environmental research. If the theory presented in Chapter 4 stating that the prices of cultured fish are discounted for pollution is correct, the price gaps between cultured and captured fish should narrow with the improvement in the physical quality of coastal water. With the completion of the Territorial Sewage Strategy, which will discharge all sewage of Hong Kong to the deep South China Sea using huge submarine sewers, the pollution loadings in coastal water should significantly improve. This would provide an opportunity to test the above prediction. In addition, this would also provide an opportunity to test the conclusion that the loss in captured coastal fish is due to overfishing, not pollution. The argument is, even with clearer water, coastal captured fish yield would not increase as far as the fish remain common property.

(3) The Planning Department announced on Christmas Eve 1993 that the plot ratios for different types of land use (residential, commercial and industrial) of Kowloon Peninsula would be further reduced for some districts like industrial and residential uses in San Po Kong, commercial use in Tsim Sha Tsui and Yau Ma Tei but relaxed for other districts such as Kwun Tong, Kowloon Bay and Cheung Sha Wan. Such zoning policies are predicated on infrastructural, environmental and strategic planning grounds. The concepts and discussions about the downzoning of industrial areas in Tsuen Wan in Chapter 5 should provide analysts with some insights. The interesting question would be whether such a comprehensive change as the plot ratio structures of Kowloon would significantly enhance the land values of the West Kowloon reclamation more than those of the Central and Wan Chai reclamation, which does not get the benefit of a similar change.

(4) The ascendency of the property rights paradigm in the economics arena (as reflected in awarding the Nobel Prize to economists in the past years) is expected to exert some response (positive or negative) in the planning research and education field, which has always professed itself as being multi-disciplinary. This would provide a check against reducing the activity of planning for the people as a pure physical or architectural endeavour. To be able to articulate in terms of the property rights paradigm, however,

requires not only a readiness to listen to unfamiliar ideas, but also some operational tools. Some of the operational tools adopted here are borrowed from mainstream economics (such as the Knight-Gordon-Cheung model) and the estate surveying (such as the bid-rent curves) disciplines. It appears that planning schools would get huge returns in improving the human capital they produce, i.e. planning graduates, by more closely affiliating with the economic and surveying fields which are strong respectively on rigorous theorization and practical market penetration.

Epilogue

The influence of Pigovian economic thinking in planning is persuasive. In the executive summary of the consultancy study final report on 'Support to Industry on Environmental Matters',[4] the consultants make this statement of the 'costs of pollution' in support of the 'polluters pay principle' (i.e. the Pigovian taxation):

> These costs were previously 'externalised' (i.e. not pay for and often underwritten by society as a whole) . . . ' (Support to Industry on Environmental Matters — Final Report, The Executive Summary para 3, p. 1)

Coase's paper 'Problem of Social Cost' (1960)[5] addresses exactly this line of thought.

The Coasian paradigm of transaction costs and reciprocal nature of pollution should in this context provide policy makers with a powerful analytical and empirical alternative to the Pigovian approach. Unfortunately, as revealed in Chapter 3, Coase has been mistaken by many policy analysts as being a libertarian objecting to all government control. In fact, he does not dismiss government regulation *a priori* but argues that the costs and benefits of policy options, which include non-intervention or relaxation of existing regulations, must be carefully assessed before jumping straight to intervention. More unfortunately, Coase's followers in their analysis of zoning control have apparently been unduly influenced by Coase's casual criticism of zoning control.

The Coasian paradigm of zoning is too restrictive in focusing on externalities and tends to dismiss zoning too easily for being inefficient due to rights attenuation. On the basis of the Coase Theorem that 'the delimitation of rights is the prelude to market transactions', and Cheung's notion that institutions are the result of choice to reduce transaction costs, zoning is interpreted here as a means to assign exclusive property rights, thereby constraining rent dissipation, as well as an interventionist mechanism that attenuates private property rights. This dual character of zoning is in fact implicit in Coase's reasoning although Coase himself may be responsible for the restrictive stance of the Coasians.

Apart from assuming away the notion of time, the Coase Theorem also omits the concept of extension. Extension is brought back into property right analysis of zoning in this book. Zoning as government delineation of land boundary is demonstrated to be inherent in the assignment of exclusive rights over land, the most developed one being private property rights protected by the law. Government zoning is therefore a special case by which private property rights are attenuated. Whether this attenuation reduces the transaction costs of an unregulated land market or increases the transaction costs of the land market is a case-specific, content-specific, system-specific, and a comparative rather than categorical or universal question.

Empirical tests and case studies are carried out here for evaluating these characters of zoning within a property rights framework with reference to examples in Hong Kong. It is shown that zoning as a means for the initial assignment of rights can effectively constrain rent dissipation. As regards subsequent attenuation of private property rights, the beneficial results are inconclusive. CDA zoning does enhance the environment and property value, subject to the transaction cost constraints of land assembly. Downzoning and planning application *per se* do not appear to be correlated with environmental improvement, but failure to delineate rights clearly in rural zoning appears to retard the land market.

> The literature on regulation sometimes gives the impression that all regulation is stupid, corrupt or both. This conclusion should be avoided (Eggertsson 1990: 147).

The results of the empirical tests in this book surely support this view, as far as zoning regulation is concerned.[6]

Notes

1. See p. 41, ante.
2. Caldwell, Bruce. *Beyond Positivism: Economic Methodology in the Twentieth Century.* UK, USA and Australia: George Allen and Unwin, 1982.
3. Barzel, Yoram. *Economic Analysis of Property Rights.* Cambridge: Cambridge University Press, 1989.
4. Support to Industry on Environmental Matters — Final Report, Gilmore Hankey Kirke (GHK Hong Kong Limited) for Industry Department, Hong Kong Government, 1993.
5. See Coase, R.H. 'The Problem of Social Cost' *The Journal of Law and Economics* (October 1960): 35, also in *The Firm, the Market and the Law.* Chicago: University of Chicago Press, 1988, p. 120.

6.   For a critical appraisal of the Hong Kong planning system in terms of property
     rights concepts, see Lai, Lawrence W.C., *Town Planning in Hong Kong: A Critical
     Review.* Hong Kong: City University of Hong Kong Press, 1997c, (Chinese
     translated version [香港城市規劃檢討] published by the Commercial Press, Hong
     Kong, October 1997d). The views in *Town Planning in Hong Kong* are consistent
     with those in Lai (1997b) and this work.

Appendix One

The Use of Aerial Photographs in Planning Enforcement Against Unauthorized Development[1]

Background

In 1991, an amendment[2] to the Town Planning Ordinance was passed to extend explicitly the jurisdiction of planning legislation to the entire territory of Hong Kong. Previously, it had been presumed that the reference to 'existing and potential urban areas' in the preamble of the Town Planning Ordinance excluded the rural areas of the New Territories, that is, areas outside the designated new towns.

Under the provisions of the amended Town Planning Ordinance, the Interim Development Permission Area (IDPA) Plans[3] were produced. The IDPA plans became gradually replaced by successively refined Development Permission Area (DPA) plans[4] and then Outline Zoning Plans. In areas for which IDPA plans were produced, changes in land use, unless approved by Town Planning Board or permitted as of right (under Column 1 or the cover pages of the Notes) by the relevant statutory plans after the gazette date of IDPA, constitute an offence.

The relevant provisions including the definition of the offence, its remedies and its statutory defences are generally described as 'planning enforcement' provisions. According to these provisions, the Planning Department may either serve an Enforcement Notice[5] requiring rectification (failure to comply entails prosecution), or proceed to prosecute directly. The accused may avoid prosecution or conviction if they obtain planning permission[6], or they can show that the uses in dispute are in fact 'existing uses',[7] that is, uses that had existed 'immediately before' the date of the IDPA.

On conviction, an accused is liable to pay fines. The levels of fines have been revised upwards successively. The Consultative Paper on the Town Planning Bill (July 1996) proposes a number of further amendments, notably the penalty of imprisonment, personal liability for company directors and Cho/Tong[8] managers, and the admissibility of photographic evidence.

The planning enforcement law creates a statutory strict liability criminal offence for authorized changes in use 'being found'[9] after the date of IDPA ˜on the current owner, occupier or user's land.[10] No *mens rea* or actual conduct[11] of the accused is necessary to establish the offence and there is no provision for jury trial. The mischief[12] which the law is said to target is the uncontrolled proliferation of open storage uses on land governed by agricultural leases.

In terms of private property rights, the theme of this book, it criminalizes uses previously legitimate under the proprietor's land contract with government. It nullifies the rights of the agricultural leaseholders to put land under open storage as affirmed in the Melhado Case.[13] In that case, it was ruled that the land uses surveyed by the Indian engineers and registered as part of the agricultural leases were merely descriptive and not restrictive regarding the nature of permitted land uses. In July 1996, further amendment to the enforcement law was proposed in the draft Town Planning Bill.

The author has argued in *Town Planning in Hong Kong: A Critical Review* (Lai 1997b) that planning enforcement from the strategic planning point of view is indicative of a reactionary mentality to rural land uses in face of rapid economic and urban growth. It is also antagonistic towards the government's strategic planning policies of expanding the Hong Kong international container port. It is reactionary for it is based on the normative view that the New Territories shall remain 'green' in appearance (Photograph 17) when neither the economic nor demographic conditions permit. It is contradictory as there is insufficient 'as of right' zones to accommodate the demand for open storage generated by the building and container industries (Figure A.1.1, Photographs 18 and 19), and such demand is generated by the government's territorial planning policies.

The author has also suggested alternatives, such as a licensing system and a comprehensive update of the description of uses in agricultural leases, to the existing approach so as to punish the open storage industry. The discussion concentrates on the use of aerial photographs as evidence by the prosecution. Aerial photographs are useful materials for planning purposes. However, they have some inherent and potential limitations. These limitations become particularly significant since they are intended to be used as court evidence. Some judges have expressed metaphorically that 'the aerial photographs tell the story'. Whether they really tell the true or complete story is an issue to be discussed.

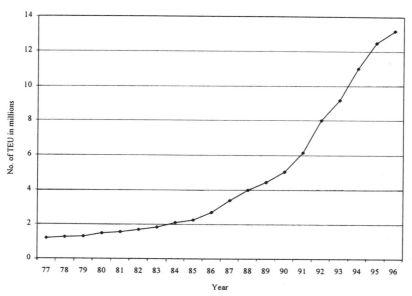

Figure A.1.1 Number of Twenty-feet Equivalent Units (TEUs) Handled in Hong Kong, 1977–1996

(Figure A.1.1 shows the rapidly growing number of containers (in TEUs) handled by Hong Kong from 1977 to 1995. Source: Hong Kong Government, *Annual Reports,* 1978 – 1997 issues).

Photograph 17 Farmland in Kam Tin East (Courtesy of the Hong Kong Government)

(The rural scenery in this photograph has been replaced by extensive open storage of containers and building materials such as that shown in Photograph 18. The physical pattern of the ponds and the fields corresponds to the irregular ownership pattern.)

Photograph 18   Container Storage Area in So Kwun Fat, 1996

The economic activities shown in this photograph, the target of planning enforcement but for its 'existing use' status, are part and parcel of those shown in Photograph 19.

Photograph 19   The International Container Port in Kwai Chung (Courtesy of the Hong Kong Government)

More of these large container berths will be constructed as planned by the Port and Airport Development Strategy.

The structure of the prosecution (previously Crown) case: Conviction on the basis of aerial photographs alone

An apparent flaw of the planning enforcement is its legislative design and the way in which prosecution is conducted. 'Existing use' or use before the gazette of the relevant statutory town plan (the Interim Development Permission Area (IDPA) Plan) is exempted by the law. However, this legal exemption often has little practical value for the defendant. The reason is that the prosecution relies almost exclusively on aerial photographs produced by the Survey and Mapping Office as evidence to prove the Crown case. Transparent plastic overlays bearing land lot boundaries as indicated in the DD plans are superimposed on aerial photographs taken at different time spots of a given site. They are then compared in three different ways when prosecution is taken:

(a) the alleged unauthorized use was not found on the date of the gazette of the IDPA ('the relevant date')and found to arise afterwards;

(b) the alleged unauthorized use was not found before the date of gazette of the IDPA and found to arise afterwards; and

(c) the alleged unauthorized use was indeed found before the date of the gazette of the IDPA but found to have dissipated before the gazette of the IDPA plan.

Before analysing the credibility of the above three situations, it should be realized that photograph aerial evidence is problematic to be treated as evidence, in two significant ways.

Firstly, it is hearsay evidence which does not fall under the exceptions to the hearsay rule in the legislation for Hong Kong's criminal proceedings or in common law.[14] Secondly, aerial photographs are susceptible to a number of interpretation problems.

The rule against hearsay

The foundation of private property rights is the rule of law. The rule of law depends on a sophisticated but logical body of rules of evidence. The rules of evidence in criminal proceedings put the onus of proof on the prosecution and exclude, other than a few exceptions, hearsay or unsworn evidence. The benefit of doubt goes to the defendant. However, in Hong Kong's planning enforcement (criminal) litigation, hearsay evidence is, doubtful as it appears, the sole basis of court decisions. The absurdity of the existing enforcement practice, and its property rights implications, is exemplified in the following examination of the use of aerial photograph evidence. In the end, the issue is not simply a matter of property rights of individual proprietors, but also a matter of justice and personal liberty of the public at large.

Evidence of a statement made to a witness by a person who is not himself called as a witness may or may not be hearsay. It is hearsay and inadmissible when the object is to establish the truth of what is contained in the statement. It is not hearsay and is admissible when it is proposed to establish by the evidence, not the truth of the statement, but the fact that it was made. The fact that a statement was made, quite apart from its truth, is frequently relevant in considering the mental state and conduct thereafter of the witness or of some other person in whose presence the statement was made. (*Subramanian* v. *Public Prosecutor* [1956] 1 W.L.R. 956, 970)

Common law exceptions to the hearsay rule

There are a number of common law exceptions to the hearsay rule:[15]
(a) admission and confession made by the accused;
(b) statements made by a person who subsequently died as to the cause of that person's death;
(c) statements made by a person who subsequently died made in the cause of that person's duty;
(d) statements made by a person who subsequently died as to matters against interest;
(e) statements made by a persons who have subsequently died concerning public rights;
(f) statements as to pedigree;
(g) statements in public documents;
(h) evidence in former proceedings;
(i) statements concerning the principle of completeness or the doctrine of *res gestae;*
(j) opinion evidence;
(k) evidence of certain business or banking transactions;
(l) statement of facts of a public nature published in works of a public nature such as histories, scientific works, dictionaries and maps.

Aerial photos produced by the government are unlikely to be 'public documents' (item (g) above) by law under the Evidence Ordinance:

> 18. Copy of document of public nature
>
> Whenever any book or other document is of such a public nature as to be admissible in evidence on its mere production from the proper custody, and no copy thereof or extract therefrom shall be admissible

in evidence in the court, provided it is proved to be an examined copy or extract or provided it purports to be signed and certified as a true copy or extract by the officer to whose custody the original is entrusted, and which officer is hereby required to furnish such certified copy or extract to any person applying at a reasonable time for the same, on payment of a reasonable sum for the same, not exceeding 50 cents for every folio of 72 words.

It is obvious that s.18 refers to written materials, not photo images.

It could be argued by the prosecution that the aerial photographs should be admitted into evidence as public documents because the photographers who took these photographs were civil servants under a duty to perform what was required.[16] If civil servants failed to perform their duties properly then they could be liable under the Civil Service Regulations which forms part of the civil servants terms of contract.

However, the case *Liliey* v. *Pettit* (1946)1.K.B. 401 held that 'a document to be receivable in evidence as a public document at common law must be one prepared for the purpose of the public making use of it and with the object that all persons concerned in it may have access thereto'. Furthermore, 'the regimental records of soldier which are kept for the information of the Crown and the Executive and not for that of members of the public who have no right of access to them are not public documents within the meaning of the rule'. In the case of *Thrasyvoulos Ioannou and Ors* v. *Papa Christoforos Demetrious and Ors* (1952) AC. 84, it was held inter alia that 'a document which is brought into existence as a result of a survey, inquiry or inquisition carried out or held under lawful authority is not admissible in evidence as a public document unless the inquiry was a judicial or quasi-judicial inquiry and the document is not only available for public inspection but was brought into existence for that very purpose'. It also stated that 'the statements in a document tendered in evidence as a public document should be statements with regard to matters which it was the duty of the public officer holding the inquiry to inquire into and to report on'.

Furthermore, the negatives of the aerial photographs, as distinct from the photographs, are the items which should be the public document but these are not available for inspection by the public as only the photographs therefrom are available for inspection.

It is of course common knowledge, that all civil servants are bound by the Civil Service Regulations and these Regulations form part of the contract between the Hong Kong government as the employer *vis-a-vis* the civil servant as the employee. However, it is unclear what liability a civil servant could face, should he commit acts which breaches these said Regulations. Prima facie it may be assumed that the liability would depend upon which of said Regulations was breached.

It is not at all clear as to what liabilities the photographers would face, should these photographers either have failed to perform or negligently perform their work. Whatever liabilities the said photographers may face would only be speculative in the absence of actual reference to the said Regulations, and examples of penalties imposed on the persons committing similar breaches of the said Regulations.

That the negatives of the aerial photographs are kept by the Survey and Mapping Offices of the Lands Department was merely for safety reasons so that prints of the aerial photographs could be produced and made available for public inspection. In this respect, no distinction was made between the negatives and the said photographs being available for public inspection.

The photographs are clearly taken with a view to show that the land photographed had or had not been 'developed' as defined by the Town Planning Ordinance. The use of these photographs were also for the benefit of the Planning Department, other government departments and the public in their study of the lands for the purpose of planning and development of the areas as a whole. It is not disputed that public interest would be affected when considering the development of such land. However, the aerial photographs were used clearly for the interest of the main and not for the sole purpose of prosecuting landowners which had breached the said Ordinance.

The aerial photographs showing the land cannot clearly show the landowners where their lands are situated in the aerial photographs unless the plastic overlays are also available. However, these said plastic overlays are not available to the public as are other materials produced by the prosecution. That would clearly mean that even if the aerial photographs are available to the public, they would have limited or little use to the landowners concerned since these owners cannot identify their lands with the said photographs. It is clear that the aerial photographs are more for the use of Planning Department than for the public unless the said plastic overlays are also available. Under these circumstances, it can be argued that the aerial photographs cannot be admitted into evidence under the common law. Straight proof is therefore required.

In other words, in order to appropriately prove the Crown case beyond reasonable doubt, the prosecution has to obtain sworn evidence from all those personnel who were involved in the aerial photograph taking and developing process. Staff movement may entail that this would become impossible in time. The draft Town Planning Bill seeks to overcome the issue of admissibility of photo evidence by legislation.[17] This statutory categorization of photographs as 'evidence of the facts stated' may well save the costs of straight proof. However, the legal drafting involved is logically problematic because photographs, unlike written documents such as records of statements or accounts, do not contain facts or concepts as denoted in terms of words or numerics but reveal only images at a point in time. The difference between words and numerics on the one hand and images (other than those involving words or numerics) on the other is one of a kind that reduces the statutory meaning of 'evidence of the facts stated'. The reason is that images, unlike words or numerics, are open to interpretation.

The aerial photographs do not tell the whole story

Other than admissibility, aerial photographs are susceptible to a number of interpretation problems.

In so far as the court is concerned in dealing with ascertaining land uses, or indeed changes in land uses, on the basis of aerial photographs, it is extremely reckless to rely on aerial photographs alone to prove, disprove, infer or assess land uses — whether or not such photographs are themselves distorted due to technical constraints; whether or not they are admissible in law as evidence tendered in court, or are taken at an altitude correct enough to reduce errors in human perception. They are often indeed neither necessary nor sufficient sources of information for most conceivable planning and development control purposes, a situation to be contrasted with radar camera photography of speeding vehicles in traffic offences.

Aerial photographs such as those produced by the Surveying and Mapping Office of course contain information, when properly interpreted, useful for planning purposes. They contain black and white or even coloured images of objects, matters and condensation during day light below the camera lens fixed to a flying aeroplane. A town planner with the relevant educational and professional training can fruitfully use aerial photographs to demonstrate prior known facts and to discover prior unknown facts.

As far as the 'demonstrative' or 'illustrative' value of aerial photographs, as often used in planning reports, are concerned, no inference is needed because the planner knows from personal experience, or from field survey and social knowledge (for example, the shape of Kai Tak runway) as to what the photographs demonstrate. As such, the photographs have no probative value and, when Hon Rhind J. in *Tse Kwei King and Cheung Kam v. A.G.*[18] and Hon. Litton V.P. in *R. v. Helen Transportation Co. Ltd., Liu Ka Sing and Chan Yuk Kwan*[19] referred to aerial photographs, in obiter (because admissibility of aerial photographs was not an issue in either), he was invoking the illustrative value of these photographs.

As regards using aerial photographs to discover prior known facts so as to adduce evidence uncorroborated by other sources of information, there is an inescapable need to draw inferences from the images revealed on the prints of the photographs. Other than technical aspects of photogrammetry, an aerial photograph interpreter must be aware of the following:

(a) As far as 'land uses' or 'changes in land uses' are concerned, inferences are made in a two-step procedure. Inferences are first made about the physical state of affairs (topography, hydrology, botany, climatology — in case clouds fly below the lens, vegetation cover and so on); followed by making inferences from entities which are conceptually distinct but related to the aforesaid, that is, the social, economic, cultural, institutional and other dimensions of land uses. Example 1: very often, identical physical settings (two pieces of vacant land) could be and are actually used for radically different purposes (market gardening after the fallow period v. open storage; playground v. vehicle parking; open space v. construction of building). Example 2: a body of water may be a fish pond, a pool of flood water, a tank of water for irrigation or cleansing. Example 3: an elegant building could be a structure of monumental value and will be conserved by government; a squatter structure will be liable to clearance.

(b) Aerial photographs show records of information collected at one point of time. Surely, some speculative inferences could be made about the history and degree of future permanency of certain objects and artifacts s like mounts, rivers, trees and buildings. However, a reasonable degree of scepticism should be reserved. In the case of planning enforcement in Hong Kong, inferences about changes in land uses from aerial photographs must be predicated on those taken consecutively at the same altitude at regular bi-weekly intervals.[20]

(c) Aerial photographs such as those used in the Crown case are taken by using a technology[21] incapable of revealing matters 'below the surface'. Below apparent trees and wild grass covers could be fallow agriculture land, marine sand, construction waste, garbage (in Hong Kong such a use is called 'controlled tips' and now described as 'landfills') or a pond. Below the apparent 'deep blue sea' could be mud flats which will become dried land after the photograph is taken. Below canopies of trees could be peaceful garden houses or tanks ready for an assault.

(d) Aerial photographs, such as those taken by the government, cannot tell 'pretend objects' or abnormal uses of real objects. The military history of World War II was replete with examples where reliance on aerial photographs alone in gathering intelligence led to strategic and tactical errors.

It is, therefore, a basic norm for the town planner that while aerial photographs are useful inputs for planning purpose, 'it does not mean that aerial reconnaissance methods can replace ground methods entirely. Their principal advantage is that they can simplify or facilitate the information gathering requirements so that the necessary ground work can be speeded up and at the same time made more productive' (Strandberg, 1967: viii).[22]

'Ground methods' in the Hong Kong planning practice as referred to by Professor Strandberg, include site visits and surveys conducted by trained survey officers supervised by qualified surveyors or planners. It should be noted that ground surveys are themselves susceptible to problems about inferences. Suffice it to say that such ground surveys must always be carefully conducted and results properly interpreted. Unfortunately, the prosecution often fails to produce convincing evidence of ground surveys. In many court cases, basic land surveying equipment like compasses and theodolites were not even contemplated by those professionals responsible for the enforcement surveys.

The logic of the prosecution case

Returning to the three ways of prosecution, the first approach is patently illogical. It is incumbent upon the prosecution to prove beyond reasonable doubt that the alleged authorized use had not been in existence before the the relevant date, but only came into being afterwards. The first approach informs the court nothing about the state of affairs before the relevant date. The second approach sounds more logical but given that aerial photographs only show images of physical attributes at specific times, there are reasonable doubts that an 'existing use' could perhaps be present between the times when the two photographs were taken. In a criminal proceeding, the benefit of doubt should be given to the defendant. The third approach is outrageous if the arguments against the second approval are valid. Arguable, it may be said that a change in the intensity of use may be 'material'. However, it does not appear in the existing body of planning law that such an interpretation is correct.[23]

The prosecution process can be totally 'fictional'. It is often the case that neither the judge, the prosecution nor the defendant (and of course the lawyers) knows personally whether an alleged unauthorized use or development is indeed really 'existing' or otherwise. The judge does not know for obvious reasons. The prosecution does not 'know' because the prosecution team was established after the relevant date. The defendant may not know for he may well have acquired land after the relevant date. Therefore, the court is asked to decide a conviction or an acquittal on the basis of hearsay evidence alone. The counsels of both sides in the litigation may well be very eloquent and the judge's statement extremely learned. However, is this alone consistent with the spirit of the rule of law, not to mention human rights, where the evidence is based on photograph images of a few snapshots?

To make matters worse, the prosecution often has neither accurate DD plans nor record of site surveys conducted or assisted by land surveying experts. This affects the accuracy of the plastic overlays and the reliability of evidence collected by field officers. These factors sometimes affect the determination of the relevant 'planning unit' in the prosecution case. The DD plans are at best *topological* description[24] of land ownership. The point about land surveying is of utmost importance in the New Territories as there is hitherto no public document or record indicating boundaries of zones and agricultural lots accurately.

The inefficiency of the existing and proposed legislation

With a defendant who is resourceful and convinced of his innocence, the magistrate court may need at least ten full-day hearings of the evidence of the Crown, the defendant and the expert witnesses of both sides alone. In the Keen Lloyd Limited Case,[25] it took three years for a case to be taken to the High Court from the date of serving of enforcement notices. The present legal arrangements benefit the lawyers (employed by the government and the defendants) and the expert witnesses most. It wastes the time of both the court and defendants. It opens immense opportunities for rent-seeking by professionals and bureaucrats.

If open storage is indeed an intolerable social evil, then the legal drafter should have written the law in such a way that the tricky issues of hearsay evidence and messy defence of 'existing use' should not be allowed in the ordinance. A summary offence procedure such as that adopted for traffic offences should have been adopted to replace the practice of solely relying on aerial photography in arguing their cases. Instead of the impractical defence of 'existing use', a more efficient and equitable alternative is to issue land use certificates to land users after a comprehensive ground-level land use survey of the rural areas.

As argued above, the legislative attempt to categorize photographs as being evidence of facts is unable to avoid the interpretation problems surrounding photograph images. Aerial photographs could be used to facilitate the survey but should not be used as the sole evidence of uses.

Notes

1. The research of this appendix is sponsored by a research grant provided by the University of Hong Kong and is partly based on the author's expert witness statement for the Keen Lloyd Limited Case (see note 25 post).
2. Town Planning (Amendment) Ordinance 1991 (4 of 1991).
3. S.26, Town Planning Ordinance.
4. S.20, Town Planning Ordinance. S.20(2) dictates that only for areas previously covered by IDPA plans prepared under s.26 can DPA plans be produced. This means that enforcement provisions cannot be extended to cover New Towns or the old urban areas for where Outline Zoning Plans were the first statutory plans prepared. 1991.

5. S.23(1), Town Planning Ordinance. This can be served on the owner, occupier or a person who is responsible for the alleged unauthorized development. The follow-up option to an 'Enforcement Notice' may be a 'Stop Notice' under s. 23(2) or a 'Reinstatement Notice' under s. 23(3).

6. S. 7(c), s. 21(c), s. 23(4A)(a)(ii), and s. 9 (d) of Town Planning Ordinance.

7. S. 7(a), s. 21(a), and s. 23(9)(b) of Town Planning Ordinance.

8. Cho or Tong is the body corporate for a 'clan'.

9. This is definitely the situation for offences committed under s. 23 (6) where the offence is 'where there is or was unauthorised development'. The wordings of 'no person shall undertake or continue development' in s. 20(7) and s.. 21 (1) seem to suggest requirements of certain acts to form the *actus reus* of the offence. However, in the majority of the cases, it seems that only the situation of land as seen in aerial photographs or ground photographs matters.

10. This is expressed clearly for s. 23 offences. The usual practice for s. 20(7)(1) and 21 (1) is against the user.

11. See note 9, ante.

12. See Consultation Paper on Town Planning Bill, July 1996, Hong Kong: Hong Kong Government, pp. 1–15.

13. *A.G.* v. *Melhado Investment Ltd.* [1983] HKLR 327.

14. The court has been advised to accept the Crown case in a number of key cases without reference to this legal point, such as *Tse Kwai King and Cheung Kam* v. *A.G.* (1993, MP No. 1509), *A.G.* v. *Tang Yuen Lin* (Magistracy Appeal No. 1300 of 1994), *Regina* v. *Way Luck Industrial Ltd.* (Magistracy Appeal No. 1396 of 1994), *Regina* v. *Tang Ying Yip* (Magistracy Appeal No. 864 of 1994), *Regina* v. *Helen Transportation Co. Ltd., Liu Ka Sing and Chan Yuk Kwan* (Magistracy Appeal No. 303 of 1995) and *Regina* v. *Power Straight Ltd., Dragon Friend Ltd.* (Magistracy Appeal No. 644 of 1995). In the Helen Transportation Case, the expression 'the photographs tell the story' was made.

15. The common law exceptions are extracted from Bruce, Andrew and McCoy, Gerard, *Criminal Evidence in Hong Kong*, 3rd edition, Hong Kong: Butterworths, 1995.

16. The arguments for and against this point were adapted from the ruling on admissibility for TMS 4262/94, 4266/94, 4267/94, 4269/94, 4270/94, 4271/94, 4272/94 unreported magistracy cases.

17. Section 79(1) of the draft Town Planning Bill reads: 'Any photograph, publication, record or other document purporting to be a photograph, publication, record or other document, or a copy of a photograph, publication, record or other document, executed, signed or issued under this Ordinance and purporting to be signed or initialled by any person employed in the administration of this Ordinance shall in any proceedings, in the absence of evidence to the contrary, be admissible as evidence of the facts stated therein, and it shall not be necessary to prove the signature or initials of the person purporting to sign or initial the photograph, publication, record or other document.'

18. See note 14.

19. See note 14.

20. Certain categories of temporary uses of less than two weeks are exempted. Therefore, logically, intervals of photograph taking exceeding two weeks cannot preclude possibility of such exempted uses.

21. The government does not use infra-red or ultra-violet remote sensing techniques for taking aerial photographs.

22. Below are some selected extracts from other relevant literature on aerial photographs and remote sensing; they support the view that great care should be taken in aerial photograph interpretation and that ground surveys are indispensable:

Bagley, J.W. *Aerophotography and Aerosurveying.* **New York and London: McGraw-Hill Book Company, 1941:**

Ch. VI Reading and Interpretation of Aerial Photographs

160. Field trip to get experience — 'It is important to become acquainted with the appearances of objects by experience. Study of photographs should be accompanied by field trips with the photographs in hand and direct identification of objects pictured. As many different types of terrain as practicable should be studied, and familiarity gained with all types such as tropical jungles, deserts, arid lands, New England scenes, farm lands of the Middle West, mountains and plains. The character of suburban areas and of sections of cities can be determined accurately after proper study of types.' (p. 111)

163. Detection of objects behind camouflage. — 'Camouflaged or hidden objects may in many instances be detected by evidence surrounding or near them. Travel to and from a military object such as a big gun may lead to the detection of its emplacement by paths and signs of tracking and the clearing of the site.' (p. 113) 'Collections of large quantities of materials unless well concealed will betray their character in one way or another.' (p.114)

Falkner, Edgar. *Aerial Mapping: Methods and Applications.* **Boca Raton, Ann Arbor, London and Tokyo: Lewis Publishers, 1995:**

Ch. 20 Field Verification

'Often the validity of photogrammetric mapping relies on the mapper to institute to judicious and standardized procedural operations. In order to ascertain that the mapping is in fact reliable, there are corroborative field survey strategies that can be applied.'

Sites Prone to inaccuracy:

'Examples of situations which can cause the compiler to lose stereo contact with the terrain include:

Areas in dense shadows

Areas obscured by patches of vegetation

Areas of limited image contrast such as high radiometric reflections off pavement.'

'The accuracy of any points located under these conditions are automatically subject to intolerable errors.' (p. 193)

Hallert, B. *Theory of Photogrammetry.* **New York, Toronto and London: McGraw-Hill Book Company, 1960:**

Ch. 1 The Basic Principles of Photogrammetry, 1–7 Photo Interpretation

'Photo interpretation as a separate technical branch has in reality little to do with measurement procedures, properly speaking, and many authorities consider that should be classified as a branch within photography. The art is not include, in photographic technical literature, however, and it would therefore seem desirable that be considered a branch of photogrammetry because of the importance that photo interpretation has for this science as a whole.'

'Experience is the first prerequisite of photo interpretation. Good general skill can only be acquired after long and intensive training under varied circumstances Special "photo interpretation key books" are of much value in this connection. During World War II special photo interpreters were trained. Their task was to pick up items of interest from a strategical and tactical viewpoint aerial pictures.' (p. 71)

Howard, J. A. *Aerial Photo-Ecology*. London: Faber and Faber, 1970:
Ch. 14 General Principles
'The procedure recommended in photo-interpretation, particularly at management level, is as follows: (a) scan the photographs monocularly and/or stereoscopically, (b) select stereo-pairs of photographs representative of the types vegetation being evaluated, (c) check these types in the field against the photographs, (d) delineate the types on all the photographs, and possibly take a representative sample of the photographic types and check these in the field to ensure typing has been carried out correctly, (e) adjust previous typing and complete all typing, (f) plan and carry out whatever field survey is needed for obtaining additional data.' (p. 154)

Kilford, W.K. *Elementary Air Survey*. London: Pitman Publishing Limited 1979:
Ch. 11 Some Notes on Data Collection from Air Photos and Other Imagery
'Legal and administrative boundaries are not seen on an air photograph, and their locations needs investigation on site or on maps. Place, and other names need the same treatment. Physical boundaries are readily seen and fences may be distinguished hedges by their shadow, straightness and thickness.' (p. 261)
'We must remember, however, that we are only dealing with deductions and probabilities and that even a garden will not necessarily indicate a house — perhaps there is a float above a shop, or the garden is being cared for by a small shopkeeper, by a warehouse caretaker or even by the local authority. A large number of people in the street may suggest the presence of a shop or shops, which will also often have a wider pavement in front. Thus to achieve any certainty, the interpretation of building uses, especially in an urban area, would almost certainly need to be aided by sample site visits, though low-flown photos might reveal much from the elevations disclosed by the leaning effect, and obliques would probably show even more in this way.' (p. 262)

Spurr, S.H. *Photogrammetry and Photo-Interpretation*. New York: The Ronald Press Company, 1960:
Ch. 14 Principles and Technique of Photo — Interpretation
'The Human Factor in Photo-interpretation: In contrast to map making, which is an objective problem susceptible to machine solution and production,

photo-interpretation has a substantial subjective element in it. While images may be measured on the photograph, and while such pictorial elements as tone and texture can be referred to a standard scale for naming and quantifying, the basic question of "What is it?" requires human experience and intelligence for its answer.' 'Because of the difficulty of dealing of such objective human elements, there is a good deal of words and nonsense in the literature of photo-interpretation. Nevertheless, it cannot be denied that the visual ability of the observer, his intelligence, and the ways and means by which he arrives at a decision are of basic importance in the solution of the photo-interpretation problem.'
'The human factor in photo-interpretation may be subdivided into (1) visual acuity, and (2) mental acuity. Colwell (1954) has ably summarized the status of knowledge of these.' (p. 246)

Lellesand, Thomas M. and Keifer, Ralph W. *Remote Sensing and Image Interpretation.* **New York, Chichester, Brisbane, Toronto and Singapore: John Wiley & Sons, Inc., 1987:**
Ch. 1 Concepts and Foundations of Remote Sensing, 1.1 Introduction
'In short, we use sensors to record variations in the way earth surface features reflect and emit electromagnetic energy. The data analysis process (g) involves examining the data using various viewing and interpretation devices to analyze pictorial data, and/or a computer to analyze digital sensor data. Reference data about the resources being studied (such as soils maps, crop statistics, or field-check data) are used when and where available to assist in the data analysis. With the aid of the reference data, the analyst extracts information about the type, extent, location, and condition of the various resources over which the sensor data were collected.' (p. 3)
'As we have indicated in the previous discussion, rarely — if ever — is remote sensing employed without the use of some form of reference data.'
'Reference data are often referred to by the term ground truth.' (p. 24)

Reeves, R.G.L. (eds.) *Manual of Remote Sensing* (vol. 1). **Virginia: American Society of Photogrammetry, 1975:**
Ch. 2 History of Remote Sensing, Author-Editor: William A. Fischer Manual of Remote Sensing
'In 1941 the President's Office of Emergency Management established a National Defense Research Committee (NDRC) as a funded research and development agency. In December 1941, a Camouflage Section headed by Dr. Arthur C. Hardy was organized under NDRC.' (p. 36)
Ch. 13 Ground Investigations In Support Of Remote Sensing, Author-Editor: Keenan Lee Test Sites
'Meaningful interpretation of most remote sensor data is dependent on ancillary data and a knowledge of the geographic area of which the data are being interpreted. The more the user-interpreter knows about the area over which the remote-sensor data were obtained, the better his interpretation.'
'Some of the ancillary data must be obtained during the acquisition of the airborne or space borne remote-sensor data; others can be obtained before or afterward.

When large areas are being remotely sensed, as by space borne instruments, it is impractical, if not impossible, to obtain ground data from the entire area; rather, data from small selected portions of the area are more easily and effectively gathered.' (p. 805)

Reeves, R.G.L. (eds.) *Manual of Remote Sensing* (vol. 2). Virginia: American Society of Photogrammetry, 1975:
Ch. 14 Fundamentals of Image Interpretation
Co-author-Editors: Estes, John E. and Simonett, David S.
'Most problems in image interpretation require the interpreter to have at his command knowledge derived not from the images themselves but from the relevant field or fields of study.' (p. 871)

Strandberg, C.H. *Aerial Discovery Manual.* New York, London and Sydney: John Wiley & sons, Inc., 1967:
Preface
'Dr. Luna B. Leopold, former Chief Hydrologist, U.S. Geographical Survey, has said, "Making photographic surveys from the air, scientists can do in an hour or two what might otherwise take 10 days." '
'This does not mean that aerial reconnoissance methods can replace ground methods entirely. Their principal advantage is that they can simplify the information-gathering requirements so that the necessary ground work can be speeded up and at the same time made more productive.' (p. vii)

23. It is argued in the Way Luck Industrial and Helen Transportation Cases that the question of change of use is one of fact and degree. However, some general principles can be found in the English planning law regarding the legal meaning of 'material change in use'.
The following changes do not necessary constitute 'material changes':
(a) changes in the intensity of use (from 8 caravans to 27 caravans — *Guildford UDC* v. *Penny* [1959] 2Q.B.112, [1959]2 All ER111);
(b) changes in the content of storage (from coal to oil — *East Barnet UDC* v. *British Transport Commission* [1962] 2Q.B.484, [1961]3 All ER 878);
(c) changes in the frequency of use (from part-time to full-time — *Peake* v. *Secretary of State for Wales* [1971] 22P. & C.R. 889).
The following changes do constitute 'material changes':
(a) if the change involves a substantial increase in the burden of services which a local authority has to supply (Per Lord Evershed in *Guildford UDC* v. *Penny* [1959] 2Q.B.112, [1959] 2 All ER111); or
(b) if the change is 'material' from the planning point of view.
See Telling, A.E. and Duxbury, R.M.C. *Planning Law and Procedure*, London: Butterworths, 1993.

24. Leung, S.C. 'The ABC of Land Parcels,' *Journal of the Hong Kong Institute of Land Surveyors*, 1984, 26.

25. *Keen Lloyd Limited and Cheung Kam Tong* v. *A.G.* (1996, Magistracy Appeal No. 266).

Appendix Two

A Technical Note on the Government's Housing Demand Concept Used in the Long-Term Housing Strategy

There is no doubt that the government has through years of efforts achieved the policy goal of meeting the basic housing needs of the people in Hong Kong. However, this does not entail that the methodology of reserving and allocating land to attain such a need-based goal will always satisfy the market demand for housing. This appendix aims to elaborate on this point as revealed in the government's Long-Term Housing Strategy (LTHS). The analysis throws light on the nature of Hong Kong's planning system as a development rights rationing system.[1] This system rations development rights by regulating the pace and extent of the release of government land, and the relaxation of development restrictions on the land already allocated. Such regulation manifests itself in district planning through re-zoning, as forward planning activities, planning permission, and development control functions of the government.

The government's housing demand estimation for the announced LTHS is radically conservative. According to the technical report for the Assessment of Housing Demand for LTHS,[2] 'housing demand' is conceived by the government to be a fraction of 'housing need'. Housing need is assumed to be satisfied once a household is accommodated in a self-contained housing unit built of permanent materials.

'Housing need is defined as the number of existing or potential households on need of "adequate housing", i.e. self-contained living quarters made of permanent materials...' (p. 3 Executive Summary, Assessment of Housing Demand, Working Group on Housing Demand)

'For one reason or another, not all households with housing needs intend to acquire separate accommodation. The second step (having derived 'housing need' defined above), therefore, is to convert the housing needs of individual components into 'housing demand' by applying a factor (and hence housing demand becomes a fraction of the so-called housing need) known as the

Accommodation Generation Rate (AGR). Housing demand is defined as the number of existing and potential households with housing needs who *intend to* seek separate accommodation.' (p. 3, ibid.) (Brackets and italics mine)

The above perception of need or demand makes little sense in terms of economic theory. The methodology depends critically on the erroneous assumption that demand is a fraction of need. Need, in turn, is defined by the government in terms of the fulfillment of the so-called adequate housing. The concepts in terms of supply and demand theory are characterized in Figure A.2.1. The vertical N* and D* functions stand respectively for housing 'need' and housing 'demand' conceived by the government. Neither N* nor D* is responsive to price, an economic fundamental which cannot be denied. They are instead assumed to be price-inelastic and are fixed quantities mechanically derived from the government's housing policy criteria. The government then matches D* with an identical amount of housing units which it describes as housing 'supply'. Such supply, or S*, is in fact a kind of 'planned supply'. Graphically, planned supply S* shares the same vertical curve as D*. Any gap between S* required to match D* for a year in future and the existing stock of housing units is to be bridged by new land supply made available by the planning procedures. The downward sloping D_m and upward sloping S_m are the standard market-demand-and-supply curves for housing units. These market-demand-and-supply curves bear a functional relationship with price, but they have no role in the government's adopted approach to quantify housing demand. As land supply in Hong Kong is heavily regulated and controlled by the government, the market price of housing is determined by the actual demand D_m and planned supply S*. The latter is identical to

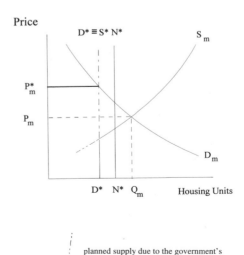

planned supply due to the government's
restrictive land and planning policies

Figure A.2.1 Planned and Actual Supply and Demand of Housing Units in Hong Kong

D*. The resulting market price P*$_m$ would be much higher than that, P$_m$, achieved in a free market characterized by D$_m$ and S$_m$ or a completely regulated land market where D* equals S* at all prices. The government's demand estimates, according to Figure A.2.1, would always be much smaller than the actual demand at all price levels.

The government's approach may also be simplified by the cartoons in Figure A.2.2. The government in effect presumes that all existing self-contained housing units built of permanent materials are homogeneous in quality. All households that have already been accommodated in these units are expected to have zero demand for housing. Four such households (A, B, C and D) are drawn in Figure A.2.2. The government's planned supply will only cater for those new households generated by the existing households in the family cycle or immigration. Two such households (E and F) are shown in Figure A.2.2 without any roofs over their heads. They constitute what the government calls 'need'. 'Demand', according to the reduction ratio AGR mentioned above, is considered as a portion of 'need'. Assuming that the ratio is 50%, the government's estimated demand in Figure A.2.2 will be one household. Accordingly, the government will plan to supply land for the building of one extra unit (say for E but not for F). When the land for building this extra unit is reserved in the town plan, the government will be able to sit back and relax, as there is no more unsatisfied housing 'demand'. However, this approach has a lot of problems. To begin with, the assumption about 'adequate housing' (N* in Figure A.2.1 and households A, B, C and D) is alarmingly unrealistic. The primeval standard perceived by the government, that is, 'self-contained

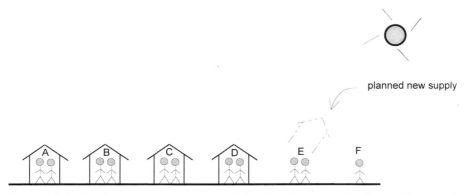

Figure A.2.2 The Government's Concept of Matching Demand with Planned Supply of Housing Units

Concepts of the government:
1.   A, B, C and D have no housing demand.
2.   E and F have housing needs but only E has 'demands'. Accordingly, land for building a unit for E is planned for.
3.   The quality of the existing housing units does not matter, in so far as they are 'self-contained' and built of permanent materials.

units built of permanent materials', which may be suitable planning public housing in the early 1970s, is no longer useful for planning public or private housing in post-industrial Hong Kong. The reason is that as soon as a household (A, B, C or D) becomes satisfied in terms of basic housing needs, it would seek to upgrade its living environment through 'trading up' (to HOS in case of public rental tenants, or to larger private housing units for those outside the public housing sector) when economic conditions permit.

In the private housing sector, the upward mobile households would seek to move into (then trade up within) comprehensively planned housing estates in locations of good accessibility, and for those who are financially most capable, they will seek to move into 'luxurious' units (greater than 1000 sq. ft.).

One should not fail to note that while per household income in Hong Kong has been rising in the past few decades, the space and environmental standards for the bulk of low-to-middle income households (in public or private sectors) in Hong Kong are poor. (The civil servant or equivalent staff quarters are special cases). It is in fact a wrong assumption that as soon as a household has met the minimal 'adequate housing' standard as adopted in the government's planning, it will remain satisfied with its existing accommodation. This assumption is inconsistent with the economic assumption of insatiable wants. When such wants are backed by income, they will manifest in terms of demand for better housing. Besides, the government has ignored the fact that existing housing units are heterogeneous in terms of quality, such as size, location, design and management.

As the government ignores the demand generated by the households that are already housed in self-contained units of permanent materials (and plans land supply according to new or future households only), high housing price becomes a natural means to ration inadequate quality housing to resourceful households. A comparison between Figure A.2.3 and Figure A.2.2 will reveal

All households (A to G) have demand for housing or re-housing.

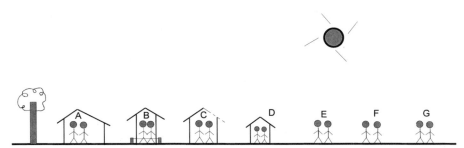

Figure 3   Actual Supply and Demand of Housing Units

Actual Housing Conditions:
1.   The location, size and other qualities of the existing housing units vary.
2.   There are many more new households than estimated.

the problems of the government's housing planning methodology. Figure A.2.3 shows some existing housing units of varied quality, and latent new households who have not been recorded in census or estimated in population forecasts. All households, whether or not they are adequately housed in terms of the government's criteria, have housing demands as depicted by D_m in Figure A.2.1.

Secondly, housing demand at any time is a function of real income, interest rate and price combined, rather than a constant or fixed quantum 'worked out' by planners. The government's presumption that 'demand' is a fraction of need is therefore highly misleading for planning purpose, as it tends to underestimate the land required. The concept of 'demand' in the government's planning makes no reference to real economic factors such as income, prices and mortgage rates. Instead, it is 'constructed' according to policy considerations and the 'aspirations' of the households surveyed. It is felt that this approach is unreliable, as it cannot gather useful information for an economic analysis of demand conditions. This problematic judgement about housing needs will lead to a drastic underestimation of demand and supply, providing that there is a sustained economic and population growth.

Thirdly, the government's housing model is using a stock concept. This means that the quantity of a sufficient stock of housing land is derived from a given number of housing units. As argued above, this approach tends to underestimate demand, and therefore supply. Furthermore, it ignores the practical realization of the already underestimated land stock that has been reserved in long-term plans for the supply of housing units actually needed. The efficiency of such flow of units into the housing market depends critically on that of the current planning, land administration and building procedures. In these respects, there is much room for improvements.

Lastly, one should not confuse housing demand with the issue of speculation in the property market or high housing prices. The curbing of speculation or the suppression of prices through administrative measures will not reduce demand. Indeed, if property prices are falling in real terms (for both nominal asking prices and mortgage rates), demand will increase along the aggregate housing demand curve.

If the government is committed to fight the problems posed by speculation or high property prices, must be even more concerned with creating, or enabling (through a more permissive policy towards change in use) the realization of more land supply. The above analysis also suggests that a realistic estimation of land supply to bring housing price down requires a proper understanding of consumer behaviour and market fundamentals. These two aspects are essential for formulating and achieving a better housing strategy. It is, however, beyond the scope of this appendix to discuss either the problems of the existing zoning policies or an alternative method to estimate housing demand. Suffice it to say, the received economic theories have much to offer in these key policy areas.

Photograph 20   Ma Hang Public Housing Development

Luxurious and residential development is shown on the left and Stanley Mount is on the right.

Photograph 21   'Woodside' High-Rise Homeownership Site, Quarry Bay

This site of high scenic value was chosen as an ad-hoc response to escalating property prices. It adjoins the Quarry Bay Country Park, and involves the deletion of zones for low-rise school development as well as the destruction of an old building of architectural interest, which was once owned by Swire. Such re-zoning is unlikely to be available to private developers although the government could obtain huge premiums from selling the land for private development. Subsidized housing, however, is handled differently. Upon completion, it will screen off the ridge-line of Mount Butler. Hence it is an inefficient, from an economic point of view, and undesirable, from the planning point of view, use of urban-country park fringe land.

▓▓ **Notes**

1. See Lai, Lawrence W.C., *Town Planning in Hong Kong: A Critical Review*, Chapter 5, Hong Kong: City University of Hong Kong Press, 1997c. Chinese translated version [城市規劃檢討] published by Commercial Press, Hong Kong, October, 1997d.

2. Working Group on Housing Demand, *Technical Report on Assessment of Housing Demand (1995/96–2005/06)*. Hong Kong: Hong Kong Government, January 1997. The Working Group includes representatives of the Housing Branch, Financial Services branch, Housing Department, Census and Statistics Department, Planning Department, Rating and Valuation Department, and the Housing Society.

Glossary

Anarchy
A state of affairs in which competition is unconstrained by property rights. See *Property Rights*.

Coase Theorem
(a) Clear delineation of property rights is a prelude to market transaction.
(b) Where property rights are clearly delineated, resource allocation is the same irrespective of property rights in the absence of transaction costs.
(c) Where property rights are clearly delineated, the Pareto condition will always be satisfied in the absence of transaction costs.
[Cheung 1990: 10–12]

Common Property Rights
A system of property rights in which the opportunity to appropriate a good is determined by the order of discovery.

Communal Property Rights
A system of exclusive property rights under which each person has an exclusive right to use a good once it is appropriated within an area with restricted entry. [Alchian and Demsetz 1974: 22]

Comprehensive Development Areas
This refers to:
(a) land so designated in statutory town plans i.e. Outline Zoning Plans/ Development Permission Area Plans;
(b) land governed by lease conditions requiring submission of master layout plans for building development; and
(c) land developed for 'estate' type housing.

Cost
The value of alternatives.

Development Control
The process through which the property rights assigned by forward planning are enforced by the government planner. See *Forward Planning*.

Economics
The social science that investigates maximization behaviour subject to constraints.

Exclusive Property Rights
Any system of property rights other than communal property rights.

Extension
Physical space, considered as a single concrete continuum, as contrasted with the abstract conceptual space of mathematics. [Runes 1960: 105]

Externalities
Uncompensated effects due to transaction costs.

Firm
An organization in which the exchange result of division of labour is ordered. Examples: family, tribe, commune, church, company, political party, government.

Forward Planning
The process through which the government planner assigns or reassigns property rights over land. See *Development Control*.

Good
Any object or service having value.

Government
A monopoly firm of violence which supplies protection by enforcing property rights within a state.

Government Planner
Whether he or she is officially called a 'planner' is immaterial: in the case of Hong Kong, the Land Authority can be regarded as a Planning Authority which assigns property rights by contract (lease) whereas the Planning Authority assigns/reassign property right by legislation.

Government Zoning
An area with its boundary delineated by the government. See *Planned Zoning.*

Institutions
Mechanisms of transactions including the market and the firm.

Land
Space and its content, if any.

Land Use Planning
The process of allocating land to different uses in accordance with a plan. It is carried out by individuals, private firms and government.

Market
A state of affairs in which the exchange result of division of labour is based on voluntary contract.

Market Price
The price actually paid by the consumer and received by the supplier in a voluntary transaction. See *Value.*

Modes of allocation of resources
(a) violence;
(b) rationing according to age, queueing etc;
(c) price competition in the market;
(d) non-price competition in the market or in firms; and
(e) rank and order within a firm.

Planned Zoning
A kind of government zoning through which the planner specifies the type and/or intensity of use for a clearly delineated area. See *Zoning.*

Planner, Land Use
One who determines types and intensity of land uses for zones.

Planning
The profession dealing with the techniques, activities, procedures and management of government interventions in spatial and socio-economic affairs in terms of the policy issues of
(a) the concern for efficiency in resource allocation in the presence of 'market failure', namely the existence of externalities, problems of providing public goods and the existence of monopoly under the profit mechanism in the process of industrialization and urbanization;

(b) the desire for equity in income, wealth distribution and opportunity; and
(c) a general acceptance of Pigovian micro-economic and Keynesian macro-economic management in Western countries.

Private Property Rights

The most developed form of exclusive property rights. The owner of a good can freely:
(a) use it;
(b) derive income from it; and
(c) alienate or transfer it in whole or in part to another person.
   [Cheung 1974: 53–71]

Property Rights

Rules of competition. See *Common Property Rights* and *Exclusive Property Rights*, which include *Communal Property Rights* and *Private Property Rights*.

Public Goods

Goods not transacted in the market due to high transaction costs of pricing. They are transacted by the state, which taxes its citizens for payment.

Rent

Value of a good or service.

Rent Dissipation

Value of a good being reduced by the costs of competition.

State

An entity with a government and territory with restricted entry.

Transaction Costs

Costs that exist in a state of affairs involving transactions, i.e. more than one person, other than the costs of production, including:
(a) costs of competition;
(b) costs of delineating and enforcing property rights;
(c) costs of information;
(d) costs of bargaining; and
(e) costs of contract formation.

Value

The maximum price the consumer is willing and able to pay when required. See *Market Value*.

Zero Transaction Costs
A state of affairs in which time or dimension is assumed away. [c.f. a frictionless world]

Zone
An area with its boundary delineated by some organizations. Examples: a freehold lot, leasehold lot, licensed area, planned zone.

The dedication of a certain area to a particular use [Abercrombie 1933:139]

Zoning
The process of delineating a zone.

Bibliography

Abercrombie, Professor Sir Patrick. *Town and Country Planning*. London, New York, Toronto: Oxford University Press, 2nd ed. 1933.

Abercrombie, Patrick. Hong Kong: Preliminary Planning Report. London: Professor Sir Patrick Abercrombie, September 1948.

Anderson, Terry L. and Hill, P.J. 'The Evolution of Property Rights: A Study of the American West.' *Journal of Law and Economics* 18 (No. 1, 1975): 163–179.

Angello, Richard J. and Donnelley, Lawrence P. 'Property Rights and Efficiency in the U.S. Oyster Industry.' *Journal of Law and Economics* 18 (October 1975): 253–262.

———. 'Prices and Property Rights in the Fisheries.' *Southern Economic Journal* 42 (No. 3, 1975): 253–262.

———. 'Externalities and Property Rights in the Fisheries.' *Land Economics* 52 (November 1976).

Alchian, Armen A. 'Some Economics of Property Rights.' *Il Politics* 30, (No. 4, 1965): 127–149.

Alchian, Armen A. and Demsetz, Harold. 'Production, Information Costs, and Economic Organization.' *The American Economic Review* 62 (December 1972): 777–795.

———. 'The Property Rights Paradigm.' *Journal of Economic History* 3 (No. 1, 1973): 16–27.

Alexander, Ernest R. *Approaches to Planning,* 2nd ed., 2nd printing. USA: Gorden and Breach Science Publishers, 1993.

Anderson, Terry. 'The New Resource Economics: Old Ideas and New Applications.' *American Journal of Agricultural Economics* 64 (No. 5, 1982): 928–934.

Anderson, Terry and Hill, Peter J. 'Property Rights as a Common Pool

Resource.' in Baden, John and Stroup. Richard ed. *Bureaucracy versus Environment.* Ann Arbor, Michigan: University of Michigan Press, 1981.

Atiyah, P.S. *The Rise and Fall of The Freedom of Contract.* Oxford: Clarendon Press, 1979.

Atwood, James R. 'An Economic Analysis of Land Use Conflicts.' *Stanford Law Review* 21 (January 1969): 293–315.

Avrin, M.E. 'Some Economics Effects of Residential Zoning in San Francisco.' in Ingram, Gregory K., eds., *Residential Location and Urban Housing Markets.* (pp. 349–376) Cambridge: Ballinger, 1977.

Babcock, R.F. *The Zoning Game.* Madison: University of Wisc. Press, 1966.

Bagley, J.W. *Aerophotography and Aerosurveying.* New York and London: McGraw-Hill Book Company, 1941.

Ball, Simon and Bell, Stuart. *Environmental Law.* London: Blackstone, 1991.

Bartik, Timothy J. 'Measuring the Benefits of Amenity Improvements in Hedonic Price Models.' *Land Economics* 64 (No. 2, May 1988): 172–183.

Barzel, Y. 'A Theory of Rationing by Waiting.' *The Journal of Law and Economics.* Vol. 17, No. 1 (April 1974): 73–95.

———. 'An Economic Analysis of Slavery.' *The Journal of Law and Economics* (April 1977): 87–110.

———. 'Property Rights and Resource Allocation in the Competition for Monopoly Gain.' Unpublished manuscript, December 1986.

Baumol, William J. 'On Taxation and the Control of Externalities.' *The American Economic Review* (June 1972): 307–322.

Baumol, William J. and Oates, Wallace E. *The Theory of Environmental Policy.* Englewood Cliffs: Prentice-Hall, 1975.

Baysinger, B.D. and Butler, H.N. 'The Role of Corporate Law in the Theory of the Firm.' *The Journal of Law and Economics* (April 1985): 179–181.

Becker, G.S. 'A Theory of Competition among Pressure Groups for Political Influence.' *The Quarterly Journal of Economics* (August 1983): 371–400.

Becker, G.S. and Stigler, G.J. 'Law Enforcement, Malfeasance and Compensation of Enforcer.' *Journal of Legal Studies,* 1984.

Becker, L.C. *Property Rights: Philosophic Foundations.* London: Routledge and Kegan Paul, 1977.

Beckerman, Wilfred. *Pricing for Pollution* (Hobart Paper 66). London: Institute for Economic Affairs.

Benjamin, Daniel K. 'Circumstances of Time and Place: Environmental Aspects of the California Coastal Plan.' *The California Coastal Plan.* San Francisco: Institute for Contemporary Studies (1976): 51–65.

Bennett, J. and DiLorenzo, T. 'Political Entrepreneurship and Reform of the Rent-seeking Society.' in Colander, D. ed., *Neoclassical Political Economy: The Analysis of Rent-Seeking and DUP Activities.* Cambridge, Mass.: Ballinger, 1984.

Benson, Bruce. 'Rent Seeking from a Property Rights Perspective.' *Southern Economic Journal* 51 (No. 2, 1984): 388–401.

Berki, R.N. *The History of Political Thought: A Short Introduction.* London, Melbourne and Toronto: Rowman and Littlefield, 1976.

Boast, R.P. 'Transferable Development Rights.' *New Zealand Law Journal* (October 1984): 339–342.

Bottomley, Anthony. 'The Effect of the Common Ownership of Land upon Resource Allocation in Tripolitania.' *Land Economics* Vol. 40 (February 1963): 91–95.

Bristow, M. Roger. 'Planning By Demand: A Possible Hypothesis About Town Planning in Hong Kong.' *Asian Journal of Public Administration* (December 1981): 192–223.

———. *Land Use Planning in Hong Kong: History, Policies and Procedures.* London: Oxford University Press, 1984.

Bromley, Daniel W. 'Property Rules, Liability Rules, and Environmental Economics.' *Journal of Economic Issues* XII (March 1978): 43–60.

———. 'Entitlements, Missing Markets, and Environmental Uncertainty.' *Journal of Environmental Economics and Management* 17 (1989): 181–194.

Bruce, Andrew and McCoy, Gerard. *Criminal Evidence in Hong Kong,* 3rd edition. Hong Kong: Butterworths Asia, 1995.

Buchanan, James M. and Tullock, Gordon. 'Polluters' Profits and Political Response: Direct Controls Versus Taxes.' *American Economic Review* 65 (March 1975): 139–147.

Burton, John. 'Externalities, Property Rights and Public Policy: Private Rights or the Spoliation of Nature,' in Cheung, Steven, N.S. ed. *The Myth of Social Cost* (Hobart Paper 86). London: The Institute of Economic Affairs, 1978.

Calabresi, G. and Melamed, A.D. 'Property Rules, Liability Rules and Inalienability: One View of the Cathedral.' *Harvard Law Review* Vol. 10 (April 1985): 1089–1128.

Caldwell, Bruce. *Beyond Positivism: Economic Methodology in the Twentieth Century.* UK, USA and Australia: George Allen and Unwin, 1982.

Campbell H.F. and Lindner R.K. 'The Production of Fishing Effort and the Economic Performance of Licence Limitation Programs.' *Land Economics* 66 (No. 1, 1990): 56–66.

Carn, Neil G. 'Is Highest and Best Use a Justification for Zoning?' *Appraisal Journal* (April 1984): 177–182.

Chan, Peter P.F. 'Aquacultural Development in Hong Kong.' *Fishery Bulletin* 1 and 10 (November 1988).

Cheung, Steven N.S. 'Private Property Rights and Sharecropping.' *Journal of Political Economy* 76, No. 6 (December 1968): 1107–1122.

———. 'Transaction Costs, Risk Aversion, and the Choice of Contractual

Arrangements.' *The Journal of Law and Economics* Vol. 12, No. 1 (April 1969): 23–42.

———. 'The Structure of a Contract and the Theory of a Non-Exclusive Resource.' *The Journal of Law and Economics* 13 (April 1970): 49–70.

———. 'The Enforcement of Property Rights in Children, and the Marriage Contract.' *The Economic Journal* 82 (June 1972): 641–657.

———. 'The Fable of the Bees: An Economic Investigation.' *The Journal of Law and Economics* 16 (April 1973): 11–33.

———. 'A Theory of Price Control.' *The Journal of Law and Economics* 17 (April 1974): 53–71.

———. 'Roofs or Stars: the Stated Intent of a Rents Ordinance.' *Economic Inquiry* (March 1975): 1–21.

———. *The Myth of Social Cost* (Hobart Paper 82). London: The Institute of Economic Affairs, 1978.

———. 'Economic Explanation: Let Us Ride with the Surging Tide.' Inaugural Lecture delivered on 26 October 1982. *University of Hong Kong Supplement to the Gazette February 28, 1983.* Hong Kong: University of Hong Kong, 1983.

———. 'The Contractual Nature of the Firm.' *The Journal of Law and Economics* (April 1983): 1–21.

———. *Thus Spake the Tangerin Seller* [賣桔者言]. Hong Kong: Hong Kong Economic Journal, 1984. (Chinese publication)

———. *The Future of China* [中國的前途]. Hong Kong: Hong Kong Economic Journal, 1985. (Chinese publication)

———. 'Coase, Ronald Harry' in Eatwell, John, Milgate, Murray and Newman, Peter ed. *New Palgrave: A Dictionary of Economics* Vol. 1, London: Macmillan, 1991, pp. 455–457.

———. 'Common Property Rights.' in Eatwell, J., Milgate M. and Newman, P. eds. *The New Palgrave.* London: Macmillan, 1987, pp. 504–505.

———. 'Transaction Costs and Economic Organisation.' in *The New Palgrave.* London: Macmillan, 1987, pp. 55–58.

———. *On the New Institutional Economics* (Discussion Paper Series No. 118). Hong Kong: Department of Economics, the University of Hong Kong, 1990.

Choi, Po-King and Ho, Lok-Sang eds. *The Other Hong Kong Report 1993.* Hong Kong: Chinese University Press, 1993, pp. 175–191.

Chau, K.W., Lai, W.C. Lawrence and Ho, C.W. Daniel. 'Political Risk, Rental Yield and the Methods of Development/Investment Appraisal and Valuation Techniques Used in Hong Kong.' in *PRRES Conference Proceedings.* Melbourne: RMIT, 1995, pp. 929–937.

Chow, Shuk Fun, Bessie. 'Forestry in the New Coasian Institutional Economics,' unpublished B.Sc. (Surveying) dissertation, Department of Surveying, the University of Hong Kong, June 1994.

Coase, Ronald, H. 'The Nature of the Firm.' *Economica.* n.s. 4 (November 1937): 386–405.

———. 'The Federal Communications Commission.' *Journal of Law and Economics* Vol. 2 (October 1959): 1–40.

———. 'The Problem of Social Cost.' *The Journal of Law and Economics* Vol. 3 (October 1960): 1–44.

———. 'The Lighthouse in Economics.' *Journal of Law and Economics* 17 (October 1974): 357–376.

———. *The Firm, the Market and the Law.* Chicago: University of Chicago Press, 1988.

———. *The Institutional Structure of Production.* Sweden: Royal Swedish Academy of Science, 1991.

Colander, D. ed. *Neo-classical Political Economy: The Analysis of Rent-Seeking and DUP Activities.* Cambridge, Mass.: Ballinger, 1984.

Commons, John R. *Legal Foundations of Capitalism.* New York: Macmillan, 1924.

Consultative Paper on the Town Planning Bill, The. (June 1966)

Cooke, Philip. *Theories of Planning and Spatial Development.* London: Hutchinson, 1983.

Crecine, John P., Davis, Otta A. and Jackson, John E. 'Urban Property Markets: Some Empirical Results and Their Implications for Municipal Zoning.' *Journal of Law and Economics* Vol. 7 (1967): 79–99.

Crone, Theodore M. 'Elements of an Economic Justification for Municipal Zoning.' *Journal of Urban Economics* 14 (1983): 168–183.

Dahlman, C.J. 'The Problem of Externality.' *Journal of Law and Economics* 22 (1979): 141–162.

Dales, J.H. 'Land, Water, and Ownership.' *Economics of the Environment,* 2nd ed., edited by Robert Dorfman and Nancy Dorfman. New York: W.W. Norton, 1977.

Davies III, J. Clarence and Barbara S. Davies. 'Federal Standards and Enforcement.' from *Economics of the Environment,* 2nd ed., edited by Robert Dorfman and Nancy Dorfman. New York: W.W. Norton, 1977.

De Alessi, Louis. 'The Economics of Property Rights: A Review of the Evidence.' *Research in Law and Economics* 2: 1–47.

Deacon, Robert T. 'An Empirical Model of Fishery Dynamics.' *Journal of Environmental Economics and Management* 16 (1989): 167–183.

Delafons, J. *Land Use Control in the United States.* Cambridge: MIT Press, 1969.

Demsetz, Harold. 'The Exchange and Enforcement of Property Rights.' *Journal of Law and Economics* 7 (October 1964): 11–26.

———. 'Towards a Theory of Property Rights.' *American Economic Review* Vol. 57 (May 1967): 347–359.

———. 'Information and Efficiency: Another Viewpoint.' *Journal of Law and Economics* 12 (1969): 1–22.

————. 'The Private Production of Public Goods.' *Journal of Law and Economics* 13 (1970): 293–306.

————. 'Economic, Legal and Political Dimensions of Competition.' UCLA Department of Economics Discussion Paper 209, September 1981.

Dickson, A. 'A Critical Review on American Zoning System.' *Land Economics* 62, No. 4 (November 1986): 201–230.

Dunham, Allison. 'City Planning: An Analysis of the Content of the Master Plan.' *Journal of Law and Economics* Vol. 1 (1958): 170–186.

————. 'A Legal and Economic Basis For City Planning.' Columbia Law Review 58 (1958): 650–671.

————. 'Promises Respecting The Use of Land.' *Journal of Law and Economics* Vol. 8 (1965): 133–165.

Dunlop, John Thomas. *Planning and Markets: Modern Trends in Various Economic Systems.* McGraw Hill, 1969.

Dupout, Diane P. 'Rent Dissipation in Restricted Access Fisheries.' 119 *Journal of Environmental Economics and Management* 19 (1990): 26–44.

Duxbury, Robert. 'Planning Compensation: Some Recent Cases.' *Journal of Valuation* Vol. 3, No. 3 (1985): 324–331.

Dworkin, Roald. *Taking Rights Seriously.* London: Duckworth, 1991.

Dwyer, D.J. 'Land Use and Regional Planning Problems in the New Territories of Hong Kong.' *Geographical Journal* 152 (July 1986): 232–242.

Eggertsson, Thrainn. *Economic Behaviour and Institutions.* Cambridge: Cambridge University Press, 1990.

Ellickson, R.C. 'Alternatives to Zoning: Covenants, Nuisance Rules and Fines as Land Use Controls.' *The University of Chicago Law Review* 40 (No. 4, 1973): 681–781.

Falkner, Edgar. *Aerial Mapping: Methods and Applications.* Boca Raton, Ann Arbor, London and Tokyo: Lewis Publishers, 1995.

Farnworth, T. 'Hong Kong Planning Law and The 1990 Amendment Bill'. (1991): 8–13.

Fei, Hsiao-tung [費孝通] *Peasant Life in China: A Field Study of Country Life in the Yangtze Valley.* London: Routledge, 1947.

Fischel, William A. 'A Property Rights Approach to Municipal Zoning.' *Land Economics* 54 (February 1978): 64–81.

————. 'Equity and Efficiency Aspects of Zoning Reform.' *Public Policy* 27 No. 3 (Summer, 1979): 301–331.

————. 'Externalities and Zoning.' *Public Choice* 35 (1980): 37–43.

————. *The Economics of Zoning Laws: A Property Rights Approach to American Land Use Controls.* Baltimore: Johns Hopkins University Press, 1987.

————. 'Zoning and Land-Use Control.' in *The Economics of Zoning Laws.* Baltimore: John Hopkins University Press, 1985, Chapter 9.

Fisher, Anthony C. and Peterson, F.M. 'The Environment in Economics: A Survey.' *Journal of Economic Literature* 14 (March 1976): 1–33.

Freeman III, A. Myrick. *Air and Water Pollution Control: A Benefit-Cost Assessment,* Table 9.1, p. 170.

————. 'On Estimating Air Pollution Control Benefits from Land Value Studies.' *Journal of Environmental Economic Management* 1 (No. 1, May 1974): 74–83.

Fullenbaum, Richard F., Carson, Ernst, W. and Bell, Frederick W. 'On Models of Commercial Fishing: A Defense of the Traditional Literature' *Journal of Political Economy* 80, No. 4 (July/August 1972): 761–768.

Fung, Bosco C.K. 'Enforcement of Planning Controls in Hong Kong.' *Planning and Development* 4 (No.1, 1988): 21–26.

Gifford, Adam Jr. 'Rent Seeking and Nonprice Competition.' *Quarterly Review of Economics and Business* 27 (No. 2, 1987): 63–70.

Goetz, Michael L. and Wofford, Larry E. 'The Motivation for Zoning: Efficiency or Wealth Distribution?' *Land Economics* 55 (No. 4, 1979): 472–485.

Goldberg, Victor P. 'Commons, Clark, and the Emerging Post-Coasian Law and Economics.' *Journal of Economic Issues* X (December 1976): 877–893.

————. 'On Positive Theories of Redistribution.' *Journal of Economic Issues* XI (March 1977): 119–132.

————. 'Toward an Expanded Economic Theory of Contract.' *Journal of Economic Issues* X (March 1976): 45–61.

Gordon, H. Scott. 'The Economic Theory of a Common-Property Resource: The Fishery.' *Journal of Political Economy* (April 1954): 124–142.

Gould, J.R. 'Extinction of a Fishery by Commercial Exploitation: A Note.' *Journal of Political Economy* 80, No. 5 (September/October 1972): 1031–1038.

Grant, Malcolm. *Urban Planning Law.* London: Sweet and Maxwell, 1982.

Grieson, Ronald E. and White, James R. 'The Effects of Zoning on Structure and Land Markets.' *Journal of Urban Economics* 10 (1981): 271–285.

Grigalunas, Thomas A. and Opaluch, James J. 'Assessing Liability for Damages Under CERCLA: A New Approach for Providing Incentives for Pollution Avoidance?'. *Natural Research Journal* 28 (No. 3, Summer 1988): 509–533.

Gulezian, R.C. *Statistics For Decision Making.* Philadelphia: W.B. Saunders Company, 1979.

Hall, Peter. *Great Planning Disasters.* London: Weidenfeld and Nicolson, 1980.

Hallert, B. *Theory of Photogrammetry.* New York, Toronto and London: McGraw-Hill Book Company, 1960.

Han, Zhi. 'The Impact of Transportation Improvement on the Gradient of Residential Property Prices: A Study on Tolo Highway,' unpublished B.Sc. (Surveying) dissertation, Department of Surveying, University of Hong Kong, June 1994.

Harlett, Graham. *Urban Land Economics: Principles and Policies.* London: Macmillan, 1979.

Harris, Jack C. and Moore, William Douglas. 'Debunking the Mythology of Zoning.' *Real Estate Review* 13 (Winter 1984): 94–97.

Hayek, Friedrich von A. *The Road to Serfdom.* Chicago and London: University of Chicago Press, 1944.

————. *Individualism and Economic Order.* Chicago and London: University of Chicago Press, 1948.

————. 'Housing and Town Planning.' in *The Constitution of Liberty.* London: Routledge, 1960: 340–357.

Heikkila, Eric. 'Using Simple Diagrams to Illustrate the Economics of Land Use Zoning.' *Journal of Planning Education and Research* 8 (No. 3, 1989): 209–214.

Helpman, Elhanan and Pines, David. 'Land and Zoning in an Urban Economy: Further Results.' *American Economic Review* 67 (December 1977): 982–986.

Herd, W.M. 'The Balance of Private and Public Interests in the Control of Non-conforming Uses.' *University of Queensland Law Journal* 12, No. 2 (December 1982): 29–40.

Hirsch, Werner Z. 'The Efficiency of Restrictive Land Use Instruments.' *Land Economics* 53 (May 1977): 145–156.

————. *Law and Economics: An Introductory Analysis.* Chapter IV, 'Economic Analysis of Zoning Laws.' New York: Academic Press, Inc. 1979.

Hirshleifer, J. 'Economics from a Biological Point of View.' *The Journal of Law and Economics* (April 1977): 1–52.

————. 'The Economic Approach to Conflicts.' UCLA Department of Economics Discussion Paper 220, Janaury 1984.

————. 'Conflicts and Settlement.' UCLA Department of Economics Working Paper, January 1985.

Holmes, P.R. and Lam, Catherine W.Y. 'Red Tides in Hong Kong Waters — Response to a Growing Problem.' *Asian Marine Biology* 2 (1985): 1–10.

Home, Robert. *Planning Use Classes.* Oxford: BSP Professional Books, 1989.

Hong Kong Fish Marketing Organization. *Annual Report 1988–89,* p. 6.

Hong Kong Fisheries Newsletter 4, No. 2: 2.

Hong Kong Government. *Annual Report on Hong Kong for the Year 1946,* p. 28.

————. *Marine Fish Culture Ordinance,* 1982.

————. *Town Planning Glossary,* u.d. p.S.6.

Hong Kong Government Environmental Protection Department. *Hong Kong Environment,* 1986 to 1992 issues.

Hong Kong Government Fisheries Department. *Annual Department Report,* for the period 1 May 1946 to 31 March 1947, p. 3.

Hong Kong Government Information Services Department. *Hong Kong 1973–*

1997. Hong Kong: Hong Kong Government Printer, 1973–1997 (various issues).

Hong Kong Government. Planning, Environment and Lands Branch. Report of the Task Force on Land Supply and Property Prices, Hong Kong: Government Printer, 1994.

Hong Kong Government Planning Department. *Town Planning in Hong Kong — A Quick Reference.* Hong Kong: Planning Department, 1995.

Hong Kong Government Planning, Environment and Lands Branch. *Consultation Paper on Town Planning Bill.* Hong Kong: Government Printer, July 1996.

Hong Kong Government Rating and Valuation Department. *Property Review: A Review of the Hong Kong Property Market.* 1981–1993 issues.

Hong Kong Institute of Fishery Limited. *Fishery Bulletin,* No. 6, June 1987.

Hong Kong Institute of Planners Working Group on the Review of Town Planning Ordinance. 'Issues of Town Planning Legislation in Hong Kong.' *Planning and Development* 4 (No. 1, 1988): 2–7.

Hong Kong Legislative Council. *Marine Fish Culture Bill,* 2 January 1980, p. 288.

Hong Kong *Sing Tao Daily News.* 27 August 1989, p. 34.

Hong Kong University Fisheries Journal 1 (December 1954): 63–65.

Howard, J.A. *Aerial Photo-Ecology.* London: Faber and Faber, 1970.

Ip, Ying Yee. 'Effect of Transportation Improvement on Land Rent Gradient: An Empirical Study of KCR Electrification Impact on Shatin — Tai Po Residential Gradient,' unpublished B.Sc. (Surveying) dissertation, Department of Surveying, University of Hong Kong, June 1992.

Jackoboice, George. 'Paying for Pollution.' *Window* 1 issue 20, (13 November 1992): 50–51.

Jacobs, Jane. *Life and Death of Great American Cities.* Harmondsworth: Penguin, 1964.

Janicke, Martin. *State Failure: The Impotence of Politics in Industrial Society.* Translated by Alan Braley. Cambridge: Polity Press, 1990.

Jowell, Jeffrey. 'Bargaining in Development Control.' in *Journal of Planning and Environmental Law* (1977): 414–433.

Kaser, Michael Charles. *Planning and Market Relations:* Proceedings of a conference held by the International Economic Association at Liblice, Czechoslovakia, 1971.

Keung, John K.Y. 'Physical Planning and National Development: A Study Exemplified by Reference to Hong Kong.' Unpublished M.Sc. thesis, Department of Town Planning, UWIST, 1980.

Kilford, W.K. *Elementary Air Survey.* London: Pitman Publishing Limited, 1979.

Klein, Benjamin, Crawford, Robert G. and Alchian, Armen A. 'Vertical Integration, Appropriable Rents, and the Competitive Contracting

Process.' *The Journal of Law and Economics* (October 1978): 297–326.

Klein, B. and Leffler, K. 'The Role of Market Forces in Assuring Contract.' *Journal of Political Economy* (August 1981): 615–641.

Klosterman, Richard E. 'Arguments For and Against Planning.' *Town Planning Review* 56 (No. 1, 1985): 5–20.

Knapp, Kim. 'Private Contracts for Durable Local Public Good Provision.' *Journal of Urban Economics* 29 (1991): 380–402.

Knight, F.H. 'Some Fallacies in the Interpretation of Social Cost.' in Stigler G. and Bouldings K. eds. *Readings in Price Theory*, pp. 160–179. American Economic Association by R.D. Irwin, 1952.

Kuhn, Thomas S. *The Structure of Scientific Revolutions.* Chicago: University of Chicago Press, 1962.

Kwong, Jo Ann. *Market Environmentalism: Lessons for Hong Kong.* Hong Kong: Chinese University Press, 1990.

Lafferty, Ronald N. and Frech III, H.E. 'Community Environment and the Market Value of Single-Family Homes: The Effect of the Dispersion of Land Uses.' *Journal of Law and Economics* Vol. 21 (1978): 381–394.

Lai, Lawrence W.C. 'The Formation of Squatters and Slums in Hong Kong: From Slump Market to Boom Market.' *Habitat International* 9, (No. 3/4 1985): 251–260.

———. 'The Role of Land Use Planning — An Economic Exposition.' *The Hong Kong Surveyor* 3 (No. 2, 1987): 6–9.

———. 'Rent Seeking.' *Hong Kong Economic Journal Monthly* [信報月刊] 166 (January 1991): 46–48.

———. 'Some Economic Consequences of Lowering Industrial Plot Ratios.' *Hong Kong Economic Journal Monthly* [信報月刊] 166 (January 1991): 98–99. (Chinese publication)

———. 'The Pricing of Lighthouses and Roads: Transaction Costs, Public Goods and Planning Intervention.' *Planning and Development* 7 (No. 1, 1991): 36–40.

———. 'Some Economic Aspects of Agriculture in the New Territories.' *Planning and Development* 7 (No. 1, 1991): 42–44.

———. 'The Effect of MRT on Land Values Rekindled — An Empirical Survey of the Impact of Mass Transit Railway on Office Rental Structures and Locations in Hong Kong.' *Journal of Property Valation and Investment* 9 No. 2 (February 1991): 123–136.

———. 'Coase and Land Use Planning.' *Hong Kong Economic Journal Monthly* [信報月刊] 170 (May 1991): 62–63. (Chinese publication)

———. 'Road Pricing and Coase's Lighthouses.' *Hong Kong Economic Journal Monthly* [信報月刊] 176 (November 1991): 29–31. (Chinese publication)

———. 'Ronald Coase and Town Planning.' *Planning and Development* Vol. 8, (No. 2, 1992): 28–30.

———. 'Marine Fish Culture and Pollution — An Initial Hong Kong Empirical Study.' *EKISTICS* Vol. 59 No. 356/357 (September/October–November/December 1992), pp. 349–356, also in *Asian Economic Journal* Vol. VII (No. 3, 1993): 333–351 and *Planning and Development* Vol. 9 (No. 2): 11–20.

———. 'The Effect of MRT on Office Decentralisation: a Hong Kong Empiricial Study' Sydney: Proceedings of the Third Australasian Real Estate Educators' Conference, 26–29 January, 1993.

———. 'Two Tales of the Fish: Pollution or Dissipation [魚的迷蹤].' *Hong Kong Economic Journal* [信報月刊] 194 (May 1993): 93–94. (Chinese publication)

———. *Essays on Real Estate* [資產變法], Hong Kong: Sing Tao, November 1993. (Chinese publication)

———. 'The Economic Justifications for Manning — the Similarities and Differences of the Works of von Hayek and Coase', *Hong Kong Economic Journal Monthly* [信報月刊] 200 (November 1993): 62–63.

———. *Doubts on Private Property Rights* [私有產權的疑惑], Hong Kong: Qin Jia Yuan Publishing Co., December 1993. (Chinese publication)

———. 'Urban Renewal and the Land Development Corporation' in *The Other Hong Kong Report.* Hong Kong: The Chinese University Press, 1993, pp. 175–191.

———. 'Property Rights and Zoning, *Ekistics* 61 (No. 336 May/June 1994 and No. 337 July/August 1994): 156–169.

———. 'The Economics of Land Use Zoning: A Literature Review and Analysis of the Work of Coase.' *Town Planning Review* 65 (No. 1, 1994): 77–98.

———. 'The Hong Kong Solution to the Overfishing Problem: A Study of the Cultured Fish Industry in Hong Kong', *Managerial and Decision Economics*, Vol. 16, No. 5 (September–October)1995: 525–535.

———. *Essays on Economics and Public Affairs* [經濟暢論], Hong Kong: Hong Kong Economic Journal, 3rd ed. March 1995. (Chinese publication)

———. 'Evaluating Office Decentralization of a Financial Centre,' *Australian Land Economic Review* 3 (No. 1, 1997a): 13–24.

———. 'Property Rights Justifications for Planning and a Theory of Zoning.' *Progress in Planning,* 48 (No. 3, 1977b): 161–246.

———. *Town Planning in Hong Kong: A Critical Review.* Hong Kong: City University of Hong Kong Press, 1997c. (Translated Chinese version [香港城市規劃檢討] published by Commercial Press, Hong Kong, October 1997d.)

———. 'The Leasehold System as a Means of Planning by Contract: The Hong Kong Case,' unpublished research monograph, Department of Real Estate and Construction, the University of Hong Kong, August 1997e.

———. 'Reflections on the Abercrombie Report 1948: A Strategic Plan for

Colonial Hong Kong,' unpublished research monograph, Department of Real Estate and Construction, the University of Hong Kong, August 1997f.

Lai, Lawrence W.C. and Lam, Ken. 'A Guide to the Culture of *Ophrocephalus maculotus*.' Fishing Farming International (September 1996): 54–55.

Lai, Lawrence W.C. and Lam, Ken. 'Pond Culture of Snakehead in Hong Kong: A Case Study of an Economic Solution to Common Property Resources.' *Aquaculture International* December 1998, forthcoming.

Lai, Lawrence W.C. and Yu, Ben T. *Water Pollution: A Fatal Mistake and Fish Story?* (Occasional Discussion Paper No. 1). Hong Kong: Department of Surveying, University of Hong Kong, 1992.

Lam, Catherine W.Y. 'Pollution Effects of Marine Fish Culture in Hong Kong.' *Asian Marine Biology* 7 (1990): 1–7.

Lam, Catherine W.Y.; Lui, P.H. and Fong, M.F. 'Marine Water Quality in Hong Kong.' Technical Report No. EP/TR3/88. Hong Kong: Environment Protection Department, Hong Kong Government, 1988.

Lawson, Rowena M. *Economics of Fisheries Development.* London: Frances Printer, 1984.

Lean, William. *Aspects of Land Economics.* London: Estates Gazette, 1966.
————. *Economics of Land Use Planning.* London: Estates Gazette, 1969.

Lellesand, Thomas M. and Keifer, Ralph W. *Remote Sensing and Image Interpretation.* New York, Chichester, Brisbane, Toronto and Singapore: John Wiley & Sons, Inc., 1987.

Leung, S.C. 'The ABC of Land Parcels.' *Journal of the Hong Kong Institute of Land Surveyors* (1984): 26.

Leslie, Margaret. 'In Defence of Anachronism'. *Political Studies* 18, No. 4 (December 1970): 433–47.

Levy, John M. *Urban and Metropolitan Economics.* New York: McGraw Hill Book Co., 1985.

Lin, S.Y. 'Fish Culture in Ponds in the New Territories of Hong Kong.' *Journal of the Hong Kong Fisheries Research Station* 1, No. 1 (February 1940): 161–192.

————. 'The Fishing Industries of Hong Kong: A General Survey.' *Journal of the Hong Kong Fisheries Research Station* 1, No. 2 (September 1940): 153–155.

Linowes, P.R. and Allensworth, D.T. *The Politics of Land Use: Planning Zoning owe Private Development.* New York: Praeger, 1973.

Mandelker, Daniel R. *Planning and Control of Land Development.* Charlottesville: Michie Co., 1990.

Mark, Jonathan H. and Goldberg, Michael A. 'Land Use Controls: The Case of Zoning in the Vancouver Area.' *AREUEA* Journal 9 (1981): 418–435.

Martin, Robyn. 'A Critical Review of the Town Planning Ordinance.' *Planning and Development* 4 (No. 1, 1988): 8–13.

Maser Steven M., Riker, William H. and Rosett, Richard N. 'The Effects of Zoning and Externalities on the Price of Land: An Empirical Analysis of Monroe Country, New York.' *Journal of Law and Economics* 20 (April 1977): 111–132.

McAuslan, P. *Land Law and Planning: Case Materials and Text.* London: Widenfeld and Nicholson, 1975.

————. *The Ideologies of Planning Law.* Oxford: Pergamon Press, 1980.

McConnell, R. Shean. 'The Implementation and the Future of Development Plans.' *Land Development Studies* (1987): 79–107.

Melville, D.S. and Morton, Brian. *Mai Po Marshes.* Hong Kong: World Wild Fund, 1984.

Mendelsohn, Robert. 'Estimating the Structural Equations of Implicit Markets and Household Production Functions.' *Rev. Econ. Statist.* 66 (No. 4, November 1984): 673–677.

Mendelsohn, Robert and Nordhaus, William D. and Shaw, Daigee. 'The Impact of Agriculture: A Ricardian Approach.' *American Economic Review* April 1992.

Mercuro, Nicholas and Ryan, Timothy P. 'Property Rights and Welfare Economics: Miller et al. v. Schoene Revisited.' *Land Economics* 56 (No. 2, 1980): 203–212.

Mills, David E. 'Is Zoning a Negative-Sum Game?' *Land Economics* 65 (No. 1, 1989): 1–12.

Mills, David E. 'Zoning Rights and Land Development Timing.' *Land Economics.* Vol. 66, (No. 3, 1990): 283–293.

Misczynski, Dean J. 'Land-Use Controls and Property Values.' in Hagman, Donald G. and Misczynski, Dean J. ed. *Windfalls for Wipeouts: Land Value Capture and Compensation.* Chapter 5 (pp. 75–109) Washington: Planners Press, 1978.

Montgomery, David M. 'Markets in Licenses and Efficient Pollution Control Programs.' *Journal of Economic Theory* 5 (1972): 395–418.

Moor, N. *The Planner and the Market.* New York: Longmans, 1983.

Moore. T. 'Why Allow Planners To Do What They Do? A justification from economic theory.' *American Institute of Planners Journal* 44 (1978): 387–398.

Mynors, Charles. 'The Planning and Compensation Act 1991: (3) Development Plans, Minerals and Waste Disposal.' *The Planner* Vol. 77, No. 32 (13 September 1991): 7–9.

Nabli, M.K. and Nugent, J.B. 'The New Institutional Economics and its Applicability to Development.' *World Development* 17 (No. 9, September 1989): 1333–1347.

Nelson, R.H. *Zoning and Property Rights: An Analysis of the American System of Land-Use Regulation.* Cambridge: MIT Press, 1977.

Ohsfeldt, Robert L. 'Assessing the Accuracy of Structural Parameter Estimates in Analyses of Implicit Markets.' *Land Economics* 64 (No. 2, May 1988): 135–146.

Ostrom, Elinor. 'Institutional Arrangements and the Commons Dilemma.' in Vincent Ostrom, David Feeny, Hartmut Picht ed. *Rethinking Institutional Analysis and Development: Issues, Alternatives, and Choices.* San Francisco: International Center for Economic Growth, 1988.

Ostrom, Elinor. *Governing the Commons: The Evolutions of Institutions for Collective Action.* US: Cambridge University Press, 1990 (6th printing, 1995).

Oxley, M.J. 'Economic theory and Urban Planning.' *Environment and Planning* A7 (1975): 497–508.

Palmquist, Raymond B. 'Estimating the Demand for the Characteristics of Housing.' *Rev. Econ. Statist.* 66 (No. 3, August, 1984): 394–404.

Pearce, B.J. 'Instruments for Land Policy: A Classification.' *Urban Law and Policy* 3 (1980): 115–155.

———. 'Property Rights vs. Development Control: A Preliminary Evaluation of Alternative Planning Policy Instruments.' *Town Planning Review* 52, (No. 1, 1981): 47–60.

———. 'The Changing Role of Planning Appeals' in Cross and Whiteheads eds. *Development and Planning.* Policy Journals, 1989.

Peltzman, Sam. 'Toward a More General Theory of Regulation.' *The Journal of Law and Economics* 19 (August 1976): 211–240.

———. 'The Growth of Government.' *The Journal of Law and Economics* (April 1977): 209–287.

Petersen, I. 'Co-operatives and Marketing.' *Hong Kong Business Symposium,* compiled by J.M. Braga (1957): 221–225.

———. 'A Brief Account of the Administration of the Fishing Industry in Hong Kong.' *Hong Kong Fisheries Bulletin* 1 (October 1970): 1–4.

Pigou, A.C. *The Economics of Welfare.* 4th ed. London: Macmillan, 1932.

Pines, David and Sadka, Efraim. 'Zoning, First-Best, Second-Best and Third-Best Criteria for Allocating Land for Roads.' *Journal of Urban Economics* 17 (March, 1985): 167–183.

Pogodzinski, J. Michael and Sass, Tim R. 'The Economic Theory of Zoning: A Critical Review.' *Land Economics* 66, (No. 3, August 1990): 294–314.

———. 'Measuring the Effects of Municipal Zoning Regulations: A Survey.' *Urban Studies* 28, (No. 4, August 1991): 597–621.

Pope, R.D. 'A History of Letter A/B Land Exchange Policy.' *The Hong Kong Surveyor* Vol. 1, No. 1 (May 1985): 7–9.

Popper, Karl. 'Falsification and the Methodology of Scientific Research Programmes.' in Lakatos, I. and Musgrave, A. ed. *Criticism and Growth of Knowledge.* Cambridge: Cambridge University Press, 1970, p. 181.

Posner, Richard A. 'Taxation by Regulation.' *Bell Journal of Economics and Management Science* 2 (Spring 1971): 22–50.

————. 'Theories of Economic Regulation.' *Bell Journal of Economics and Management Science* 5 (Autumn 1974): 335–358.

————. 'The Social Costs of Monopoly and Regulation.' *Journal of Political Economy* 83 (August 1975): 807–827.

Reeves, R.G.L. eds. *Manual of Remote Sensing* (vols. 1 and 2). Virginia: American Society of Photogrammetry, 1975.

Regan, Donald H. 'The Problem of Social Cost Revisited.' *The Journal of Law and Economics* (1972): 427–437.

Reuter, Frederick H. 'Externalities in Urban Property Markets: An Empirical Test of the Zoning Ordinance of Pittsburgh.' *The Journal of Law and Economics* 16 (October 1973): 313–349.

Richards, J., 'The Status of Fisheries in Hong Kong Waters.' Hong Kong Agriculture and Fisheries Department, unpublished manuscript, 1980.

Rosen, Sherwin. 'Hedonic Prices and Implicit Markets: Product Differentiation in Pure Competition.' *J. Polit. Econ.* 82 (No. 1, January/February, 1974): 34–55.

Runes, Dagobert D. ed., *Dictionary of Philosophy*. Totowa, New Jersey: Littlefield, Adams and Co., 1960.

Sager, Tore. 'Why Plan? A Multi-Rationality Foundation For Planning.' *Scandinavian Housing and Planning Research* 9, No. 2 (August 1992): 129–147.

Sams, Garry. 'Compulsory Purchase Compensation: Third RICS Discussion Paper.' *Journal of Valuation* 3 (1985): 427–434.

Samstag, Tony. 'Fishing Industry Turns to Farming.' *Fishery Bulletin* 7 (July 1986).

Samuelson, Paul A. 'Diagrammatic Exposition of a Theory of Public Expenditure.' *Review of Economics and Statistics* 36 (1955): 350–356.

————. 'Aspects of Public Expenditure Theories.' *Review of Economics and Statistics* (November 1958): 332–338.

Schneider, Keith. 'Making Farming Pay: Company Applies New Methods to Develop Crops of the Future.' *Fishery Bulletin* 7 (July 1986): 2.

Scott, Anthony. 'The Fishery: The Objectives of Sole Ownership.' *Journal of Political Economy* LXIII (February/December 1955): 116–124.

Segerson, Kathleen. 'Institutional Markets: The Role of Liability in Allocating Environmental Resources.' in *Proceedings of AERE Workshop on Natural Resource Market Mechanisms*. Association of Environmental and Resource Economists, June 1990.

Siegan, Bernard H. 'Non-Zoning in Houston.' *The Journal of Law and Economics* 13 (1970): 71–148.

————. *Land Use Without Zoning*. Lexington: D.C. Heath, 1972.

Smith, Carl T. 'Wan Chai — In Search of An Identity' in Sinn, Elizabeth ed. *Between East and West: Aspects of Social and Political Development in Hong Kong*. pp. 47–93, 1992.

————. *A Sense of History: Studies in the Social and Urban History of Hong Kong*. Hong Kong: Hong Kong Educational Publishing Co., 1995.

Smith, Vernon L. 'On Models of Commercial Fishing: The Traditional Literature Needs No Defenders.' *Journal of Political Economy* 80, No. 4 (July/August 1972): 776–778.

Sorensen, Anthony D. and Auster, Martin L. 'Fatal Remedies: The Sources of Ineffectiveness in Planning.' *Town Planning Review* 60 (No. 1, January 1989): 29–44.

Sorensen, Anthony D. and Day, Richard A. 'Libertarian Planning.' *Town Planning Review* 52 (October 1981): 390–402.

Sowell, Thomas. *Knowledge and Decisions*. New York: New Books, 1980.

Spurr, S.H. *Photogrammetry and Photo-interpretation*. New York: The Ronald Press Company, 1960.

Staley, Samuel. *Planning, Uncertainty and Economic Development in Hong Kong: A Critical Evaluation of the Comprehensive Review of the Town Planning Ordinance*. Hong Kong: Hong Kong Centre for Economic Research, University of Hong Kong, 1992.

Staley, Samuel R. *Planning Rules and Urban Economic Performance: The Case of Hong Kong*. Hong Kong: The Chinese University Press, 1994.

Stewart, M. 'Markets, Choice and Urban Planning.' *Town Planning Review* 44 (1973): 203–220.

Stigler, George J. 'The Economics of Information.' *Journal of Political Economy* 69 (June 1961): 213–225.

————. 'The Theory of Economic Regulation.' *Bell Journal of Economics and Management Science* 2 (Spring 1971): 3–21.

Strandberg, C.H. *Aerial Discovery Manual*. New York, London and Sydney: John Wiley & Sons, Inc., 1967.

Stull, William J. 'Land Use and Zoning in an Urban Economy.' *American Economic Review* (June 1974): 337–347.

————. 'Community Environment, Zoning, and The Market Value of Single-Family Homes.' *The Journal of Law and Economics* 18 (October 1975): 535–557.

Sullivan, Arthur M. *Urban Economics*. Homewood: Irwin, 1990.

Szczepanik, Edward F. 'Economic Survey of Hong Kong Fishing Industry.' Manuscript, Hong Kong: Department of Economics, University of Hong Kong, December 1957.

Telling, A.E. and Duxbury, R.M.C. *Planning Law and Procedure*. London: Butterworths, 1993.

Thrower, Stella L. *Hong Kong Country Parks*. Hong Kong: Hong Kong Government Information Services Department, 1984.

Tiebuot, Charles 'A Pure Theory of Local Expenditure.' *Journal of Political Economy* 64, No. 5 (October 1986): 416–424.

Tregear, T.R. and Berry, L. *The Development of Hong Kong and Kowloon as Told on Maps.* Hong Kong: Hong Kong University Press/Macmillan, 1959.

Tullock, G. ed. *Exploration in the Theory of Anarchy.* US: Centre for the Study of Public Choice, 1972.

Tullock, G. 'Rent Seeking and Zoning', unpublished research paper, 1994.

Turvey, Ralph. 'Optimization and Suboptimzation in Fishery Regulation.' *American Economic Review* 54 (1964): 64–76.

Umbeck, J. 'Might Makes Rights: A Theory of the Formation and Initial Distribution of Property Rights.' *Economic Inquiry* Vol. 20 (January 1981): 38–59.

Usher, D. *The Economic Prerequisites to Democracy.* Oxford: Basil Blackwell, 1981.

Warner, S.B. *Streetcar Suburbs: The Progress of Growth in Boston, 1870–1990.* Cambridge, Mass.: Harvard University Press, 1962.

White, Michelle J. 'Suburban Growth Controls: Liability Rules and Pigovian Taxes.' *Journal of Legal Studies* (1979): 207–230.

Wigglesworth, John Michael. 'Planning Legislation as a Necessary Charade: A Personal View.' in *Planning Legislation Report Proceedings of CAP Cyprus Seminar,* 1982, pp. 133–142.

———. 'Planning Law and Administration in Hong Kong: With Particular Reference to the Position in the United Kingdom', unpublished Ph.D. thesis, University of Hong Kong, January 1986.

Wihlborg, C.G. 'Outer Space Resources in Efficient and Equitable Use: New Frontiers for Old Principles.' *The Journal of Law and Economics* (April 1981): 23–43.

Williamson, Oliver E. *Markets and Hierarchies: Analysis and Antitrust Implications.* New York: Fress Press, 1975.

———. *The Economic Institutions of Capitalism.* New York: Fress Press, 1985.

Willis, K.G. *The Economics of Town and Country Planning.* Oxford: Granada Publishing, 1980.

Willoughby, P.G. 'Let The Land-Owner Beware.' *Hong Kong Law Lectures* (1978): 145–230.

Wilson, James A. 'Fishing for Knowledge.' *Land Economics* 66 (No. 1, 1990): 12–29.

Wolf, C.J. 'A Theory of Non-Market Failure: Framework for Implementation Analysis.' *The Journal of Law and Economics* Vol. 30 (October 1987): 107–139.

Wong, Sydney Chun Cheung. 'Zoning Control and Property Right in Hong Kong', unpublished M.Sc. dissertation, University of Wales Institute of Science and Technology, September 1986.

Working Group on Housing Demand. *Technical Report on Assessment of Housing Demand (1995/96–2005/06).* Hong Kong: Hong Kong Government, January 1997.

Wu, Rudolph S.S. 'Marine Fish Culture in Hong Kong: Problems and Some

Possible Solutions.' *Fish Farming International* 12, (1985): 12–13.

———. 'Marine Pollution in Hong Kong: A Review.' *Asian Marine Biology* 5 (1988): 1–23.

Yang, Xiaokai. 'Development, Structural Changes, and Urbanization.' *Journal of Development Economics* 34 (1990): 199–222.

Yang, Xiaokai and Borland, J. 'A Microeconomic Mechanism for Economic Growth.' *Journal of Political Economy* 99 (1991): 460–482.

Yang, Xiaokai and Ng, Yew-Kwang. *Theory of the Firm and Structure of Residual Rights* (Discussion Paper No. 141). Hong Kong: School of Economics, University of Hong Kong, 1993.

Yu, Ben T. 'Potential Competition and Contracting in Innovations.' *The Journal of Law and Economics* (October 1981): 215–238.

———. 'An Economic Analysis of a Social Contract.' Unpublished manuscript, October 1984.

———. 'An Analysis of Hong Kong's Political Reforms from the Theory of Rent Dissipation.' *Hong Kong Economic Journal Monthly* [信報月刊]. (December 1986): 20–22. (Chinese publication)

———. 'The Value of a Nobel Prize', *Hong Kong Economic Journal Monthly* [信報月刊]. 1987. (Chinese publication)

Index

Terms